FOOD ON THE PAGE

COOKBOOKS AND AMERICAN CULTURE

MEGAN J. ELIAS

PENN

UNIVERSITY OF PENNSYLVANIA PRESS

PHILADELPHIA

Published by
University of Pennsylvania Press
Philadelphia, Pennsylvania 19104-4112
www.upenn.edu/pennpress

Printed in the United States of America
on acid-free paper

1 3 5 7 9 10 8 6 4 2

Library of Congress Cataloging-in-Publication Data

Elias, Megan J.
Food on the page : cookbooks and American culture / Megan J. Elias.
1st edition. / Philadelphia : University of Pennsylvania Press, 2017
Includes bibliographical references and index.
LCCN 2016055355 / ISBN 9780812249170 (hardcover : alk. paper)
LCSH: Cookbooks—United States—History. / Food writing—United States—History. /
Food—United States—History. / Food habits—United States—History. /
Cooking, American—History.
LCC TX644 .E45 2017 / DDC 641.300973—dc23 LC record
lccn.loc.gov/2016055355

CONTENTS

FOOD ON THE PAGE

INTRODUCTION

WORDS ABOUT FOOD

I ONCE BOUGHT A secondhand copy of a *Fannie Farmer Cookbook* in which a previous reader had written and underlined the word "no" next to a recipe for soft custard. I myself have since made clear my allegiance to a particular chocolate pudding recipe through spine wear as I opened the book to it many times and through glops of batter dropped on the page, expressing my own version of "yes."

The little direct evidence of cooking that occurs in physical cookbooks comes in the form of such personal annotations and stains. These marks do not often show up in archived cookbooks for the practical reason that libraries look for the cleanest copies they can get. Because of this, researchers seldom encounter this kind of evidence. Even when notes and stains show up, it can be difficult to know what to make of them. They can be read for clues to women's lives, but the stories they tell tend to be very particular. As in my case, I like *Fannie Farmer*'s Denver Chocolate Pudding quite a lot.[1]

Cookbooks are full of words about food, but they don't really tell us what people eat. I first became interested in the history of American cookbooks when I realized this limitation. Trying to figure out what Americans had eaten in the past, I found that cookbooks could not tell me what I wanted to know. That certain recipes recur again and again over a generation or more both on restaurant menus and in cookbooks may suggest that someone has cooked them, but there is no way to be sure.

And yet cookbooks are far from mute. American cookbooks have long been remarkably voluble on the subject of national cuisine—what it was, what it wasn't, if it was bad or good, and what it could become. Cookbook authors provide a surprising amount of commentary that is distinct from kitchen lore, touching on the cultural meanings of cuisine.[2] In other words, cookbooks, like any other genre of literature, have something to tell us about our times. When we encounter trends in literary genres, we seek explanations in historical context—romanticism in reaction to industrialization, for example. Equally, we look to see which previous traditions contemporary authors are drawing upon. It is time we did the same for food writing. Why were there so many books about Southern cooking after the Civil War? Why are there so many big pictures of raw vegetables in contemporary cookbooks? Why do such a lot of twenty-first-century cookbooks eschew something—wheat or meat, for example—in times of plenty?

This book is about how American writers have defined their national foodways in cookbooks and magazines. In food studies, scholars commonly use the term "foodways" to refer to the combination of what people ate, how meals happened, and what diners thought about food—which dishes were considered normal, what materials were deemed edible, which preparations are appropriate to which groups. I trace how those definitions have changed over time, incorporating ideas from mainstreams and subcultures while also influencing cultures. When we read cookbooks for what they have to say about national foodways, we hear voices that have long been disregarded, the voices of people, many of them women, who understand that every meal is at once a cultural statement and a performance of self.

Examined from this perspective, cookbooks provide a lively range of opinions about and prescriptions for American food and, by extension, American culture. Each theme in cookbooks and each voice in this discourse emerges from a background of previous themes and voices. Tracing that genealogy, we can understand that ideas about food are not mere fads but instead part of an extended discourse that involves ideas about national identity—who is an American—as well as what is good and bad taste. Contemporary critics identify some kinds of food as "processed" not because of any objective truth, for example, but because of how writers have defined the natural and the unnatural in American foodways over the course of the twentieth century.

Writing About American Food

Many different kinds of writers have written about American food, from the first European arrivals in North America, curious about what they could eat, to the latest food blogger reposting recipes with a tweak or two, to the historians, anthropologists, and sociologists who are now using food as a lens to understand American society.

Long before 1796, when the first cookbook was published in the United States, diary keepers and letter writers commented on food—praising and criticizing individual cooks as well as what were perceived as national habits.[3] Traveling from Boston to New York in 1704, for example, Sarah Kemble Knight endured a meal of pork and cabbage with a sauce so purple that she thought it had been cooked in her host's dye kettle. To accompany this was "Indian" bread, meaning cornbread. Knight, "being hungry, gott a little down, but my stomach was soon cloy'd" or clogged and "what cabbage I swallowed serv'd me for cudd the whole day after."[4]

Englishman Andrew Burnaby, who toured the southern colonies during 1759 and 1760 found happier fare. He reported that soruses, a bird "rather bigger than a lark," was such "delicious eating," that when they were in season, "you meet with them at the tables of most of the planters, breakfast, dinner, and supper."[5] Because there was an inn in every town of the Northeast and a tradition of hospitality throughout the plantation colonies, letters and journals of travelers in the eighteenth and early nineteenth centuries were regularly punctuated with such commentary. While Knight complained of a single bad cook, Burnaby commented more generally on regional foodways.

Cookbook writers contributed to this conversation in America beginning in 1796 by producing a kind of literature that was both reflective and formative of their own culture. Cookbooks are typically categorized as prescriptive literature in that they set out rules that the reader must follow for success. While a collection of recipes that includes no commentary is very lightly prescriptive, the collections of recipes and household guidance that were the norm through most of the nineteenth century more forcefully claimed their authors' knowledge and readers' ignorance. Cookbook author Mary Randolph, for example, began *The Virginia Housewife*, first published in 1824 with a lecture on "the good government of a family," rather than food, and peppered her text with absolutes such as "blancmange must never be served without raspberry cream or syllabub to eat with it."[6]

Words about food help us to understand what we are eating—is our blancmange correctly served?—to place it in our particular cultural context, and to situate it in relation to what other people are eating. Words even help us to taste the food on our plates because we are creatures of culture, swayed by expectations and suggestive language.

It is common knowledge that the sense of smell is largely responsible for our experience of taste, but it is less commonly recognized that our interactions with words about food also determine how we taste what we eat. A study reported in 2013 by researchers at Cornell University's Food and Brand Lab offers evidence of the phenomenon. Participants in the study were given snacks—yogurt, cookies, and chips—that had been packaged with or without a label reading "organic." The majority found the "organic" snacks tastier than those not labeled with the high prestige term, despite the fact that all were identical and all were organic.[7] The concept is also familiar from the world of wine connoisseurship, in which the tradition of "blind" tasting—not being told anything about a wine before first tasting it—derives from the fear that any kind of descriptors bias judgment.

When we read cookbooks and food magazines, we are not reading blind. Our senses are typically captivated by images and adjectives that are designed to make us act on our consumer impulses—to get up and make something to eat. Cookbooks are aspirational texts. Sometimes we aspire to make just one recipe; at other times we more broadly reach for the lifestyle and values presented in a book.

Illustrations of kitchens and table settings help to establish the class culture or subculture of the cuisine. Mary Randolph, for example, also gave advice about tableware that helped establish particular objects, such as cruets and pickle vases, as normal and correct. Her reader learned much more than cooking; she learned a material culture that extended out of the kitchen into the marketplace for domestic goods.

In the food magazines that emerged in the twentieth century, advertisements reinforced those messages, begging us to associate a particular recipe with a kind of car or wine. We subconsciously ask ourselves—is that me? Is that someone I want to be? Publishers and advertisers hope that we say "yes" to either question, but the second is more likely to prompt us to new purchases. Recognizing these moves and tracing their history helps us to see food for what it is—not just sustenance, but language.[8] By presenting readers with particular foodways as their own national cuisine, American cookbooks provide commentary on national norms while also helping to construct that culture.[9]

Methodology

Excellent sources for ideas about food, cookbooks also exhibit both change and continuity over time. Like any other type of literature—detective fiction or coming-of-age novels, for instance—cookbooks express the anxieties and assumptions of an era. Individual authors share those concerns across their distinct texts, forming trends in the genre.

Apart from a bibliography of American cookbooks that covered the era from 1742 to 1860 and a few books and articles that detailed the history of a specific theme, I found that there was no comprehensive history of American cookbooks.[10] Nor was there any broad analysis of what American cookbooks had to say about national cuisine. My book is an attempt to solve both of these problems at once. It is a history of American cookbooks, but equally a history of the discourse defining American food that we find in those books.

The time period covered by this book, the late eighteenth century to the present day, is long. This posed challenges for coverage, but it also allowed me to trace a kind of family tree of cookbooks, to show how one theme developed in reaction to another and how we ended up with our contemporary understandings of what American food is. When I told people that my book was about American food, many of them said "Oh, are you going to explain why it's so bad?" My answer was that I was going to explain why some people *think* it is so bad and how it became acceptable, even laudable to say so.

This book is organized around ideas rather than around famous books or authors.[11] I encountered these ideas by applying myself patiently to the Library of Congress catalog, using the search terms "American" and "cooking" and looking only for books published in English in the United States. As I read through lists, decade by decade, I took note whenever a new term popped up and recurred. One of the first terms to catch my eye, for example, was "economical," which occurred frequently in cookbook titles through the last quarter of the nineteenth century. If I thought I was seeing a trend emerging, I tested it by searching across decades. Thus, for instance, I found twenty titles with the term "natural" during the sixty years between 1900 and 1960, but 151 in just twenty years between 1960 and 1980. In order to better understand the reach of a trend, I also searched for cognates or related terms, for example, looking not just for natural, but also for "health" and "organic."

Usually, more than one new theme emerged at a time. So, for example, I began to see more books about slimming at the same time that I encountered more books promoting commercial products. These convergences seemed to require analysis—were the separate trends in conversation with each other? Did their simultaneous emergence signal the diversification of cookbook subjects?

In the same spirit, as soon as I noticed what I thought was an increase in Southern titles, I checked to see whether there were any comparable phenomena for other regions. I assumed I would find similar books about New England or the Midwest, but I did not. Where I had originally thought I might be looking at the rise of regionalism in thinking about American food, I found I was really observing something else—culinary contributions to the legend of the Lost Cause.[12]

Numerically, the books that appear in this study do not represent the majority of the books published at any given time. It probably will not surprise anyone to know that although publishers offered more vegetarian cookbooks in the 1970s than ever before, these titles were still vastly out-numbered by cookbooks for carnivores. What matters to me is that vege-tarian cooking suddenly seemed like a new and interesting idea to enough people that authors wanted to write about it and publishers felt safe taking risks on these books.

In a few cases, what I already knew about cultural history shaped my searches. I knew that food had been an important element in the 1960s counterculture, for instance. The food term "granola" has even been used to describe the lifestyle. So I searched for cookbook titles that used the term "hippie," and was surprised to find very few.[13] I did find overtly countercul-tural cookbooks, but most of them were published in the 1970s and did not use the term hippie in their titles. My archival searches challenged what I thought I knew again, when I discovered a health food movement in the late 1940s that seemed to have only an indirect connection to a later incarnation.

Books often led me to other books as writers referenced each other. Thus when I read in Lucy Horton's *Country Commune Cooking* that all commune kitchens had Edward Brown's 1970 *Tassajara Bread Book* on their shelves, I knew I needed to devote some time to that text. I ordered a second hand copy and it arrived in the mail redolent of patchouli, as if to mark its authen-ticity as an artifact of an era.[14]

I had no idea that some of the categories I identified existed until they emerged in my review of archival catalogs. I had not anticipated finding lots of American history cookbooks in the 1970s, for example, but it made sense to me once I considered the contemporary context—the bicentennial and the ongoing nuclear arms race, which both foregrounded national identity in popular culture.

Once I identified what seemed to be a new idea in American cookbooks, I read as widely in that category as I could. Because I had regular access to collections at both the New York Public Library and the Fales Collection at New York University, there were not many books I wanted to look at that I couldn't find. I made special trips to three other significant archives—the Li-brary of Congress, the Schlesinger Library at Radcliffe Institute, and the So-phie Newcomb College Collection at Tulane University—to expand my re-search in special areas, such as corporate cookbooks and Southern cookery.

Within thematic categories, I chose the books with the most to say, or those that most eloquently expressed a particular idea about American cooking. I refer directly to only a small number of the hundreds of books that I read, but each one helped me to understand all the others. As I read through books within a category, I noticed repeated tropes as well as repeated flavors. These repetitions helped me to recognize categories and to understand their contours.

In day after day of reading cookbooks and food magazines as I researched the material in this book, I certainly experienced the power of words about food. Constantly made hungry by descriptions of food in my research texts, I decided one day to catalog my cravings. As I sat in the New York Public Library one winter morning, in the space of one hour I craved blue cheese, Irish soda bread, rye bread, café *brûlot*, anisette, macaroons, fish and chips, Yorkshire pudding, fish stew, mortadella, and a peanut butter sandwich. Some of these foods I have never even tasted. Ravenous as this book has made me, then, it has also taught me how evocative a literature food writing is, suggesting at every turn of the page pleasures yet unknown.

CHAPTER 1

THE BEST-FED PEOPLE
IN THE WORLD

AMERICAN COOKBOOKS
IN THE NINETEENTH CENTURY

IN THE FIRST AMERICAN cookbook, published in 1796, Amelia Simmons struck a note that would continue to resound over the next two hundred years: "This treatise," she explained, "is calculated for the improvement of the rising generation of Females in America."[1] During Simmons's lifetime, American women's skill in the kitchen was supposed to grow from the new-lywed's stumbling incompetence to the seasoned housekeeper's expertise. In later generations, the American woman would be compared unfavorably to her counterparts abroad, to men, and even to her own grandmother in kitchen affairs.

Little is known about Amelia Simmons herself, but she seems to have had knowledge of well-to-do foodways, probably as a professional cook. Simmons's *American Cookery* set itself apart from similar English books previously published in North America by including recipes for originally American foodstuffs such as corn and turkey. Her book was not only the first American cookbook, it was also first in a soon-to-expand market for kitchen guidance. Before Simmons's generation, cookbooks—like most books—had belonged to the economic elite. In the early years of the nine-teenth century, as a middle class emerged, cookbooks appeared too, to serve this new market.[2]

The antebellum era in America was a time of migration and cultural transformation. New communication and transportation technologies made it possible for Americans to keep in touch culturally while moving farther away from older settlements. Cookbooks helped ease these transi-tions and simultaneously became part of expanding markets across the con-tinent. If a woman carried a cookbook published in Philadelphia with her on the Oregon Trail in the 1840s, for example, she could expect to enjoy flavors of the old home in the new. Foodstuffs might be different in the West, but her cookbook would give her guidance for preparations that would look familiar. As entrepreneurs established towns and trade routes, a new edition of her Philadelphia book could find its way out west in the years after she settled. For all their potential mobility, however, cookbooks published be-fore the Civil War tended to show little in the way of diversity.

Before the Civil War, American publishers produced approximately 265 books with recipes, not all of them cookbooks.[3] This number includes works primarily concerned with gardening, cheese making, brewing, winemaking, and husbandry, as well as some humorous pieces such as *The Hasty Pudding*, an ode to the joys of cornmeal mush.[4] Of the recipe books published before the war, only twenty-six overtly referred to America or the United States in their titles and only nine referred to particular regions—Virginia, the Caro-linas, Philadelphia, and New England.

"America" and the United States became more popular terms in cook-book titles in the 1840s and 1850s, while regional references in titles are equally spread over the period, beginning with one of the first successful American cookbooks, Mary Randolph's *The Virginia Housewife: or Methodi-cal Cook*, first published in 1824.[5] By the 1840s, publishers offered American audiences a few German, French, and Spanish cookbooks, both in those languages and in translation.

A noted twentieth-century cookbook collector, Louis Szathmary, wrote in 1974 that his collection of American cookbooks included "a few" works from the 1700s and almost three hundred from the nineteenth century, but more than five thousand published since 1900.[6] As Szathmary's accounting suggests, in the 1870s, the American publishing industry began a phase of expansion that continued well into the twentieth century. One of the results of this expansion was the diversification of American cookbooks as a genre. The cookbooks published after the Civil War built upon models established before the war but also introduced new themes that in turn shaped early twentieth-century writing about food. Three of these new themes were community, Southern regional identity, and progressivism.

From Compendiums to Tastemakers

Antebellum era cookbooks were most often household manuals, helping readers to get rid of moths and to care for the sick as well as teaching them how to cook contemporary Anglo-American fare. Authors organized texts around foodstuffs, including both raw materials and finished goods, rather than meals. Randolph's *Virginia Housewife*, for example, began with a chapter on soups, but followed this with chapters on beef, lamb, mutton, and pork. Chapters on fish and poultry (including eggs) were followed by chapters on sauces, vegetables, puddings, and cakes. By beginning with soups and saving chapters on desserts till the end of the book, authors loosely followed the outline of the typical middle-class dinner meal.

This format assumed that the reader already understood the basic grammar of the meal—what the accepted order and composition of courses was.[7] It also suggested that dinner was the meal most in need of planning, which was certainly the case through the nineteenth century. Breakfast and lunch were private meals, most often composed of leftovers from a previous night's dinner. Even when specific foods became associated with these meals, they were seldom occasions for entertaining guests, so the nineteenth-century housewife had much less cause to think about them.

Exemplifying the encyclopedic impulse, well-known editor Sarah Josepha Hale titled her 1857 cookbook, *Mrs. Hale's receipts for the million: containing four thousand five hundred and forty-five recipes, facts, directions, etc. in the useful, ornamental, and domestic arts, and in the conduct of life. Being a complete family directory. Relative to accomplishments, amusements, beauty, birds, building, children, cookery, courtship, dress, etc. economy, etching, etiquette, flowers, gardening, Grecian painting, phrenology, potichomanie, poultry, riding, swimming, surgery, domestic temperance, trees, etc. woman's duties, words of Washington, etc.* The hodgepodge of her title encompassed most of the enthusiasms and anxieties of mid-nineteenth-century America.[8]

Economy was a common theme in antebellum cookbooks. Lydia Maria Child, for example, in her very popular 1829 *The Frugal Housewife*, laid out a plan of moderation in all things.[9] Echoing the tones of an almanac, she prefaced a list of household hints with the words, "IF you would avoid waste in your family, attend to the following rules, and do not despise them because they appear so unimportant: 'many a little makes a mickle.'" The emphasis was on economy and thrifty management of the entire home, not just the kitchen.

Child differentiated her book from its predecessors and competitors by identifying its audience as ordinary folk. Calling it a "cheap little book of economical hints," she avowed her "deep conviction that such a book is needed." Although her material was "of the common kind," she argued, "It is such as the majority of young housekeepers do not possess." Child explained that cookbooks had been mostly written for the wealthy, whereas she had written for the poor.

Child's understanding of poverty, however, was belied by her description of girls' education: "When quite young, they are sent to schools where no feminine employments, no domestic habits can be learned; and there they continue until they 'come out' into the world."[10] This kind of academic education and formal entry into the social world were features of upper-middle-class life. The working poor, who could seldom provide schooling for any of their children, were least likely to arrange for girls to learn anything *but* housekeeping. Child's insistence that her book was for practical use, however, reflected her experience as an editor who had learned that this notion would appeal to book buyers.

Child and others like her wrote for a generation of American women who were taking on roles different from those modeled by their own mothers. As American households transformed from productive centers, where everything from homespun cloth to sausages was made, to repositories of consumer culture, families increasingly bought food outside the home in its raw or semiprepared state and processed it in the kitchen. The colonial era housewife had little need to think of "economy" when she had grown all the vegetables, churned the butter, and slaughtered the hog herself. She could be clever about how she managed her resources, but they seldom had a cash equivalent in her experience. In the antebellum era, in contrast, middle-class husbands gave their wives budgets with which to feed the family and impress guests. This brought the concept of economy in its financial sense into woman's sphere of work.

As food became a consumer good, private fine dining, in contrast to family meals or public feasting, was an important part of middle-class life. Housewives now entertained with elegant meals, a new phenomenon that required guidance. Style began to matter just as much as substance.[11]

Mary Randolph capitalized on both trends—toward economy and in pursuit of style—when she published what can be considered the first regional, as well as the first American cookbook, *The Virginia Housewife*, in 1824.[12] The book's subtitle "Methodical Cook," and its opening epigraph, "Method Is the Soul of Management," spoke to the middle-class woman manager of a household that consumed market goods. When she wrote the book, Randolph was locally renowned as the mistress of the Queen, a popular boarding house in Richmond. By identifying herself with Virginia, where she had grown up the child of a wealthy plantation owner, Randolph drew on common associations of the South with lavish hospitality, made possible through the use of enslaved labor. Those who aspired to elite lifestyles would have been attracted by Randolph's instructions for managing staff and her many rules for proper culinary performance.

Although she associated her book with a single southern state, Randolph in fact included recipes of many regions and nations, such as polenta and ropa vieja. These inclusions reveal that American cuisine was never so xenophobic or bland as its critics often suggest. Alongside directions for preparing this multicultural cuisine, Randolph assured her readers that careful management was "an art that may be acquired by every woman of good sense and tolerable memory." For the reader ready to embark on this business, Randolph had choice recipes for cologne and dish soap as well as pies and soup, attentive to the total household, not just the dining room.

Randolph's book both echoed the preexisting models of cookbooks published in her time and participated in establishing culinary norms for the elite and those who strove to entertain in the finest manner. While there were other more countercultural cookbooks in the antebellum era, such as temperance cookbooks and a few books that advocated a vegetarian diet, the majority remained true to alcohol-consuming and carnivorous American foodways.[13] The cookbooks of early nineteenth-century America offered much practical advice but very little diversity in style of presentation and scant paragraphs of commentary on the culture that they served. With the end of the Civil War, however, came a transformation in cookbook styles.

In the mid-nineteenth century, innovations in printing and commercial advertising, as well as the transportation of goods—books among them—expanded the American reading audience. Most notably, the mechanization of typesetting speeded up production and thus made it easier to publish more books. The introduction of wood pulp paper in the 1850s also brought down the costs of production. Railroad networks brought these cheaper books to readers outside the Northeastern cultural centers. More people could both find and afford books.

Postwar industrialization brought rising incomes while the introduction of public schools and universities brought rising literacy rates. Together these trends produced a larger cohort of readers and book buyers, a group largely found in the middle class. The growth of a market for ever-increasing categories, types, and styles of household goods also helped create a demand for manuals and magazines that could help middle-class women and their servants manage the new abundance.

Nineteenth-century readers seem to have appreciated books that helped them navigate the daily business of life. Etiquette guides and books of house plans joined with the popular new monthly journals and magazines to keep readers up to date with contemporary fashions and values. While there are no collected sales figures for cookbooks in the nineteenth century, the trade journal *Publishers Weekly* appears to have listed cookbooks as "domestic economy" texts, a category that showed a marked expansion at the beginning of the twentieth century.[14]

The Grolier Club of New York, a society of self-described bibliophiles, included *Mrs. Lincoln's Boston Cookbook* on its list of "100 influential American books printed before 1900."[15] It was the only cookbook on the list. These books clearly spoke to the reading class, those middle-class Americans involved in a wide range of self-improvement projects extending from intellectual enrichment to modern housing design. Servants, who tended to have low levels of literacy and little leisure, did not often read cookbooks. Instead, the books served as guides for women of the employer class in directing kitchen staff but also in establishing their own membership in a socioeconomic cohort.[16]

Many domestic commodities tied middle-class women to the world of commerce. Cookbooks gave women another way to connect the private and public sphere by showcasing food fashions from around the country and offering advice for perfect meals and management.[17] For middle-class women, culinary work was descriptive and imperative rather than hands-on. Most of the owners and readers of cookbooks did not regularly cook whole meals for their families. Literate and with access to disposable income, the cookbook purchaser was most frequently a woman of the urban or small town middle class, a person unlikely to be found stirring pots or stoking fires to feed her family. She might enter the kitchen on the cook's night out, or to prepare special treats for family occasions, but she was usually only responsible for choosing her family's menu, not for making her choices edible.[18]

When she read cookbooks, then, the middle-class housewife did so as a reader, rather than as a worker. She may have taken inspiration from what she read to request new dishes from her hired cook, but she would also have

read for interest and to keep current with the latest fashions in food. Introductions set a tone and helped the reader see herself as part of a particular
culture with assumptions and expectations in common with social peers.

At the turn of the century the American middle class became tastemak-
ers, never entirely displacing elites, but flexing economic muscle in a way
that made publishers and other producers of consumer goods pay attention.
Because they existed between classes, Americans who had some disposable
income but could not be truly careless with money had more cause to think
about distinction than either the very rich or the poor. Unable confidently
to assume propriety, the middle class was the perfect market for items such
as cookbooks that provided social guidance.[19]

Cookbooks identified and promoted particular foodways as belonging
to particular cultures. Readers could aspire to belong to these cultures or
reassure themselves that they were already adhering to the culinary practices of their chosen group. That this discourse largely ignored working-
class people does not mean that they had no distinct foodways, but only that
cookbooks as a genre primarily spoke for and to the middle class.[20]

Cookbooks also contributed to a new focus on American regional histories and identity in the late nineteenth century. Following the rupture of the
Civil War, many American writers turned new attention to regional cultures.
Mark Twain, Helen Orne Jewett, and Kate Chopin, among others, portrayed
local lives, often in times of transition, creating a rich body of literature that
celebrated the particularities of American culture. This era is also notable
for the emergence of the historical profession in America. Following the
lead of German scholars, American historians began to publish works based
on archival research into primary sources, rather than syntheses of secondary works. This semiscientific approach to history gave new importance to
local stories, those not yet found in chronicles of the ages.[21]

Historical writing was a manifestation of a growing interest in America
as a unique entity in the world's past, present, and future. Expanding across
the continent and, at the end of the nineteenth century, into the Caribbean
and Pacific, the American presence in the world seemed newly noteworthy.
Cookbook writers participated in this emergent genre, writing history while

also valorizing particular foodways. They included introductory essays to their books to place each set of recipes in a cultural context. Far beyond just making a case for why a particular book was worth buying, these essays often tried to explain American regional or national food cultures historically. The ubiquity of introductions can be a little puzzling if we think that cookbooks exist to show people how to cook, but seem less odd when we think about the place of cookbooks in the nineteenth-century home.

The authors of cookbooks after the Civil War wrote for and about a nation recovering from trauma. The authorial collectives who produced community cookbooks staked the nation's future on bolstering local networks within a broader cosmopolitan American culture. Authors of Southern-themed books, by contrast, offered reconnection to regionalism as a route to recovery, while cooking school teachers in the North asserted a progressive cuisine that included national and regional flavors, a knitting together of disparate parts without loss of local identities.[22]

Community Cookbooks

Community cookbooks offer a unique problem for the historian of American food writing because they include almost no commentary, yet they are so numerous and so national a phenomenon that they cannot be dismissed. By noting patterns of recipe inclusion over time and across place, it is possible, however, to discern a collective statement about American food culture specifically and social life more generally.[23]

Community cookbooks were works compiled by women of middle-sized towns or small cities, congregations, or clubs, generally for a charitable purpose such as repairs to a local church building. While they bore titles that were intimately regional and seemed to promise access to local kitchens, such as *How We Cook in Los Angeles* (1894), these books were much more remarkable for their similarities than for their differences. It turned out that how "we" cooked in Los Angeles was a lot like how "we" cooked in Peoria. Many community cookbooks used recipes borrowed from popular published books, marking their contributors as connected to a national

print food culture rather than reliant on local traditions.[24] They followed
the model of the encyclopedic antebellum cookbooks in that they were organized around ingredients and dishes rather than meals. This pattern began to change in the early twentieth century, as the introduction of electric
toasters and coffeepots, as well as of lunch parties, caused authors to think
about meals other than dinner. The 1908 Sonoma County, California, community cookbook, *The Reappear*, for example, included not only the usual
sections for soup, meat, vegetables, pies, and puddings but also a chapter of
"breakfast and luncheon dishes."[25]

Because the audience for a community cookbook was the same as its
producers—books were sold locally, not distributed nationally—the books
served both as recipe exchange and as social performance. They represented the accumulated cooking knowledge and the tastes of the women of a
particular group. Community cookbooks also allowed women to appear in
public—in print form—achieving small-scale fame both collectively and in-
dividually. When an individual woman chose a recipe or recipes to share in
her community's cookbook she represented both her group and herself for
public consumption. She could choose to appear frugal, extravagant, world-
ly, clever, or like everyone else, thereby calibrating her conformity (or lack
thereof) to her peers.

Community cookbooks published during the late nineteenth century
and early twentieth century shared a palate, or a set of flavors, and a meth-
odology that allows us to see what a large number of white, middle-class
people considered their proper cuisine. A later collector of these recipes
referred to them usefully as "the fare of ordinary well-to-do families. They
include neither the quite fanciful dishes indulged in by the very rich nor the
rather Spartan fare of the very poor."[26] The books discussed here were chosen for geographic diversity and also for their accessibility; all these books
have been digitized, which offers me a rare opportunity as a scholar to share
my archival resources with the reader.[27]

Many community cookbooks included more than one recipe for the
same dish. These duplicates, however, are usually almost identical when differences in phrasings are taken into account. Looking closely at these repeti-

tions is a good way to understand what community cookbook authors wanted to say about American food. Among many repetitions, two particular recipes—lemon pie and Lobster Newburg—represent the broad common theme that American food is at once simple and traditional but also lavish and fashion-driven. This contradictory nature has frustrated critics who feel the need to identify one coherent American cuisine.

A significant number of American women contributing to community cookbooks in the late nineteenth century chose to be represented by recipes for lemon pie. Lemon pies consist of a pastry crust filled with a lemon curd. Some recipe writers included meringue toppings, others did not. Some followed the tradition of the Shaker Lemon Pie and also included thin slices of lemon, peel still on, candied and mixed into the curd. Far more than apple or any other pie, lemon appeared and reappeared across time and space.

Of the nine pie recipes included in *Par Excellence*, produced in 1888 by women in Chicago, three were lemon. The Albion, Michigan, *Collection of Tested Recipes* (1890), a typical community cookbook, offers fifteen recipes for pie, five of them for lemon pie and none for apple, that supposed classic of American cooking. Lemon pies remained popular into the twentieth century and across the country: of the fourteen pies included in the 1908 *Baptist Cookbook* from Albany, Georgia, two were lemon pies and one was an apple lemon custard. Of forty-three pies included in the 1914 *Hamilton Cook Book* from Hamilton, Ohio, six were lemon. Other pies that turned up frequently, though not as often as lemon, were mincemeat and raisin. Mincemeat was a pie with ancient roots in Anglo-American fare. Like mincemeat, raisin pies were very economical because the main ingredient could be stored for long periods. Raisin pie was also commonly known as funeral pie because even if someone died in the dead of winter, most cooks had raisins on hand to make a pie for the bereaved to share with visitors.

Because lemon pie is not an especially difficult or expensive dish to make, we can probably take its ubiquity as a sign that it was something people actually made and enjoyed during this period. That so many people wanted to be associated with it suggests that it signified belonging in middle-class

American culture. Farmers did not grow lemons in America with any commercial success until the late nineteenth century, when developments in both agriculture and transportation made it possible to get them to a wider market. Their flavor had certainly been known and valued, however, before they became more common. According to legend, Shaker Lemon Pie, an early nineteenth-century recipe, uses a whole lemon precisely because Shakers considered it immoral to waste any part of such an expensive fruit. To identify lemon pie with white mainstream American cooking was to identify the local culture with technological progress in terms of food transportation and with democratization of ingredients and flavors. Where lemons had once been associated with wealth, middle-class families could now afford them.

Lobster Newburg was another consistently popular recipe found in most community cookbooks of the turn of the century, but its presence tells a different story. However far away from the ocean a community was, its cookbook compilers were likely to include this recipe in their collection. Lobster Newburg mixes chopped lobster meat with butter, cream, sherry, and beaten egg yolks. It is often seasoned with cayenne and nutmeg, making it similar to recipes for deviled crab and deviled lobster that were also popular in community cookbooks. Judging by when recipes appeared where, the trend seems to have begun along the East Coast and spread inland, appearing more often farther from the shore after the end of the nineteenth century. Lobster's status rose in post-Civil War America for two reasons—technological developments and domestic tourism. As Eastern urban elites began summering in coastal Massachusetts and Maine, the taste of fresh lobster meat, previously a poor man's food, came to be associated with wealth. Simultaneously, for those who could not afford a seaside second home, canned lobster was becoming more widely available because of improvements in preserving and transportation.[28]

The 1905 *Youngstown Cook Book*, published by the ladies of the First Presbyterian Church of Youngstown Ohio, included Lobster Newburg made with a freshly boiled lobster, while the 1915 Benson, Nebraska, *Woman's Club Cook Book* did not specify whether the meat was fresh or canned.

Lobster Newburg at first glance is everything a lemon pie is not. It is rich and creamy where lemon pie is tart and crusty, pretentious where lemon pie is humble. Even its name seems to refer the reader or diner to another place, ill-defined in this case since Newburg was spelled various ways. In fact, Newburg did not refer to any actual place, but rather to a person. The dish was supposed to have been created for a valued customer at Delmonico's in New York, the city's and perhaps the nation's most famous restaurant. Lobster Newburg's legendary origins at Delmonico's marked the dish as urban cosmopolitan food.[29]

Because Delmonico's catered to New York's wealthy business class, Lobster Newburg could also be seen as the food of powerbrokers. To include Lobster Newburg in a cookbook produced by the women of a small town congregation in Ohio was in fact to do some of the same democratizing work the lemon pie also did. Not only did it require an ingredient that was hard to get, but it tasted of the kind of economic and cultural capital that might also seem distant from middle-class Midwestern households. The woman who contributed a Lobster Newburg recipe staked her claim to sophistication.

The late nineteenth century in America was a period of urbanization across the country that involved not just the construction of taller, more closely spaced structures, but also the widespread adoption of urban cultural markers. Opera houses flourished, general stores transformed from dusty aisles of everything useful into department stores gleaming with towers of all that was luxurious, and a vastly expanding print culture brought inland from the coasts descriptions of galas and feasts that could be re-created on a smaller scale in growing towns.[30]

Lobster Newburg reflected an urbanizing mass culture. It was also, and not coincidentally, a recipe often prepared in a chafing dish. From the late nineteenth century until about 1920, chafing dishes enjoyed tremendous popularity in middle-class American homes. Numerous books and book chapters celebrated chafing dishes and the gadgets themselves were some of the first electric home appliances. Between 1900 and 1940, the Library of Congress lists forty-nine books dedicated in part or full to chafing dish cookery. Although chafing dishes had originally appeared with oil lamp warmers, like present day buffet trays, they were quickly included in the trend to electrify domestic goods, along with coffeepots and toasters. Their popular use prefigured the fondue trend of the 1960s. Both middle-class women and men used chafing dishes to prepare meals for guests at the table, making a spectacle of cooking and taking it out of the hands of the kitchen staff.

Although Welsh rarebit (with many alternate spellings) was the archetypal chafing dish recipe, Lobster Newburg was also closely associated with the appliance. If fresh lobster was used, it would have been boiled by a servant ahead of time. If canned lobster was used, no servant was required. Supplied with pieces of lobster, cream, sherry, eggs, and a few seasonings, a hostess or host could whip everything up quite easily. A 1904 collection of recipes compiled by Cora Wood "from the experience of chafing dish enthusiasts" described the process for making "Lobster a la Newburg" in a few steps: "cut the lobster in small pieces, put in the blazer, and add the cream and sherry before lighting the alcohol lamp. When the mixture is heated add a large tablespoonful of corn-starch . . . add a pinch of cayenne pepper, and salt to taste. Cook until the sauce is sufficiently thickened, then add two egg yolks."[31]

Lobster Newburg was a not an everyday dish because of its ingredients and its associations with urban glamor. It represented emergent middle-class culture and marked this cuisine as one of worldliness and lavishness but also undergirded by the modern technology that made possible inland transportation of lobster, the print culture that made its reputation national, and, in many cases, the new technology of the chafing dish as well as a new perspective toward the formalities of traditional dining.

American cuisine, as represented by lemon pie and Lobster Newburg and compiled in community cookbooks, was marked by abundance and variety of ingredients. While assuming plenty, this cuisine also depended on the use of leftovers, including many iterations of timbales, croquettes, fritters, and meat or vegetable salads that required precooked materials. It was not a cuisine, however, of stews or of casseroles, which are two other ways to use leftovers.

Community cookbook cuisine was based in northern European, especially English foodways, but had dropped many elements of colonial and antebellum American food culture such as meat pies and sausage making. It also
included ingredients that were natively American—corn—and strictly of the
era—graham flour. It took up and dropped dishes, like the Lady Baltimore
Cake that became famous after the 1906 Owen Wister novel, *Lady Baltimore*,
and faded by the 1920s. Salads began to appear in the early twentieth century
and had earned their own chapters by the 1910s. With salads came dressings,
and as these appeared, dessert sauces began to vanish. The American cuisine
constructed in these books was not static, but moved in trends across regions
simultaneously, uniting regions even in the process of transformation.

The work that community cookbook writers did to construct a unified
American middle-class cuisine both paralleled and enabled the rise of the
consumer food industry that began to take shape after the Civil War. Attempting to create national markets for food products, corporations invested time
and money in cookbooks to introduce and facilitate use of their products. As
the next chapter discusses, these cookbooks had to offer something new as
well as reinforce a sense of common cuisine in order to appear simultaneously safe and exciting. The American foodways assumed by authors of community cookbooks offered corporate cookbook authors guidelines even as they
themselves constructed a norm and manufactured traditions. The cookbooks
produced in the South in the aftermath of the Civil War, in contrast, com-
bated the standardization of ingredients with a combined celebration of the
regional and the traditional. Where community cookbooks propagated food
fashions, Southern cookbooks advocated a timeless cuisine.

Southern Cookbooks

While community cookbooks typically did not live up to their apparent
promise to introduce readers to a distinct local food culture, the Southern
cookbook trend of the postwar years took regionalism as its organizing
theme. Although a few antebellum cookbooks had professed a Southern
identity, most notably Randolph's *The Virginia Housewife*, the emphasis had

not been especially common. After the war, however, Southern cooking became a significant genre. A brief sampling from the catalog of the Library of Congress reveals that between 1865 and 1885, the American public was offered *The Dixie Cookbook, Mrs. Porter's New Southern Cookery, Verstille's Southern Cookery, Dixie Cookery,* and the *Southern Household Companion,* among more than a dozen related titles. A similar search for cookbooks associated with New England revealed only one title, while a search for anything identified with the West or Midwest as regions turned up nothing.

Southern-themed cookbooks certainly captured the imagination of publishers. The long history of this genre since the Civil War suggests that readers responded to it enthusiastically. Southern cookbooks prefigured the merging of travel writing and recipe writing that became popular in the second half of the twentieth century; they took the reader on a journey.[32]

Southern cookbooks typically included scenarios of antebellum abundance and pleasure, focusing entirely on the foods served to the wealthy minority in their homes. The story and character of the South that authors of these books offered readers was part of the legend of the Lost Cause. This legend of southern honor framed the War as a contest between the noble South, steeped in tradition and honoring relationships between people, and the brutal North, focused on technological progress and financial gain. Southern-themed cookbooks painted an amiable picture of slavery in the region's history and established their own legend of the Lost Cuisine.[33]

Food writers defined Southern food culture as marked both by luxurious use of labor and by lavish generosity with materials. The image of the groaning board, the table laden with food to the point of collapse, was especially associated with the South. Although food writing about New England and about the Pennsylvania Dutch often emphasized plenty, writing about Southern food generally suggested excess in a way not applied to other regions. Cookbook authors presented recipes for foodstuffs or preparations such as canvasback duck or okra gumbo that were regionally specific, but Northern cookbooks also often included these foods, diluting the claim to Southern exceptionalism. Further complicating matters, Southern cookbooks included many dishes that were not strictly Southern, such as roast beef, Boston Brown Bread, Irish stew, and macaroni, which were overtly associated with other regions and nations. Martha McCulloch Williams noted that her book included recipes from France, Germany, and the Philippines. Essentially, however, she claimed that her sense of "how things ought to taste," came from her "Mammy's" cooking. Rhetoric, rather than foodstuffs, marked these books as Southern.[34]

Southern cookbook writers presented the region as a temporal space—the past—as well as geographical location. These writers may have expected their recipes to be used, but they also offered them up as history—mementos of a glorious time that had passed. To eat the food of the South, these books suggested, was to relive Southern history without the distasteful parts. This allowed readers who were nervous about modernity to escape into another time, which the authors promised was stress-free and unchanging.

Southern women cookbook writers contributed powerfully to this legend and, by writing history through this medium, established themselves as active voices in postwar cultural politics. Not yet voting and largely not active in the progressive movements in which many Western and Northern women were involved, they spoke through cookbooks, a genre obviously associated with conservative ideas of womanhood. Northern women also used cookbooks as a way to access cultural authority—as we will see, Fannie Farmer is an example of this—but they did so mostly outside the realm of national politics. Southern women's cookbooks directly supported the politics of Jim Crow by making white supremacy delicious to a national audience.

To establish their version of the South, writers had to construct alternate histories. In 1877, the year Reconstruction ended, Marion Cabell Tyree, in *Housekeeping in Old Virginia*, directly connected Southern culture to the Cavaliers of English history, claiming them as the cultural forebears of southern gentility. Virginia, she argued, "has always been famed for the style of her living. Taught by the example of . . . numerous adherents of King Charles, who brought hither in their exile the graces and luxuriousness of his brilliant court."[35] The Cavaliers were the more attractive to Tyree as they had been in conflict with Puritans, whose culture was strongly associated with the American North, where English Puritans first settled in the 1620s and 1630s.

Tyree's reference to the Cavaliers was common in Southern writing, a habit that stemmed from the antebellum popularity of the romantic writings of Sir Walter Scott. Antebellum Southern gentlemen adopted long ringlets, floppy hats, and swordplay that referred to this era as part of their creation of a cultural mystique of their own. Civil War songs like the *Southrons' Chaunt of Defiance* and *Ye Cavaliers of Dixie* also explicitly referenced this imaginary connection. Cookbooks gave women a chance to join in this rhetoric.[36]

Tyree made no mention of the American Civil War, instead referring to the American Revolution as the turning point in Southern history. During the Revolution, she explained, Southerners rejected the king but not the royal sense of style. As Southern women managed revolutionary wartime households, they created a new culture that adopted aspects of New England traditions in the process of preserving what was best about their own. Because of this experience, Southern cooking, according to Tyree, blended "the thrifty frugality of New England with the less rigid style of Carolina." Tyree seems to have used the revolution as a coded way to talk about the Civil War. By doing this she could identify her region with the winners while recognizing war as the defining event in her culture.[37]

Tyree's use of the modifier "old" to describe the cuisine in her book is a rhetorical trick that other Southern cookbook writers also used to separate their South from the South of the Civil War. By presenting Southern cooking as historical cooking, they made the past a specialty consumable in the present rather than part of a continuum of American culture.

Silas Weir Mitchell, who wrote the introduction to Celestine Eustis's 1904 *Cooking in Old Creole Days*, cleared away the clouds of innuendo and directly addressed the war in his first sentence as perhaps only a Northerner (he was from Philadelphia) could do: "A friend of mine, in the South, once said to me, that the surrender at Appomattox had brought about two serious calamities—an end to dueling and the disappearance of the colored cook. We may at least agree with him that the latter result is a matter deeply to be deplored by all who, like myself, remember the marvelous skill of the Southern cooks."[38]

Mitchell, a neurologist and novelist, was the inventor of the "rest cure" that inspired Charlotte Perkins Gilman's most famous story, "The Yellow Wallpaper." He was, in other words, a typical Progressive-Era Northern intellectual, yet the romance of the Lost Cause suffused his contribution to the cookbook. He wrote warmly of the African American cook of his childhood to whom he attributed magical powers. Her cooking was performed alone and involved "kindly incantations" over the cooking pot. Mitchell credited "colored" cooks with special skill with a gridiron pan and, now that times had changed, asked, "What other black art there was in the kitchen where the dark mammys reigned who now can say?"[39] By presenting the South's defeat, and by implication, the end of slavery, as a cultural calamity, Mitchell collaborated in the literary redemption of the South.

In the antebellum era, Southern cooking on the grand scale was very much a black art—expressive of a dynamic mixture of African, English, and North American culinary traditions and possibilities. And the black cook was a figure of unique power in the elite household precisely because she might employ "black" or dark arts against the master's family in that she could poison their food. She was a person who, although held in bondage, must also be treated with respect.

Other cookbook authors echoed this notion that African Americans' cooking skills were based in secrecy and magic. The preface to the 1885 *The Creole Cookery Book*, for example, referred to "the occult science of the gumbo" as the "hereditary lore of our negro mammies." These terms distanced African American capabilities from modernity and assisted in creating the legend that authentic Southern food was inaccessible in the postwar world.[40]

For Mitchell, the black art of Southern cuisine simply ended with the death of slavery. Oblivious or indifferent to the fact that black women continued to cook for their own families as well as for wages, Mitchell mourned the magic of the meal prepared in bondage, as if the secret ingredient had always been the awareness of radically unbalanced power, the taste of blood and sweat.

Celestine Eustis joined Mitchell in nostalgia for an imagined time when the enslaved were happy. She blended genres in her book by including several reputedly black Creole songs to be sung in the preparation of food. Her comment on the inclusion shows her active in re-creating Southern history. "Don't be surprised," she warned readers, "by some notes of music in the pepper of the sauce (*piment de la sauce*). When the negros work well, they are happy and proud of their work and express their happiness with singing, it is the eloquence of their feelings." Their songs, which she urged her readers to sing as they cooked, serve as kind of musical condiment.[41] Now that slavery had become obsolete, Eustis suggested that to re-create the authentic flavors of the South, a white cook must don a kind of culinary blackface, acting the happy Negro while cooking.

Minerva Fox's *Blue Grass Cookbook*, also published in 1904, did not rely on the white cook to become black; instead she illustrated her books with photographs of African American women identified as cooks, although none of the recipes were attributed to individuals.[42] In his introduction to Fox's book, her brother John took the reader on an imagined journey through space and time to the Kentucky of the prewar era. This was also potentially a journey across class as Fox slid the reader into the role of master.

"Out in the fields," he began, "the song and laughter of darkies make gay the air." The reader, addressed directly, was sleeping late when awakened by a "black boy in a snowy apron" who "in his kindly black paws" offered a silver goblet that seems, from Fox's description, to be a mint julep. "You" ate a huge, rich breakfast, rode around the plantation, returned for a wonderful dinner (lunch) and more juleps. The centerpiece of the dinner, which included ducks, venison, and turkey, was a Kentucky ham, cooked in champagne and brown sugar and "spiced deeply."[43]

Fox praised the hospitality of the South, where people intended to visit a home for a day and ended up staying twenty years. His South was one that sucked people into leisurely lives, a place where purposefulness and industry were beside the point. The "you" of his anecdote had no obligations elsewhere; the purpose of life was pleasure. The Kentucky of Fox's introduction was a place outside of time, steeped in tradition yet immune to history. Fox acknowledged that none of this would be possible without the labor of slavery, particularly "the turbaned mistress" of the kitchen, known as Aunt Dinah.[44]

"But for Aunt Dinah," Fox asked, "Would the master have had the heart for such hospitality? Would the guest have found it so hard to get away?" And then, most important, "Would Kentucky have sent the flower of her youth, forty thousand strong, into the confederacy[?]." Acknowledging Kentucky's peculiar history of supporting both sides in the Civil War, Fox also asked, "Would she have lifted the lid of her treasury to Lincoln, and in answer to his every call sent him a soldier practically without a bounty and without a draft? . . . I think not."[45] All Kentucky's strength exerted both to defend and to defeat slavery, were in Fox's history, the result of African American cooks' un-free labor.[46]

Williams, writing in 1913, also gave credit for the strength of Southern resistance during the war to food prepared by black cooks: "We might have been utterly crushed but for our proud and pampered stomachs. . . So here's to our Mammys—God bless them! God rest them!" To deepen the sense of Mammy as icon rather than person, Williams's description employed the language of monument and statuary: "My individual Mammy was in figure an oblate spheroid—she stood five feet, one inch high, weighed two hundred and fifty pounds, had a head so flat buckets sat on it as of right."[47] Seemingly built to serve, this Mammy belonged to a bygone era.

The historical past presented by each of these cookbook writers is one that is determinedly disconnected from the present. There are threads of connection but also a fundamental disjuncture that must not be explained by the writer. In her 1913, *Dishes and Beverages of the Old South*, Williams also provided readers an alternate version of Civil War history. She wrote, "It was through being the best fed people in the world that we of the South country were able to put up the best fight in history, and, after the ravages and ruin of the civil war, come again to our own."[48] Her easy elision of the causes of the war and the bitter fact of defeat helped to create a new version of American history in which the former Confederacy was eternally honored as morally pure though militarily outmatched. Williams's cookbook, like most of the Southern-identified cookbooks of the era, offered readers an invitation to travel not just through space, but also through time, to a reimagined "Old South" to which the war would never really come. In this Old South, furthermore, slavery did not actually exist because the food that was the soul of the nation was prepared with love, rather than because of bondage.

Abby Fisher, a former slave, who published her own cookbook in 1881, interestingly practiced a similar elision of the war by describing the Southern cuisine collected in her book as "old." By distancing herself from the material in this way, she might have sought to retain her dignity, although in fact her status as a former slave probably helped to sell the book. By identifying the cuisine as "Old Southern," she could make her readers less uncomfortable with the fact that their author had suffered—an unappetizing truth. Fisher's book included a list of names of respected white women who would vouch for the fact that she had really written the book and an open acknowledgment that she herself was illiterate and had dictated the book to a collaborator. If more authentication might be needed, the book contained a recipe for "plantation corn bread."[49] Fisher's decision not to include any account of her own enslavement or the day-to-day experience of working in a plantation kitchen acknowledged that there was only one story white Americans wanted to read about the South.

Among the most celebrated dishes in this cuisine of the Lost Cause were beaten biscuits, described as "the bread of the south."[50] Just as Lobster Newburg and lemon pie collectively speak the values of the community cookbook genre, this dish expresses the core themes of the Lost Meal writers.[51]

In 1894, cookbook author Jessup Whitehead insisted that for Virginia Beaten Biscuits to be correct or authentic, "There must be a maul, or Indian club 2 feet long, and a stout table for the beating." Not just any club would do, either: "The biscuit will not be right unless you have the maul made of hard maple, square shaped at the heavy end, but waving so as to make uneven hollows in the dough." Whitehead wrote for restaurant kitchens, where it might be possible to find this kind of equipment and workers of the physical stamina to use it. Martha McCulloch Williams's 1904 recipe, designated

"Old Style," called for the dough to be given "one hundred strokes with a rolling pin or mallet."[52]

Regionalist artist and writer (Maria) Howard Weeden celebrated the biscuits in a dialect poem, published in her 1899 *Bandana Ballads*. Weeden, a white Southerner, took on the voice of an African American cook to tell the story of "Beaten Biscuit." In this version the beating of the biscuits is epic: "Two hundred licks is what I gives / for home folks, never fewer, / An' if I'm 'spectin' company in, / I gives five hundred sure." The term "home folk" here refers to the employers' family, maintaining antebellum mythology that the enslaved identified slaveholders as their kin.[53] Biscuits beaten an extra three hundred times would have allowed the "home folks" to display their high social status for guests in much the same way single-purpose kitchen gadgets do today. In Weeden's imagination, the fictional cook would voluntarily add to her own work in order to increase the social status of the owning class, expressing her love for them through her physical labor. Even when the work was not actually doubled, as for company, the biscuit dough must have received an exhausting two hundred "licks" to be good enough for the master's table.

To get an idea of how long it might take to complete this work, we can turn to *Charleston Receipts*, which, although published in 1950, focuses on "time-honored dishes" and seems designed as a kind of quasi-usable museum of antebellum foodways. In this book Mrs. C. O. Sparkman gave a recipe for beaten biscuits that required fifteen minutes of kneading followed with the injunction to "beat with puttle or wooden mallet for 20 minutes." Altogether, then, beaten biscuit dough received more than half an hour of continuous hand processing in this recipe.[54]

Biscuits were not necessarily served only once a day, and indeed one of the prides of this cuisine of abundance was that no meal was ever accompanied by cold breads but by those just pulled from the oven—the hot breads for which the South was famous.

In 1948, African American food writer Freda De Knight recounted a story that illustrates what this standard meant for the cook. A cook De Knight interviewed "told me about a newly-rich matron who wanted to keep up with the Joneses and be different at the same time. So she insisted that a different type of biscuit be served at each meal." De Knight gave the cook credit for avoiding "overwork" by simply mixing up one batch of dough and altering it by cutting different shapes, cooking it in a variety of ways, and stuffing it with different fillings.[55]

Williams acknowledged that this kind of labor was not practical in the contemporary era. There were now, she noted, "sundry machines which do away with the beating," as well as several other shortcuts, which were "expedients for those who live in apartments" where the noise of beating might annoy the neighbors. However, these alternate methods did not produce the real thing. Those with room and distance from neighbors "should indulge in the luxury of a stone or marble slab [on which to beat the biscuits]—and live happily ever after, if they can but get cooks able and willing to make proper use of it." She did not suggest the reader do the work herself.[56] Emancipation and modernity, Williams implies, have robbed us of a unique culinary pleasure.

Southern regionalist cookbooks would be notable enough for their determinedly redemptionist messages, but they also stand out because they had no similar counterparts in the Northeast. While a few books celebrated New England food traditions, the best-known cookbooks published by Northerners during this era claimed national identity rather than regional specialty and were most notable for their advocacy of new ways of thinking about food, including level measurements and early adoption of the principles of nutritional science. Although both Southern and progressive cookbooks were new phenomena in the genre, Southern cookbooks claimed an antimodern stance, while progressive authors encouraged readers to learn new things about food and cooking.

The Progressive Cookbook

In the postwar period of the late nineteenth and early twentieth centuries, publishers continued to offer the reading public the kinds of large comprehensive cookbooks that had been popular before the war. These books did not focus on the cultural background of foods, but rather on providing a wide range of dishes within the common parameters of middle-class taste. In this uniformity they supported the national work of projecting American culture as a single entity on the world stage. [57] By presenting old favorite recipes in a new standardized format and including lessons from the new science of nutrition, they also joined in the spirit of progressivism that was applied to all aspects of human life during this era.[58] The most successful authors such as Fannie Farmer, Maria Parloa, and Marion Harland are still well-known names.

These progressive authors introduced a new paradigm to cookbooks by giving every recipe in a collection the same format so that readers would know what to expect. Typically listing ingredients first, this approach trained readers to assemble their materials before beginning work, a step that might actually waste time for the experienced cook with a good knowledge of her own larder but that would assist the first-time cook to gain confidence. In this way, progressive cookbooks bolstered a vision of American food as one loosely unified national cuisine because they elevated a set of nationally applicable standards over local practice. In 1897, a reviewer wrote that Farmer's book "so deals with and simplifies the rules of cookery that it must be much more a guide to the inexperienced." The reviewer compared Farmer's book to *The Cook Book by "Oscar" of the Waldorf* by Oscar Tschirky, famous chef of Delmonico's and the Waldorf Hotel. Tschirky's book "rains truffles and mushrooms and cream," and was more suited to hotel kitchens, while Farmer's was more practical for home cooks.[59]

Two of the most famous postwar cookbook authors, Farmer and Parloa, published their books as extensions of their work as teachers at the Boston Cooking School. Where the two women had used their work in cooking schools to establish new personae as experts and to set themselves up financially, their cookbooks brought fame and drew more fortune from a national audience.

The cooking-school goal, a progressive mission, was to train a large number of lower-middle-class women to prepare food that middle-class and elite families who employed them would recognize as correct. By establishing themselves as intermediaries between the classes, these famous teachers became agents of American cuisine.

As rural Americans moved into cities, vocational training programs offered those who found themselves in the working class the hope of a leg up in their competitive new surroundings. Parloa and Farmer were part of this vocational movement. The Women's Educational Association, a progressive group that advocated vocational training for working-class women (as well as expanded educational opportunities for upper-middle-class women) first opened the Boston Cooking School as part of their work.

Farmer and Parloa were populists as well as progressives because they wanted to make kitchen skills accessible to more women and thought that by providing tested rules they could give confidence to cooks of all social classes. While the cooking schools existed primarily to train working-class women, some middle-class women also took classes. Juliet Corson, who founded and directed the New York School of Cookery, in New York City, explained that she was "engaged . . . in the training of young women and girls in domestic economy, numbering among my pupils many ladies of our most prominent families."[60] The ladies of prominent families were of course not training to become household cooks.

Cooking school classes helped women of the employer class to develop their own sense of authority in the household, blending the progressive ideals for women's education with older notions of women's responsibilities to the home. Learning to cook could also help a middle-class wife get better results from her kitchen staff. For well-to-do women, cooking classes were probably also a diversion, part of the growing number of daytime activities outside the home emerging for women in cities.

The cooking school cookbooks reflected the progressive reform tradition of their era in that they valued transparency and efficiency in a world where mystery was often dangerous, taking the form, for example, of tainted meat, tubercular milk, or exploitative labor practices.[61] As Parloa explained in the introduction to her 1882 *First Principles of Household Management and Cookery*, the purpose of her work was to take uncertainty out of the kitchen for both kitchen staff and their supervisors.[62] Although she described her work this way, employers rather than cooks typically owned the books.

Later critics would charge that rooting out uncertainty was fatal to creativity. The famous food writer, M. F. K. Fisher, for example, wrote in 1954, "to be passed by quickly with a shudder of recognition, are cooking-school manuals . . . dangerously perfect, and if followed with the care their editors advise, would reduce all cooking to a standard of horrible monotony . . . avert your eyes from the baleful hygienic correctness of school manuals."[63] Parloa, however, "had seen so many failures and so much consequent mortification and dissatisfaction" in culinary work that she had been moved to concentrate attention on clear directions. When the dissatisfaction she mentioned was felt and expressed by employers it had real consequences. If a woman was to hold a position as a cook in a family well off enough to hire her she had to provide satisfaction reliably or risk being fired.

By publishing standardized measurements and step-by-step instructions for a wide range of dishes with roots in all American regional foodways, including some European dishes, these collections established in print a unified cuisine with open access to all readers. Equally essential were the actual standardized measuring cups and spoons, objects first popularized at the Boston Cooking School. Beginning in the 1870s, families could purchase these markers of efficiency.[64] The standardization of measurement echoed the standardization of preparation implicit in Parloa's and Farmer's books, which, by being wide-ranging in their selections, suggested that any dish was appropriate anywhere.

Writers in the progressive style were not always neutral on the subject of American foodways. Despite providing recipes for all the standard fare of the middle class, for example, Parloa criticized the "pies and heavy puddings of which so many people are fond." As an alternative, although not a replacement, she offered an extensive selection of what were broadly termed "desserts" in most cookbooks of the era, including a variety of mostly flourless sweets such as whips, and charlottes as well as ices and jellies. These were lighter in texture than the old favorite cakes, pies, and steamed puddings, and therefore, according to nutritional wisdom of the time, considered more healthful.

Sarah Tyson Rorer, well known as owner of the Philadelphia Cooking School and author of many cookbooks, also both criticized and enabled mainstream American foodways. Rorer favored a diet free from pork and leafy with greens. She excoriated Americans for eating their beef too rare. She declared many popular favorites—meat hash, buckwheat cakes, fried chicken, commercial sugar—abominations, but nonetheless provided clear instructions for how to serve many of the things she objected to so strongly, including bacon and pies.

It was more likely her particular approach to recipes than the vitriol of her commentary that won Rorer so many loyal readers. As a practiced teacher, she knew how to write good instructions, and as a savvy business-woman, she knew better than to keep people from the foods they loved. Rorer compared Americans unfavorably to the Japanese, who she said were much stronger than her countrymen while living on a virtually vegetarian diet, but she did not include any recipes including tofu or seaweed, going no farther than to include a little soy sauce in a few dishes.[65]

Rorer also not only provided recipes for sweets, she even enticed the readers with artfully arranged photographs of rolled wafers, macaroons, and filled sponge cake. This was wise on her part because the desserts she condemned rhetorically were becoming very fashionable. Desserts became popular as elements of women's cuisine in the late nineteenth century, appearing in venues such as tearooms and department store restaurants wherever middle-class and elite women participated in public culture. An overlooked factor of this cuisine was that the emphasis on lightness was especially tailored to the physiological realities of middle-class women at the turn of the century. Tightly corseted from bosom to hips but also newly active in the public spheres of recreation, entertainment, and commerce, the average "lady" was probably unable to comfortably digest much more than a fruit flavored bowl of whipped cream or a pineapple ice. If healthful meant conducive to mobility, then there was a certain logic to Rorer's crusade against the heavier sweets.

Although Farmer also had radically new things to say about food, she, like Rorer, simultaneously remained true to the culinary traditions of the middle class. Her 1896 *Boston Cooking-School Cook Book* represents both new science and old foodways, blended in a style that was very appealing to the turn-of-the-century housewife: three thousand copies of the book's first printing quickly sold out. Farmer's tone was unsentimental but not dour—she was enthusiastic about the new knowledge and eager to offer guidance in how to understand food rather than hand out proscriptions against eating certain things in certain ways.[66]

Farmer began with a synopsis of the latest understanding of human nutrition, becoming very technical very fast. Beginning with the simple enough statement that "food is anything which nourishes the body," she continued didactically, "Thirteen elements enter into the composition of the body: oxygen, 62 1/2%; carbon, 21 1/2%; hydrogen, 10%; nitrogen, 3%; calcium, phosphorus, potassium, sulphur, chlorine, sodium, magnesium, iron, and fluorine the remaining 3%."[67] Although Farmer did not have the terms calorie or vitamin at her disposal, she was attempting to explain the relationship between food and energy in the human body, a topic that she calculated would make her book attractive to a wide audience. Having established her fame as a cooking-school teacher, Farmer might be presumed to know what interested the women who would buy her book. The scientific tone certainly did not harm sales of this, one of America's most successful cookbooks.[68]

Although the *Boston Cooking-School Cook Book* chapters followed the usual division into elements of a late nineteenth-century American middle-class dinner—soup, meat, bread, dessert—Farmer also drew attention to the physical elements of food, introducing the book with sections on starches, oils, and what were termed "vegetable salts," before they were more widely known as vitamins. To introduce a cookbook with this scientific jargon was to portray everyday cooking as an act in step with modernity and progress, not tied to local folkways. While readers may or may not have read this section thoroughly, it gave the larger work a tone that was new in food writing. By privileging the intellect and systems over family lore and traditions, Farmer presented favorite American dishes such as corn bread and baked beans in the form of equations.[69]

This new standardized approach to daily life was in keeping with the rail-
way timetables and financial statements that marked the era. The *Wall Street
Journal*, for example, began publication in 1884 as the *Customers Afternoon
Letter*, which was a list of averages of prices, and the *New York Times* and
Harper's Weekly soon followed with financial columns. Just like the readers
of these columns, who were learning to interpret the jargon of the market,
Farmer's readers might not understand her discussion of phosphates, but
they could take heart that the material act of cooking could be mastered. It
was simply a matter of understanding elements, not of innate talent.[70]

The popularity of these progressive cookbooks stemmed from their ability to bridge cultures. Should it turn out, for example, that a Swedish immigrant cook's employers in Minneapolis had recently migrated from Virginia,
the spoon breads and baked hams they requested were demystified for her
by Farmer, Parloa, Corson, and Rorer. If she moved on to work for another
local family who had moved west from Rhode Island, she need only turn a
few pages to find recipes that would help her make the Sally Lunn or codfish
balls her new employers might request.

Cooking School director, teacher, and cookbook writer Corson intentionally sought out recipes from regions she did not know well to add to
her repertoire and to share with readers. She composed her 1886 *Miss Corson's Practical American Cookery and Household Management* in response
to criticism by John Eaton, U.S. commissioner of education, that her cooking school focused too much on French food. Denying charges of snobbery
on her own part, she explained that French cooking was what customers
wanted to learn. She herself was confident that there was no "lack of variety
or excellence in American cookery."[71] In an effort to support her claim, she
sought the help of Eaton to create a thoroughly American cookbook. She
asked him to use his position to circulate a survey about regional dishes nationally.

Corson planned particularly "to adapt some of my special methods to
the Southern and Western portions of the country." She noted that national
culture was transforming, "In consequence of marked social changes at-
tendant on the Civil War." She may particularly have been thinking about
changed relationships between cooks and employers in the post-emancipa-

tion south. Corson proposed a new version of regional foodways in which she would "combine rudimentary economical principles with the culinary excellence of local dishes." Requesting help in learning the "specialties of the local market supply, and of such dishes as hold popular favor," she was overtly constructing a national compendium that she promised would serve families but was also for "the guidance of instructors in cooking in different parts of the country." Understanding the new realities of the mobile nation, one in which old patterns of servitude were dissolving, Corson could see the use of a national cookbook.[72]

Less intent on notions of nutrition or standardized recipes than Farmer was, Corson nonetheless promised readers food that was both "wholesome and palatable." Wholesome, healthful, and nourishing were all terms used before the establishment of nutritional science to denote food that was good for, or at least not harmful to the human body.[73]

Corson's recipes were "above all to be clear and precise; to give such simple methods that a person of the most ordinary intelligence can follow them."[74] The result was a rich collection of recipes ranging from the urban sophistication of roast ducklings with orange sauce to the rural necessities of skinning rabbits. In her commentary, Corson devoted most of her attention to cleanliness, setting sanitary standards for kitchen, pantry, and foodstuffs. This representation of cooking as associated with physical danger paralleled the emerging interest in bacteriology that was foundational to the fields of nutrition and food science.

By integrating newly considered information about sanitation and nutrition into middle-class food culture, the postwar versions of the encyclopedic cookbooks also implicitly argued for a unified American cuisine by foregrounding the physiological function of food. Nutritional and sanitary requirements, after all, were the same wherever humans ate. Writing about food as fuel for the first time seemed to remove it from the realm of culture and identity and to place it in the assumed-to-be neutral world of science. While this can seem off-putting to present day readers, it had a democratizing effect then in that it seemed to open the secrets of good food to everyone, not just those who could afford the most expensive ingredients and an imported cook.

As much as the progressive authors stressed the science of nutrition, however, they seldom carried the conceit past their introductions, returning to contemporary favorite American foods prepared in the usual way with butter, milk, white flour, sugar, and plenty of salt. There were no futurist dishes, no nutrient tablets, only well-known cosmopolitan favorites such as saddle of venison, stuffed artichokes, Turkish pilaf, and chocolate bread pudding. One rare scientific-sounding dish—hygienic soup—was made with white stock, milk, butter, and oats, all familiar foodstuffs often used in the sickroom.[75]

In 1882, Parloa offered a list of the staples no American kitchen should be without, a catalog that reveals a diverse range of flavors. Alongside her basic starches, which included both barley and vermicelli, and common stimulants—coffee and tea—Parloa listed items primarily used to enhance enjoyment of food: "chocolate . . . molasses, vinegar, mustard, pepper, salt, capers, canned tomato . . . condiments [such] as curry powder . . . Halford sauce, essence of anchovies and mushroom ketchup."[76] Although Parloa seems to have advocated moderation in flavorings, noting of curry powder, that "a small bottle will last for years," she also assumed an American palate that made use of piquant and earthy flavors as well as sweet, salty, and sour.[77]

The large recipe collections reassured families adrift in an era of urbanization and high rates of mobility that they could find all desirable foods in one volume. These foods would remind migrants of home but also help new arrivals fit in socially. Parloa's recommended flavor library might even be understood as a set of status markers. The taste of curry powder, for instance, could reassure a dinner guest that she was visiting the correct kind of household for preserving and enhancing her own status.

* * *

The cookbook trends of the post-Civil War period suggested several ways to understand American foodways. Community cookbooks downplayed regional difference in an effort to cultivate a sense of what was valuable in

American cooking and promote the idea of unified cuisine in which variety was both recognized and valorized. Although community cookbooks achieved a certain level of homogenization as the same recipes appeared again and again, the repertoire remained notably broad. Southern cookbooks, on the other hand, celebrated regional foodways as uniquely authentic and valuable, not just as edible heirlooms, but as a way to keep a vanquished culture vibrant. They implicitly argued for the importance of the regional in America's cooking future while also erasing the legacy of African Americans in national foodways. By positing an inextricable link between slavery and the deliciousness of Southern food, Southern-themed cookbook writers rejected African Americans as legitimate participants in contemporary American cuisine.

Community cookbooks still exist, although national companies now frequently assist communities in putting together their recipe collections, which limits what regional quirkiness ever inhered in the genre. As in the past, fashionable foods are sure to recur in these volumes, which speak of national food culture much more convincingly than of neighborhood specialties.[78]

Southern redemptionist writing has long outlived the political and social movement to which it was aligned. A twenty-first-century example of the persistence of this style comes from *The Blue Willow Inn Bible of Southern Cooking*, published in 2005: "Guests at the Blue Willow Inn are encouraged to absorb and enjoy the slower pace of the Old South. A visit . . . should be an experience in both dining and relaxing. From being welcomed by greeters attired in antebellum dress to sipping lemonade on the front porch, guests are treated to genuine hospitality of a bygone era."[79] Here the antebellum South is offered as an experience of ease and pleasure with a stubborn failure to recognize that both aspects of pre-Civil War life were available only to wealthy whites and were the fruits of unfree labor. In this vision, authentic regional cooking is accessible only if the diner is willing to engage in a little historical reenactment.

The encyclopedic works that built on antebellum traditions seem to have faded in importance in recent years. The need to collect all possible options in one volume probably seems much less important in the age of recipe web-sites, food blogs, and digitized cookbooks. So while the Internet itself might seem a new version of the nineteenth-century compendium, it largely lacks the editorial choices that made books like Corson's and Farmer's so compel-ling to readers as guides to proper middle-class foodways.

CHAPTER 2

AN APPETITE FOR INNOVATION

COOKBOOKS BEFORE THE SECOND WORLD WAR

IN 1933, THE ANONYMOUS author of *The Frigidaire Key to Meal Planning* paused in the middle of the text to ask readers "Isn't this fascinating?" Readers were invited to think about food and cooking as noteworthy.[1] Meal planning with the new Frigidaire refrigerator was more than just useful; it was *fascinating*. Progressive cookbook writers like Fannie Farmer had helped to normalize the language of innovation as they introduced the new science of nutrition along with the use of level measurements. Farmer and her cohort helped shift culinary authority out of the home and into more professional spaces. Despite these new approaches, however, the progressives did not introduce new foodstuffs or even new processes. Neither knowledge of nutrition nor level measurement changed the basic principles or ingredients of any of the recipes Farmer and other cooking school authors included in their books.

Frigidaire's authors, in contrast, were part of a new generation of cookbook writers who gave primary importance to the element of novelty in culinary life. Farmer and her peers had continued to offer American readers their traditional favorites—Boston baked beans, chicken fricassee, corn meal Johnny cakes—as well as nationally fashionable dishes such as Welsh rarebit—a delight of the chafing dish crowd. At the turn of the century, corporate cookbooks, of which the Frigidaire guide was one, and slimming cookbooks, the other major new genre of the era, displaced popular taste as the guiding force in domestic cooking. Corporate cookbooks located authority about taste in the corporate kitchen, while slimming cookbooks emphasized the role of the expert guide in limiting one's intake. The implication that a reader would be unable to lose weight of her own accord and following her own methods has remained essential to the still thriving market in diet books.

Adaptations and substitutions for old recipes helped anchor both these corporate and slimming cookbooks to accepted cuisine, but their urgent background messages, on the one hand encouraging conspicuous consumption and on the other severely limiting consumption, depended on the idea that Americans were open to innovation in their foodways.

Corporate cookbooks were materials published by domestic goods companies to help familiarize customers with new products such as soups and self-regulating ovens. They were part of a larger shift in advertising from the panacea approach, in which advertisements claimed that a product cured all ills, to the single use model. This new model allowed corporations to expand their stable of products significantly. Now each "ill" required its own dedicated cure. Slimming cookbooks promised to cure the problem of weight by changing both how much and what kinds of food readers ate. Both kinds of cookbooks were features of an age of economic prosperity; a reader needed disposable income to buy packaged foods and household appliances, while only those who had more than they needed to eat had to worry about eating too much. Corporate cookbooks and slimming guides also appealed to readers by using language that evoked modernity and progress, another clue that their intended audience was the middle class. They contradicted each other in their assumptions about women's roles, however. Corporate cookbooks tended to promote women's freedom from traditional domestic expectations, while slimming cookbooks tied them to restrictive ideals of physical beauty and belittled their powers of self-control.

Both kinds of cookbooks used scientific language to validate their messages but also relied on familiar notions of what food was and what role it played in culture to make readers comfortable with new products or new diets. Both also crucially promised a scientifically improved "you," a notion that was new to the genre and part of the broader development of a consumer culture and of the philosophy of positive thinking.[2] Corporate cookbooks tended to make the "you" plural, however, appealing to women as family cooks, while slimming books spoke exclusively to the individual.

The concepts of substitution and calculation, which have become common in contemporary food discourse ("meal replacement" shakes and bars, for example) were important in corporate and slimming cookbooks. First World War era rationing cookbooks helped normalize these two ideas and to give them national importance. Mary Green, for example, introduced her 1917 guide *Better Meals for Less Money*, with the admonition that "With the steadily increasing cost of all staple foods the need of intelligent buying, cooking, and serving is greater than ever before."[3] Green's book was the first cookbook to appear on the *Publishers Weekly* nonfiction bestseller list, suggesting that there was a significant audience for her message that cooking is both resource management and an activity with ethical implications.[4]

Even before America entered the war in 1917, the global situation had caused inflation in food prices. Readers need not fear too grim fare, however, as Green argued that "Good meals depend not so much on expensive material as upon care and good use of ordinary material."[5] The trick was in knowing enough about both your materials and your family's expectations to be able to make satisfying substitutes. Like wartime guides, corporate and slimming cookbooks also emphasized new methods in the treatment of culinary materials. Nineteenth-century cookbooks, in contrast, had largely focused on cataloguing several of the best methods of preparing well-known dishes.

Green's recipe collection included many of the past century's most popular dishes: both roast beef and the beef croquettes that made the most of the roast's remains. And despite the high price of sugar, there were hot desserts, cold desserts, cakes and cookies, icings and fillings, frozen desserts,

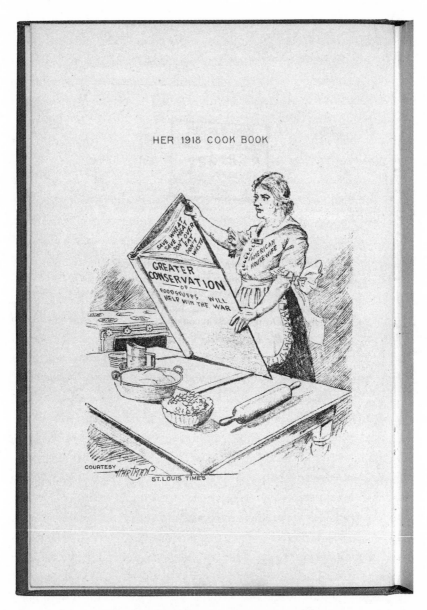

FIGURE 1. "Her Cookbook, 1918." Saint Louis County Women's Committee of the Council of National Defense, Missouri Division, *Win the War Cook Book* (St. Louis, 1918), 6.

sauces for desserts, pastries, and candies. Corporate and slimming cookbooks shared this practice of revising the familiar, though largely without the sugar.[6]

War rationing cookbooks brought women's groups into contact with state and national government agencies as they requested advice for their recipes and submitted their texts for endorsement by these same agencies. These requests helped to shift culinary authority from the home to the state, which although not changing much in the practice of daily cooking, altered the conceptual landscape of American foodways.[7]

Authors of wartime cookbooks strove for simplicity and clarity, using succinct messages and bold graphics that were reminiscent of advertising. The 1918 book, *Foods That Will Win the War and How to Cook Them* opened with two pages of guidelines in the form of public service posters. One read,

> FOOD:
> 1. Buy it with thought.
> 2. Cook it with care.
> 3. Serve just enough.
> 4. Save what will keep.
> 5. Eat what would spoil.
> 6. Home-grown is best. Don't waste it.[8]

The authors (Goudiss and Goudiss) used advertising techniques to encourage self-control in consumer behavior, even guiding readers away from the capitalist economy into self-sufficient production.

Borrowing from both the progressive cookbook writers and corporate cookbooks, *Foods That Will Win the War* included a chart of "the comparative composition of meat and meat substitutes" that enabled readers to compare many different protein sources to beef. The chart posited a rational consumer who could make choices based on analysis of value and who would willingly set aside tradition and preference for a greater good. In this sense, wartime cookbooks challenged their readers to a higher standard of civic behavior while prewar cookbooks had only offered entrée into particular class cultures. They also reinforced the notion of superior and inferior products and choices that would bolster both corporate cookbooks and slimming guides.

By using the language of substitution, wartime cookbooks reinforced a standard foodways, one in which beef, for example, was the normal protein. Salmon or lentils could do the same work for the body, but they could not automatically fulfill diners' expectations of the normal meal. The twin themes of substitution and innovation were not maintained in compendious cookbooks published after the war, but they did dominate the rhetoric of corporate cookbooks and also of the slimming cookbooks that were newly popular in the 1920s.

Corporate Cookbooks

The years between the First World War and the Great Depression were prosperous years in which industrial production of domestic goods increased markedly. Domestic goods corporations published cookbooks as a unique form of advertising and (once technology made this possible) printed them in bright colors. Technology to produce multicolored illustrations cheaply improved through the nineteenth century until, by the time the war began, Americans expected magazines to be full of brightly colored illustrations and advertisements, designed to catch the attention even of those who did not read.[9] The corporate cookbooks that included bright pictures and interesting graphics thus helped to domesticate advertising, bringing the ad, in the form of a cookbook, into the home as a permanent resident on the kitchen bookshelf.

Corporate cookbooks existed to sell products rather than to record or celebrate the foodways of a culture. In order to sell foods and appliances, however, corporations had to contextualize those products in ways that made them both comfortable and exciting. Thus they offer us an interesting record of American culinary assumptions and expectations—at least as these were interpreted by cookbook authors. The corporate cookbooks used as examples in this chapter are chosen from those that introduced popular products—refrigerators and oranges—and that also express the two themes of the genre—familiarity and exoticism—side by side.

Corporate cookbooks did the work of introducing new foods and appliances by engaging assumptions about American cooking and playing with these assumptions in ways that could inspire new purchases. As writers for the advertising agency H. E. Lesan reminded a potential client, the Borden Company, purveyors of milk, it was not enough to have a good product everyone recognized, a company needed to become associated with "unique greatness" in public opinion.[10] That motivation, shared by so many producers of domestic goods, helped to construct a national cuisine.

Although many of the new domestic goods on the market in the 1920s seemingly made household tasks easier to perform, the burden of labor was shifting from hired help to housewife. For working-class women this shift represented expansion of wage-earning opportunities and the chance for advancement beyond domestic work; for middle-class women, it was a decline in status.[11]

Along with this shift in labor practices in the home came the introduction of a distinct cuisine. At the very moment middle-class women began performing more of the labor of the kitchen, inventors and engineers and factories increased the diversity of new products for that space.[12] Middle-class women were less likely than their mothers had been to send a cook or servant to do the marketing. As servants became scarce, the woman of the house had to do her own shopping. Now that producers were dealing directly with the consumer, they could speak to her in an idiom that would not have been effective in addressing servants. Servants had little stake in the individual economy or culture of the house for which they worked. A middle-class woman charged with preparing family meals and maintaining status through social events was a more attractive target for advertising and a compelling subject for the study of marketing professionals.[13]

Although corporate cookbooks are still produced in large numbers today, the genre and its conventions were established in the period between the 1890s and 1930s. During this period, they were new and notable in the larger market for cookbooks, and also had the strongest power to influence the construction of cuisine. By the end of the Second World War, consumerism was so fully entrenched in American society that corporate cookbooks no longer had novelty. But because refrigerators were new in the 1920s and 1930s, the only guidance for how to use them was material produced by the same companies that made the appliances themselves. In 1934, for example, the Estate Stove Company offered a "built in recipe card file, with complete set of recipes," to go with its oven and stovetop combination. The existence of the recipes suggested that there were foodways specific to the appliance.[14]

Estate further promoted the idea of exclusivity to its consumers when it provided "invitations" deeming them "eligible to membership in a select organization—The Estate Cookery Club." Members received monthly bulletins, edited by a professional home economist, Ada Bessie Swan. To receive the free bulletins, Estate Stove Company range owners had only to mail in a card, thus providing the company a future opportunity to advertise directly to families who had already bought one Estate product.

While it is safe to assume that most owners of ranges and refrigerators taught themselves how the particular appliance could best serve their own needs, the only written evidence of a refrigerator cuisine in these early years—the 1920s and 1930s—existed in corporate cookbooks. Over time, community cookbooks and other kinds of food writing acknowledged the role of refrigeration in cooking by including recipes that incorporated refrigeration as a step in preparation.

Icebox cakes are a good example of this new kind of cooking. You make an icebox cake by lining up layers of wafers or thinly sliced cake with whipped cream or ice cream between them, then leaving this assembly in the freezer for several hours until the ingredients meld. An early forerunner of the ice cream cake, they only became possible with the first generation of iceboxes and gained in popularity with the introduction of electric refrigerators. The widely popular *Settlement Cook Book*, for example, had no recipes for icebox cake in its first edition in 1903, but five in its 1920 edition.[15] With household refrigeration, icebox cakes quickly became standard middle-class fare.

When refrigerators were a novelty, writing about how to use them was a way to encourage people to buy them. This kind of writing was not quite the same as advertising because its audience had already purchased the product. A book like the *Frigidaire Key to Meal Planning* ideally helped consumers use their purchase, become dependent on it, and continue to purchase refrigerators in the future. By serving refrigerator cuisine for guests, hosts might also help to create new consumers.

In-house researchers produced corporate cookbooks, often without attribution. These researchers were professionals, usually women, who had trained in the fields organized under the discipline of home economics. They might have degrees in food science or dietetics, equipment testing, or institutional management. Employers hired women trained in home economics because it added value to products to be able to say that they were professionally tested.[16]

Beginning in the 1920s, nonacademic entities like magazines and corporations established test kitchens to find out how products and appliances would perform for daily use. Workers in a test kitchen at a company like Libby, McNeil & Libby, which produced canned foods such as boneless chicken, veal loaf, dried beef, and potted ham, opened the cans and experimented with what could be made from those contents. Writers in the company's publicity department then worked with the testers to produce a collection of recipes that could be used in the kinds of homes that purchased the products. One Libby's cookbook, for example, suggested fricadillen: fried meatballs, made with bread crumbs, milk, and Libby's luncheon loaf.[17]

Recipes had to suit the class and culture of likely consumers, but they also had to appeal to a personal sense of adventure. *Foods from Sunny Lands*, published by the Hills Brothers' Company in 1925, contained an appealing example of this kind of writing. In the cookbook, Hills Brothers depicted its products—dates, shredded coconut, dried apricots—in a romanticized desert setting complete with tents, camels, and figures who might have stepped out of a Rudolf Valentino movie.[18]

Although they were actually ancient as foodstuffs, Hills Brothers' Diamond brand dried fruits and nuts were new products in that they were made newly abundant and affordable by technological developments in preservation—cold storage—and transportation—trucking and railways. Dates, in particular, had recently been introduced as a cash crop in California.[19]

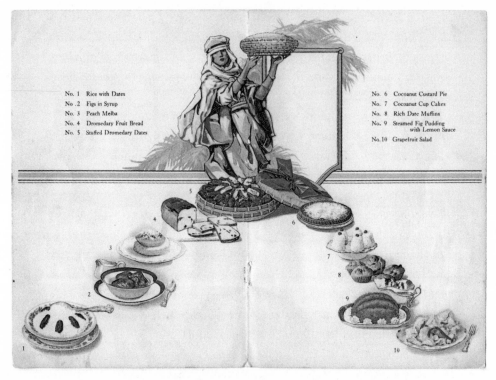

No. 1   Rice with Dates
No. 2   Figs in Syrup
No. 3   Peach Melba
No. 4   Dromedary Fruit Bread
No. 5   Stuffed Dromedary Dates

No. 6   Cocoanut Custard Pie
No. 7   Cocoanut Cup Cakes
No. 8   Rich Date Muffins
No. 9   Steamed Fig Pudding
              with Lemon Sauce
No. 10 Grapefruit Salad

FIGURE 2. *Foods from Sunny Lands*, Dromedary brand cookbook
pamphlet, Hills Brothers Company, 1925. Collection of the author.

Selling all the dried fruits and nuts together as central elements in a fantasy cuisine elevated them from the low status of staple foods to the exalted plane of luxury goods even though the very affordability that fueled the advertising was the result of their being grown in California, not in the depicted North African deserts. As recipes for "rich date muffins" and "dromedary ambrosia" (featuring "dromedary" dates) suggest, the recipes themselves were not departures from contemporary American foodways, enabling the reader to domesticate that which was perceived as exotic and simultaneously exoticize the domestic.

The spirit of experimentation was one of the central elements in corporate cuisine. Corporate cookbooks routinely privileged new processes rather than new flavors. They portrayed the history of American food as a saga of improvement over time made through intentional action rather than happy accident. Food processing companies and appliance manufacturers sold unfamiliar foodstuffs and technologies with directions to incorporate them into traditional dishes, blending past and future. The California Fruit Growers Exchange, for example, provided a recipe for two middle-class standards—white sauce and mint jelly—flavored with lemon and orange, respectively. Recipes for these sauces did not typically include citrus flavoring, but neither addition would radically alter the dishes' basic characters.[20]

The California Fruit Growers Exchange, otherwise known as Sunkist, spent a great deal of money in the early part of the twentieth century promoting citrus to the American public. Popular legend recounts how the beautiful scenes depicted on orange crates lured many of the Great Depression's homeless and destitute to Southern California in the 1930s. Sunkist began advertising in 1907 with a large budget for the time ($10,000) and saturated the market with its slogans and images. Where oranges had once been a delicacy in American culture, consumed only a few times during the year, Sunkist's efforts paid off to such an extent that, by the 1920s, orange juice became a daily feature of middle-class American life.[21]

Sunkist advertising used language that directly blended notions of nature and science to sell a product that improved on both. The 1935 California Fruit Growers Exchange, *For Vigorous Health: Sunkist Recipes for Every Day* opened with romantic imagery of fruit, "Ripened on the tree in all-year sunshine, irrigated by mountain snow waters," and immediately shifted tone in the same sentence to inform readers that "California Sunkist Oranges have a greater wealth of soluble solids."[22] While readers could easily picture sunshine and mountain streams, they were unlikely to know what soluble solids were or what their role might be in human health. The language attempted to enchant and educate at the same time, making readers privy to new, scientific ways of thinking and writing about food.

Using words that emphasized human action over natural processes, the cookbook explained how Sunkist fruit reached the consumer: "Picked every week in the year, Sunkist fruit is washed, graded, packed and rushed to you truly fresh—as Nature intended." While it was sold as "natural," Sunkist's citrus was also marketed as a product, manufactured and branded. One historian of Sunkist has described the company's product as "mass produced oranges," an intriguing way to describe fruit.[23]

Lest all oranges seem equally and naturally attractive, readers were informed, "Sunkist trademarked on the skin or tissue wrapper means dependable quality—uniform goodness and healthfulness." Improving on nature, the corporation gave the fruit a new skin, either by wrapping it in labeled paper or by stamping the skin itself with a proprietary name.

The elevation of process and package over the fruit's actual flavor echoed advertisements for many other contemporary foodstuffs produced in factories through innovative new processes. Advertising of items such as soup, biscuits, and canned meat continually assured consumers that no human hands had touched the product. Sunkist actually advertised that its fruit pickers wore white cotton gloves, whiteness being a potent symbol of purity.[24] By 1935, when *For Vigorous Health* was published, most consumers were familiar with canned fruits as a reliably safe consumer product. The freshness of unprocessed oranges could actually work against them in this market. Canned orange segments were predictable in quality and had a shelf life far beyond that of fresh oranges. Sunkist thus had to encourage consumers to believe in oranges as sanitary and simultaneously to make their freshness a virtue rather than a problem. In order to sell fruit, the California Fruit Growers Exchange, using the Sunkist brand name, had to use language already developed to sell mass-produced goods.

Marketing publications emphasized quasi-medicinal properties of citrus fruits, identifying them more as chemical compounds than fruits. Oranges and lemons, the cookbook writers assured readers, aided in digestion, prevented constipation, counteracted "tooth decay and gum troubles," promoted "the retention of calcium and phosphorus," helped infants to grow, and vanquished the dreaded (and largely imaginary) threat of acidosis. Citrus was "valuable and necessary" to health, as well as "an important flavoring ingredient." Sunkist offered no explanation, alas, of how a flavor's importance could be established.[25]

Although, according to the authors of *For Vigorous Health*, "The breakfast glass of orange juice has now become a national health habit," American consumers still had to be trained in proper citrus behavior. A section of the cookbook explained how to buy oranges and lemons, beginning with a reminder of the value of the brand label, either on the wrapper or on the fruit itself. Readers were then instructed to set aside all well-known habits of food shopping and to ask no question beyond whether the fruit bore the corporate identity marker. Shoppers were assured that "Size does not determine quality in California citrus fruits." Oranges and lemons should be judged "by the trade-mark, not by the dimensions." Nor was color, another traditional gauge of quality, meaningful. Depending on season, fruit coloration might vary, but the consumer was promised that Sunkist "fruit will always prove to be fully ripe," despite green spots that might suggest otherwise.

Sunkist's citrus management followed the consumer out of the market and back into her private home, where, in addition to a variety of recipes that blended tradition with new flavors, she was directed in proper service of the product. *For Vigorous Health* repeated for the private audience a theme that Sunkist also used in its communications with restaurant owners: orange juice must be served fresh. Sunkist strongly discouraged consumers and restaurant owners from making juice in advance of use. Instead, they were supposed to buy one of the three juicers produced and sold by the exchange and to prepare each glass fresh. Discerning customers would abandon restaurants where "stale" juice was offered. Individual consumers learned that "*Freshly extracted* orange and lemon juices furnish fruit acids needed for flavor in many drinks" and that "Orange juice should always be served fresh since flavor is lost when juice stands." The insistence on constant fresh squeezing probably stemmed from the money to be made in selling extractors and in frightening customers into thinking that any juice left over was not worth saving, necessitating the purchase of more fruit.

For Vigorous Health advised readers, "A good reamer or electric extractor and a liberal supply of oranges and lemons at all times make it possible to serve these delicious and healthful drinks . . . easily and quickly . . . whenever you wish." Electrification of private homes was still very expensive, but it was becoming more common for middle-class families. By 1928, nearly nineteen million homes were electrified, but the convenience of electrical appliances only became an ordinary feature of American homes after the Second World War, in part due to the rural electrification projects that were a lasting contribution of the New Deal.[26] Thus to suggest use of an electric juicer in 1935 was to assume a reader with a certain level of wealth. The juicer served as a status marker not only because it produced that most modern beverage—fresh orange juice—but also because it required electrification of the home, another sign of affluent modernity.

As familiar dishes developed new flavors, however, new technologies also made easier the production or preservation of old favorites. Corporate cookbooks included recipes for everyday use and also for "When you entertain," encouraging readers and consumers to make new foods and new appliances part of the semipublic persona they displayed when company came over.[27]

The language used in talking about guests frequently played on anxieties about living up to others' expectations. For example, Sunkist assured readers that "Oranges and lemons are popular with everyone, and so are well adapted for guest service," while Frigidaire decorated the end papers of its cookbook, *Frozen Delights*, with a close-up photograph of two well-dressed women being served a gelid confection by a maid in uniform.[28]

While professional home economists in the pay of corporations performed experimentation on products before they reached the market, the texts that recounted this experimentation also encouraged home cooks to approach their food as innovators. One Frigidaire cookbook, *Frigidaire Recipes*, ended with the promise that "After you have prepared a few of the recipes in this book you will be thoroughly acquainted with the technique of freezing these delicious frozen dishes. And with this fundamental knowledge you may formulate and prepare favorite dishes of your own." Following were blank pages bearing a printed heading, "Delightful Frozen Dainties of Your Own."[29] Nineteenth-century cookbooks had often included blank pages that served as a scrapbook space for the collection of new recipes or notes on recipes already attempted. Frigidaire continued this invitation to the reader to coauthor her own cookbook.[30]

Advertisements told the public that a product like canned soup was good not just because it was composed of good ingredients well prepared and cleanly packaged, but also because it could become something else. A

FIGURE 3. *Frigidaire Frozen Delights*, Frigidaire
Corporation, 1927. Collection of the author.

consumer could use it to develop her own special recipe. By the 1950s, this
art of recombination had become popular in noncorporate cookbooks, too.
Because the product was standardized, it also kept the cook in a shared context with all the other cooks of her class and status. Although food writers in
the twenty-first century might scoff at store-bought mayonnaise as "subpar,
corn-syrup-filled commercial stuff," preferring to emulsify their own, consumers of the early twentieth century were invited to join a common culture
of progress and profit through their purchase of this same product.[31] Until food manufacturers introduced stabilizers to keep their mass produced
mayonnaises fresh, home cooks had relied on boiled dressings for salads
because these were easier to make and kept longer.[32]

A 1931 Hellman's mayonnaise cookbook *Correct Salads for All Occasions*,
for example, claimed that the product was "double whipped," suggesting that

Hellman's saved women extra labor. General Foods Corporation, Hellman's parent company, had taken a substance that was familiar but also something of a treat and made it both an improved and an everyday product.[33] The strategic combination of the usual and unusual, as well as the message that preservative technologies could save labor, were also central elements in cookbooks about refrigeration, one of the most important technological innovations of the twentieth century.

Refrigerator Cuisine

In the 1920s refrigeration technology that used chemical coolants rather than ice was new. Refrigeration introduced a new object into familiar domestic space, changing how kitchens were arranged and used, and it defied the seasons, providing a taste of winter in the middle of summer heat and returning summer bounty—frozen fresh—to the table in darkest February. Among the earliest manufacturers of refrigerators, Frigidaire worked especially hard to create a mystique for its product by emphasizing the ways the appliance could make ordinary life both easier and more interesting. Both themes were employed simultaneously in Frigidaire cookbooks. The promotional cookbook, *Frigidaire Recipes*, for example, provided three recipes distinctly identified with the appliance, each bearing the name Frigidaire in its title. The recipes were for dinner rolls, cookies, and strawberry shortcake, three dishes that could be assumed to be familiar to the readers. They were dishes that were national in that they had no regional associations and "American" in that they were associated with American home life rather than restaurant fare or immigrant communities. Each dish was altered through the use of the refrigerator, with the strawberry shortcake most transformed from a traditional version of itself. Dough for the Frigidaire Rolls, made with yeast, was set to rest in the refrigerator after its first rising, and could be used as needed over the course of several days. Frigidaire Cookies were rolled into a log form and stored in the refrigerator to be sliced and baked as needed. This was a precursor to today's packaged cookie dough. Strawberry shortcake was prepared with fresh fruit poured onto sponge cake and set to cool with a topping of whipped cream mixed with egg whites, a concoction designated a mousse by the author of *Frigidaire Recipes*. The consistency of the final product, which was served from a special freezing tray, would have been very different from the shortbread or biscuits topped with fresh fruit and whipped cream that comprised the traditional strawberry shortcake. In all three recipes, the defining element—what made it "Frigidaire"—was an innovative process rather than a flavor.

A chapter about dishes made with leftovers similarly offered familiar flavors and textures of the era—scalloped vegetables, ham croquettes—but focused attention on how Frigidaire helped housekeepers turn scraps into meals. Writers of the cookbook reminded readers that leftovers were food they had already paid for and had already absorbed a certain amount of time and energy, so to waste them was to squander one's own resources. By keeping them fresh for several days, the Frigidaire offered "possibilities of labor-saving and time saving dishes," which "can be made as inviting and appetizing as when they made their first appearance."[34]

Emphasizing the significance of being able to hold foods not just over-night, but for longer periods, the book's writers argued that the refrigera-tor, a very new technology, could help housekeepers get the best value from canned goods, a somewhat older technology. Because fruits and vegetables were often "a better buy in larger cans," the writers implied, a family tended to eat the same thing every meal until the can was empty. With the use of the Frigidaire, however, these foods could "be kept two or three days before reappearing, preferably in a different form of service."[35] A newer technology in food preservation—refrigeration—supported an older one—metal cans for a kind of synergy in which innovations built upon each other.

Although it might have seemed more convenient, this new way of cook-ing required the householder to plan farther into the future and keep a list of meals in her mind at once. Rather than thinking, "We had roast beef tonight so we'll have cold roast beef for lunch," the housekeeper could now think, "Using leftover roast beef from tonight's dinner we will have creamed beef the day after tomorrow for dinner and in between have something that isn't roast beef." The result could be more day-to-day variety but also more plan-ning. To assist with this new thought pattern, Frigidaire produced its *Key to Meal Planning*. Menus for distinct meals were coded and then arranged

to make best use of refrigerated leftovers. For example, "B1" was a breakfast menu of oranges, rolled oats, toast, bacon, coffee, and milk. It could be
served on the same day as "L1," a lunch of cream of tomato soup, cottage
cheese sandwiches, and banana cream, but was not advised as partner to
"L2," which included cream of celery soup and bacon and lettuce sandwiches,
presumably because extra bacon made for B1 would be used the next day in
sandwiches for L2. Readers were advised to "select first the dinner course
and corresponding 'D' Menu. Then select any one of the 'L' and 'B' menus in
the same column." An extra feature, the "menus for left-overs" under "Dinners," suggest meals for subsequent days."[36]

Acknowledging both the practical issues of family meals and a common
yearning for exceptional experiences, *Frigidaire Recipes* set aside the grid
and folded special moments in among mundane meals of fried mush and
chicken salad. A brief chapter dedicated to ice cubes, for example, offered
recipes for colored cubes, garnished cubes, and decorated cubes. Cubes
were to be colored using food dyes, garnished by freezing fruits inside them,
and decorated with mint leaves, water cress, or candied fruit applied to the
top of a cube and secured before freezing with another shallow layer of water.
Suggestions for garnishes included cherries and an intriguing trio: orolettes,
emerlettes, and rubyettes, which were peeled grapes injected with colored
liqueurs, at the time available for sale in jars. Thus embellished, ice cubes
"not only cool beverages, but they add refreshing attractiveness." Again, the
appeal to the palate is in a novel process rather than a flavor. Consuming a
frozen grape might not be especially tasty, but consuming something made
fancy by new technology might well be.

An image printed on the frontispiece of *Frigidaire Recipes* captured this
experience as two women stand in a kitchen with an open Frigidaire behind
them. One spoons a frozen food of a bright orange color into parfait glasses
while the other, close beside her, looks on. Another woman can be seen sit-
ting on a settee facing the others. The moment is casual but also elegant as
they consume a delicate treat together in the relaxed space of a private home,
free for the moment from the presumed demands of childcare or wifely responsibilities.

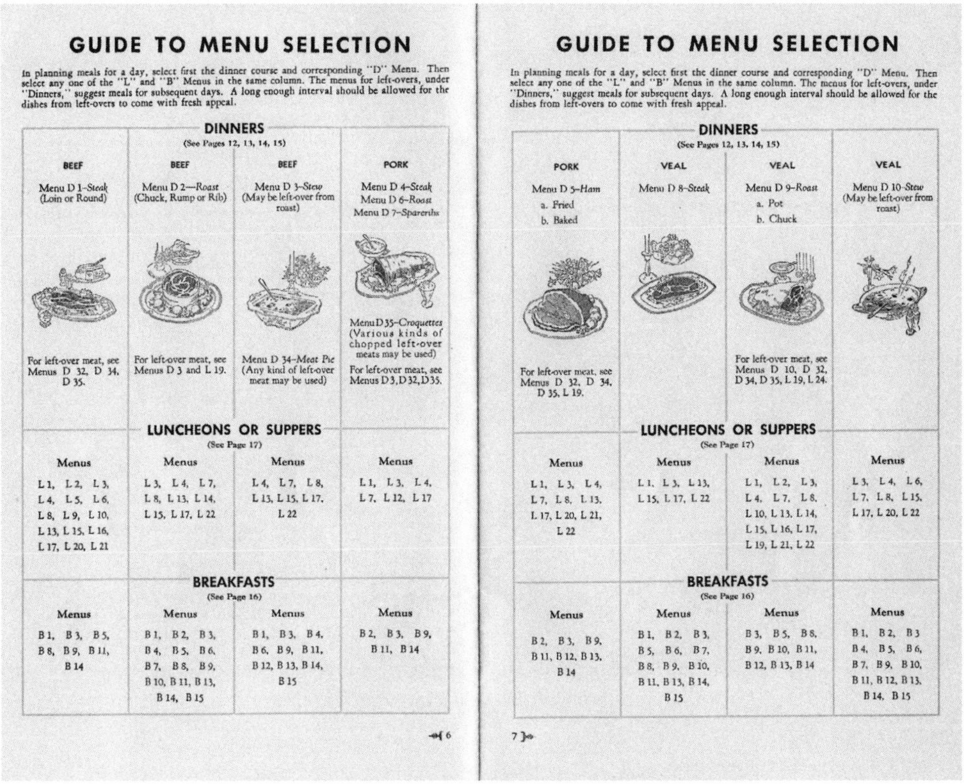

GUIDE TO MENU SELECTION

In planning meals for a day, select first the dinner course and corresponding "D" Menu. Then select any one of the "L" and "B" Menus in the same column. The menus for left-overs, under "Dinners," suggest meals for subsequent days. A long enough interval should be allowed for the dishes from left-overs to come with fresh appeal.

DINNERS (See Pages 12, 13, 14, 15)

BEEF	BEEF	BEEF	PORK
Menu D 1-*Steak* (Loin or Round)	Menu D 2—*Roast* (Chuck, Rump or Rib)	Menu D 3-*Stew* (May be left-over from roast)	Menu D 4-*Steak* Menu D 6-*Roast* Menu D 7-*Spareribs*
			Menu D 35-*Croquettes* (Various kinds of chopped left-over meats may be used)
For left-over meat, see Menus D 32, D 34, D 35.	For left-over meat, see Menus D 3 and L 19.	Menu D 34-*Meat Pie* (Any kind of left-over meat may be used)	For left-over meat, see Menus D 3, D 32, D 35.

LUNCHEONS OR SUPPERS (See Page 17)

Menus	Menus	Menus	Menus
L 1, L 2, L 3, L 4, L 5, L 6, L 8, L 9, L 10, L 13, L 15, L 16, L 17, L 20, L 21	L 3, L 4, L 7, L 8, L 13, L 14, L 15, L 17, L 22	L 4, L 7, L 8, L 13, L 15, L 17, L 22	L 1, L 3, L 4, L 7, L 12, L 17

BREAKFASTS (See Page 16)

Menus	Menus	Menus	Menus
B 1, B 3, B 5, B 8, B 9, B 11, B 14	B 1, B 2, B 3, B 4, B 5, B 6, B 7, B 8, B 9, B 10, B 11, B 13, B 14, B 15	B 1, B 3, B 4, B 6, B 9, B 11, B 12, B 13, B 14, B 15	B 2, B 3, B 9, B 11, B 14

6

GUIDE TO MENU SELECTION

In planning meals for a day, select first the dinner course and corresponding "D" Menu. Then select any one of the "L" and "B" Menus in the same column. The menus for left-overs, under "Dinners," suggest meals for subsequent days. A long enough interval should be allowed for the dishes from left-overs to come with fresh appeal.

DINNERS (See Pages 12, 13, 14, 15)

PORK	VEAL	VEAL	VEAL
Menu D 5-*Ham* a. Fried b. Baked	Menu D 8-*Steak*	Menu D 9-*Roast* a. Pot b. Chuck	Menu D 10-*Stew* (May be left-over from roast)
For left-over meat, see Menus D 32, D 34, D 35, L 19.		For left-over meat, see Menus D 10, D 32, D 34, D 35, L 19, L 24.	

LUNCHEONS OR SUPPERS (See Page 17)

Menus	Menus	Menus	Menus
L 1, L 3, L 4, L 7, L 8, L 13, L 17, L 20, L 21, L 22	L 1, L 3, L 13, L 15, L 17, L 22	L 1, L 2, L 3, L 4, L 7, L 8, L 10, L 13, L 14, L 15, L 16, L 17, L 19, L 21, L 22	L 3, L 4, L 6, L 7, L 8, L 15, L 17, L 20, L 22

BREAKFASTS (See Page 16)

Menus	Menus	Menus	Menus
B 2, B 3, B 9, B 11, B 12, B 13, B 14	B 1, B 2, B 3, B 5, B 6, B 7, B 8, B 9, B 10, B 11, B 13, B 14, B 15	B 3, B 5, B 8, B 9, B 10, B 11, B 12, B 13, B 14	B 1, B 2, B 3 B 4, B 5, B 6, B 7, B 9, B 10, B 11, B 12, B 13, B 14, B 15

7

FIGURE 4. *The Frigidaire Key to Meal Planning*, Frigidaire Corporation, 1933, 6–7. Collection of the author.

Frigidaire portrayed contemporary home life and the food that was so much a part of that life as an ideal blend of ease and glamour, with the refrigerator both "safeguarding health" and making possible the production of "frozen dainties." The salad, which would come to stand for so much in later debates about American cuisine, was portrayed as the archetype of this progressive cuisine. Frigidaire claimed that, whereas "The term 'salads' formerly implied those green leaves which could be eaten raw with a simple dressing," progress had come to the dish and "Now salads have become more varied in food combinations, more frequently a part of the meal, and in fact have

Ice Cubes Garnished with Cherries

FIGURE 5. Garnished Ice Cubes, *Frigidaire Recipes*, Frigidaire Corporation, 1928, 52. Collection of the author.

advanced to that degree of popularity that many times lunches and suppers are planned around them." Because the first rule of proper salad making was always that "the uncooked salad greens must always be cold, crisp and dry," the refrigerator was essential to proper preparation of this "advanced" dish. The use of mayonnaise dressings encouraged in *Frigidaire Recipes* also made the refrigerator a necessity because it could keep the quick-to-spoil substance fresher longer.[37]

The cocktail was another dish particularly suited to invoke appreciation for the refrigerator. This was an edible rather than a drinkable concoction, served before the main course as an appetizer. The term today is only used for fruit cocktail and shrimp or crab, all pre-dinner phenomena. Cocktails such as the crab flake, grapefruit, or oyster cocktails suggested in *Frigidaire Recipes* were supposed to be at their best when chilled.

The quality of chilliness was presented throughout the book as being particularly appetizing, as much the flavor of modernity as was the "untouched-by-human-hands" cleanliness of the Sunkist orange. A suggested "evening supper for guests" seems remarkably casual—salad, sandwiches, ice cream, cool drinks—until we reflect that the chill accompanying each item would give it a kind of sophistication that it no longer retains for twenty-first-century readers and eaters. Added to the coolness of the food, too, would be the coolness of the hostess, not warmed and flushed from working in the kitchen, but rather greeting her guests with the ease that only mechanized cuisine could supply.

Human coolness was not an incidental benefit of modern technology, but in fact one of its strongest selling points. In 1924, the American Stove Company, a major producer of gas ranges, published a guide to using its Lorain oven heat regulator, which established the product's value in terms of a homemaker's distance from her cooking tasks. The oven heat regulator enabled users to set the stove at one temperature, which the oven would maintain until the cook intervened by changing it. Previous to the introduction of oven regulators, cooks had to make frequent checks of an oven's heat level—checks that raised their own body temperatures. Coolness and convenience were two of the most common themes used to sell appliances in the 1930s.[38]

The American Stove Company encouraged readers to use the oven as a slow cooker, leaving the temperature low for a long time: "A dinner which is to be served in the evening may be prepared and placed in the oven during the early afternoon. It will be ready when [the housewife] returns to her home in the late afternoon."[39]

The implication that a woman both could and would leave her home for a stretch of approximately five hours in the day reflected the long-range impact of the women's movement and expanding entertainment and work opportunities for women in the period after the First World War. It told the reader that she would not be bound to kitchen labor, would not in fact become her family's servant, but could live a life beyond domestic duties. As a cookbook produced by Armour and Company explained, "Drudgery has been literally taken out of food preparation. Madam Home Manager's time may now well be employed along more constructive lines than in shelling peas and stringing beans." While later generations of cookbook writers like Alice Waters would celebrate the experience of shelling peas and stringing beans as a chance to connect with nature, Armour's cookbook clearly did not.[40]

Corporate cookbook writers insisted that hands-on, all-day cooking was no longer a necessary part of modern American foodways. Leisure and self-direction overshadowed work and responsibility to others. The appliance and processed foodstuffs now exercised productivity and nurturing, those virtues that had once been associated so closely with womanhood. Now the actual woman could depart her home and return, as a Frigidaire cookbook promised "with the salad prepared and chilling in Frigidaire and the dessert freezing in the freezing compartments, the hostess, herself, becomes one of the guests."[41]

New foodways that transformed a woman into a guest in her own home radically altered the long association of womanhood with domesticity. The American Stove Company did not even suggest what the newly liberated slow-cooking woman would do with her free time, implying both that the possibilities were multiple and that freedom from household work accorded women a new kind of autonomy in their daily activities. They might spend their free time in public, but the choice had been privately, personally made, belonging to the woman herself. Promising women their own time was an especially potent offer in this era of expanding, but still limited, social and cultural freedoms.

Feeling like a guest in her own home would have been especially attractive for the generation of middle-class women who came of age in the 1920s and 1930s. These were the women who found themselves performing labor that in their own memory had been performed by family servants, not by their own mothers and grandmothers. For the upper-middle- and middle-class families able to afford the new appliances, the stigma of kitchen work would have seemed to drag a woman backward from modernity into the misty recesses of time before nineteenth-century mass immigration and urbanization created an affordable servant class in towns and cities. When the work could be handed back to a servant—a mechanical one now—true modernity could be tasted.[42]

The chilled meal and the just-juiced orange were among the many foods valorized in corporate cookbooks as new and superior experiences. In the same historical moment, however, other cookbook writers—those who wrote about slimming diets—portrayed certain foods and foodways as villainous. The chilled whipped cream of a "frozen dainty" was simultaneously celebrated as modern fare in corporate cookbooks and shunned as fattener in dieting guides. Diet cookbooks became a mainstay of the genre, as diners looked for ways to navigate between their need for food and their desire for slimness. Like wartime cookbooks, both the "reducing" guides and corporate cookbooks assumed a normal cuisine that could be adjusted. The reducer would learn to substitute some foods for others, retraining her culinary expectations to avoid fattening foods. In contrast to the corporate cookbooks that encouraged the reader to boldly adopt new products and technologies, dieting cookbooks advocated a wary approach to food.

Slimming Cookbooks

Before the twentieth century in America being skinny was not associated with health. By the 1920s, however, slimness connoted both health and beauty, especially in women.[43] Until the late 1910s, plumpness was a desirable quality in both men and women because it indicated physical and economic health to observers. In 1913, the Seattle Public Library published *A List of Books for Women in the Home and in Business* that included no books about slimming, although it did list many cookbooks and books about nutrition.[44]

With transformations in ideas about women's roles in society, however, the celebration (or fetishization) of their childbearing and feeding capacities was replaced with an athletic ideal. This change occurred as family sizes were becoming smaller than they had ever been in human history. It also occurred simultaneous to the emergence of nutritional science. Like modern managerial science and the new science of psychology, nutrition seemed to give humans control over the unruly. No longer fated to plumpness, a person could potentially use the new nutritional knowledge to become slim. At least this is what numerous "reducing" diet books claimed. Professional nutritionists of this era emphasized physical health rather than bodily size, but diet guides adapted their language to the goal of losing weight.

A guide to weight loss, *Diet and Health* by Lulu Hunt Peters, remained on the nonfiction bestseller list from 1924 to 1926, keeping company with the rich and varied recipes of Fannie Farmer's *Boston Cooking-School Cook Book*, also a bestseller during those years. In response to those who had asked Peters if they would always have to stick to their diets, she wrote, "The answer is,—Yes! You will always have to keep up dieting, just as you always have to keep up other things in life that make it worth living: being neat, being kind, being tender; reading, studying, loving."[45] Like the writers of wartime cookbooks, Peters equated culinary behavior with morality, lumping dieting in with the other qualities of a being a good person and a productive member of society.

The theme of personal responsibility for weight was present in the earliest phases of the mania for slimness in American culture. Edna Sibley Tipton, for example, offered justification for her cookbook, *Reducing Menus for the Hostess of Today*, by assuring readers, "A hostess must have poise and no one can have poise if self-conscious. A fat woman is always self-conscious. How can it be otherwise?" It was a woman's responsibility to her guests not to distract them with her own corpulence, but rather, invisibly slender, to concentrate her attention on them.

Tipton claimed that it was hard for a fat woman to shop for clothes and that little children made fun of her openly in public. Appealing to female readers who hoped to benefit from women's broadened work opportunities in the period after the First World War, Tipton claimed, "Employers give preference to a slender applicant because appearance counts—trim figures are an asset." To be modern, to be sophisticated, one must be slim. Food, then, became if not an enemy outright, then a force to be maneuvered around.[46]

One of the first diet books to draw a large audience was Vance Thompson's *Eat and Grow Thin*. Originally published in 1914, it was in its 112th printing by 1931, indicating a growing market for books on this topic.[47] Thompson was a well-known theater critic and editor of an avant-garde magazine, *M'lle New York*. His diet book helped to establish the market for this genre and it also set a pattern for many other authors, such as Edna Tipton, who borrowed his list of forbidden foods for her own book, discussed here.

Subtitled "the Mahdah menus," Thompson's book channeled an apparently imaginary diet guru, Mahdah, who spoke French and was wise in the ways of dieting but was otherwise unexplained. Perhaps Thompson hoped to tap into the popular orientalism of the era, or perhaps he felt a need to distance his very real self from the advice he was giving because so much of it would be unwelcome to American readers. Thus it was Mahdah, not Thompson, who derided average American fare for consisting "very largely of fat-making foods, beginning with soup and going down through the list of gravied meats, of potatoes, macaroni, bread, butter, cream, cheese, and ending with pastries, puddings, and sweets."[48] All this would have to go. In order to lose weight, Americans must disengage themselves from their traditional cuisine. There was, however, Mahdah/Thompson promised, "no need of starving to get one's weight down. . . . One may dine and dine well if one will but dine wisely." The theme of personal choice echoed nutritionists' emphasis on the educated selection of food.

To dine wisely meant giving up all items on the "Forbidden Food" list, a concept that echoed wartime rationing. These were pork, ham, bacon, and all meat fats, breads of all kinds, all grains and cereals, rice, potatoes, macaroni, corn, and dried peas and beans, all dairy foods, cooking and salad oils, cakes, pies, puddings, ice creams, and candies, and all alcoholic drinks. Equivocating a little on this last point, Thompson, a member of the cultural elite, insisted that Mahdah's ban on alcohol came not from a moral imperative, but rather from realities about how wine reacts in the human system. Alcohol was fattening. Nevertheless, he was willing to suggest that, "One who will have his wine, in spite of this warning should not go beyond a glass or two of thin Rhine wine."[49]

The "Mahdah menus" themselves were not so startlingly different from ordinary American fare. A dinner, for example, included a first course of fish, a main dish of roast sirloin, side dishes of green beans, stewed tomatoes, and chicken salad with boiled dressing, and a fruit ice for dessert. For most of these dishes, Thompson provided no recipes, simply directing readers to "any ordinary cookbook" with the stern reminder that "it is always borne in mind that flour, sugar, milk, etc. are NOT TO BE USED." He left to the cook the complex task of rewriting traditional recipes so they would work without these basic elements of contemporary cuisine.

Thompson provided a few recipes for those dishes he thought probably wouldn't be found in the "ordinary cookbook." These recipes were assembled from cuisines other than American and included Mussels Mariniere, Turkish eggplant, a Polish-style duck dish (*barsch*), and dolmas—stuffed grape leaves. Hinting at a hidden agenda to change food culture rather than just consumption, Thompson suggested that the diet might lead the would-be-reducer "to discover that there are subtler gastronomic joys than those afforded by devouring potatoes or eating lumps of fat."[50] If readers should question whether this radical new approach were truly necessary, they had only to read his grimly titled introduction, "The Tragedy of Fat," to find the overweight portrayed as pathetic and disgusting. Food, which for centuries had served as a marker of social status, now indicated something about personal character. With modern nutritional knowledge came reassessment of behavior. Thompson claimed, "To the scientist," archetype of modern man, "there is nothing so tragic on earth as the sight of a fat man eating a potato."[51]

Popular novelist and screenwriter Fannie Hurst chronicled the transformation of her own relationship with food in the 1935 book *No Food with My Meals*. Departing from the usual encouraging tone of diet books, Hurst warned readers, "The transformation from my hitherto normal attitude toward food as a pleasant means of subsistence [is not] pretty telling." She was now slim, but dieting had not been fun and she had lost something "normal" and natural about herself in the process.[52] Regretting not only her own transformation, but perhaps that of a whole generation, she mourned, "Alas! One of the cruelest anachronisms of this whole cruelly anachronistic business is that deep within the lesser me nests regret that my palate, doubtless also leaner, has lost much of its fine gusty capacity to yearn."[53] Not only was it now "practically impossible for me to sit down wholeheartedly to a meal among whole-hearted folk," but more women were becoming like her so that it had "long since become . . . a rare spectacle [to see] an American woman partaking of a potato" in public.[54]

Hurst recalled the moment when she committed to losing weight. Lunching with a slim friend, Hurst ordered a typical meal of the era—cream of celery soup, a "grilled chop rolled around a kidney," salad "with oil dressing," an unspecified dessert, and coffee. Her friend, explaining that she was dieting, ordered just spinach. Hurst described her reaction with humorous drama: "I died that day. Of shame."[55] From that moment on, she recalled, "I set up a fundamental truth for myself. Food makes fat."[56] Food was now no longer an element of social life or individual sustenance; food was a problem.

Lulu Hunt Peters, whose *Diet and Health* went into fourteen editions in four years, similarly redefined food when she announced to readers, "Hereafter you are going to eat calories of food. Instead of saying one slice of bread, or a piece of pie, you will say 100 Calories of bread, 350 calories of pie." Like Hurst, Peters seemed to trust that changing the terminology of food would help change one's behavior toward it.[57]

Diet cookbooks of the first half of the twentieth century tended to share this extremist perspective on food: authors broadly demonized food in general but, at the same time, gave individual foodstuffs outsized powers to help or harm. Edna Tipton, for example, forbade mayonnaise, whipped cream, and cream sauces, thereby cutting her cuisine off from contemporary foodways by making it texturally less cohesive and more atomized. While these three substances became enemies of the slenderizer, Tipton found two new, modern products indispensable: "What the plump person desiring a slender figure would do without the gelatin desserts, I'm sure I don't know! . . . They can be fixed in such a variety of ways and their appearance lends such a festive atmosphere to any repast. Canned fruits are another godsend when rich ice creams must be 'passed up.'"[58] In trying to make festive and even communal the alteration of contemporary diets, Tipton celebrated the new food technologies that would often be seen as culprits in twenty-first-century debates about obesity.

Marion White, novelist and author of *Diet Without Despair, Sweets Without Sugar* (1943) and the appealingly named *Ice Cream Diets* (1946), suggested food familiar to her readers, offering substitutions and "low calorie" versions of old favorites. She planned her recipes "to fill the appetite's demand for something good to eat at an absolute minimum of calories." White thought Americans would find "good to eat" dishes such as pot roast, clam chowder, cauliflower au gratin, and devil's food cake. Noting that "thick cream soups are out, decidedly, for the woman who wants to reduce her calories," White nonetheless recognized the important place of such soups in contemporary American cuisine. She explained, "Only by courtesy do we refer to some of the following recipes as 'cream of' soups, for they are made with milk alone."[59] Cream, too, played a role in many popular desserts of the era, but White regretfully wrote, "Cream is the forbidden ingredient in any diet menu, and though it enriches and smoothes and moistens our desserts we must avoid it." Her trick was to "turn to white of egg instead of cream," approximating beloved textures in recognition of a shared national palate.[60] Calories might be reduced without altering cuisine.

In a short section entitled "Drug-Store Luncheons for the Business Girl," White addressed profound changes occurring in American foodways. As women joined the workforce in increasing numbers, fewer and fewer people of any age could be found at home at lunchtime. Cheap and speedy establishments like drug store lunch counters emerged to feed the white-collar worker. Food encountered in such a setting was likely to be limited in variety and high in fat. White offered guidance to the woman who found herself caught up in two national trends—the gender integration of the workforce, and the fashion for slenderness. Providing the reader with calorie counts for each of several meals she would likely find, White could send her off into the world, both employed and reducing. The menus she assumed would be available included the following dishes as examples of common commercial foodways of the time: "frankfurter on a roll with mustard, coffee or tea, small ice cream," "corned beef sandwich on rye bread (crusts cut) with mustard, glass of milk," and "bacon and tomato sandwich on toast, Russian dressing, tea or coffee, Danish pastry." The "business girl" was also cautioned to "Avoid the heavy soda fountain mayonnaise," when other condiments were available.[61]

*   *   *

Although only one page in her larger book, White's guide to drugstore lunches represented a new trend in writing about food in which meals were portrayed as part of a larger life that was lived in public as well as in private, dependent on circumstances and institutions as much as on personal taste or, as in the nineteenth century, a hired cook's abilities. First World War cookbooks had helped to make this change by presenting food as a resource of the wider community and the resourceful cook as a hero. Corporate cookbooks also emphasized the theme of market choice in their cookbooks while inviting readers to become agents of modernity in their own homes. Slimming cookbooks demonized food, but they did so in the name of improving the dieter's public persona, helping her to transform from a laughed-at fatty to an admired slim person.

The discourse introduced in corporate cookbooks and diet cookbooks persisted even after other themes arose. *Betty Crocker's Picture Cookbook*, a corporate cookbook produced by General Mills first in 1950, became one of the bestselling cookbooks in American history.[62] Today, recipes on food packaging are an abbreviated but ubiquitous kind of corporate cookbook, as are the many recipe sites sponsored by food and appliance companies. Frigidaire, which has expanded beyond refrigerators to a wide range of kitchen products, does not feature recipes on its website, but its rival company Kitchen Aid supports a cooking blog, the *Kitchenthusiast*. This site showcases recipes by authors who have their own blogs or who have published books, blending community and corporate cookbook models.

Just as corporate interventions into food writing are now so ubiquitous as to be almost unnoticed, the persistence of dieting cookbooks is such that the genre dominates the industry. Six of the *New York Times* top ten bestselling cookbooks in September 2016 were about diet modifications for improving health.[63] Despite the prominence of blogs and recipes sites as guides for cooking, major diet trends do seem to coalesce around cookbooks. Rory Freedman and Kim Barnouin, for example, the two women who self-iden-tify as the Skinny Bitches, note that their thrilling rise to international fame began with their cookbook: "What a whirlwind this has all been! It feels like only yesterday that we decided to write *Skinny Bitch* and now," they have become bestselling authors with multiple books and DVDs.[64]

Diet cookbooks use the terms plan and program to set themselves apart from other recipe collections, and frequently include promises for radi-cal life alteration, rhetoric uncommon in cookbooks not concerned with weight. Bestselling author and doctor Dean Ornish's book, *The Spectrum Diet*, for example, in its subtitle promises "a scientifically proven program to feel better, live longer, lose weight, and gain health."[65] The language of novel-ty and improvement that has become so commonplace in commercial food writing first appeared in the corporate cookbooks and slimming guides that were published in the first thirty years of the twentieth century. By the late 1920s, this obsession with control and progress, whether technological or physical, had earned a crowd of critics whose voices would in turn make a major impact on the way Americans think and write about food.

GOURMET IS A BOY

MIDCENTURY COOKBOOKS AND FOOD MAGAZINES

WRITING ABOUT FOOD IN the context of lifestyle notably marked the next development in American food writing, the emergence of the gourmet perspective. Gourmets placed high value on both cooking and eating, drawing attention to a more extended culinary experience than one typically found in a cookbook. Gourmet cookbooks celebrated French cuisine, but they went beyond the usual unreflective assumption that French food was fancy food to evangelize for the French cook's general approach to cooking and eating. They argued that French food was honest while American food was overly showy and full of tricks.

Gourmets particularly blamed the corporatization of American cuisine—seen in books like *Frozen Delights*—and diet fads for all that they did not like.[1] They also hated nutritionists and those who included nutritional information in cookbooks. For the gourmet, food was above all an experience, not an equation. However often the gourmet railed against nutrition or commercialism or reducing diets, however, he always emphasized individual experience; cookbooks in those hated genres had naturalized this theme for American readers.

When it began publication in 1941, *Gourmet* magazine was a boy. If this statement makes no sense to us today, it is because our ways of thinking about food, gender, and culture have shifted since that time. Yet that declaration has been very important to the ways in which American food writers have portrayed their national cuisine.

The announcement of *Gourmet*'s gender came in an exchange between the editors of the magazine and an enthusiastic reader, printed in the April 1943 issue. L. B. Beardsley of Billings, Montana, wrote, "Boy, she sure is some magazine," to which the editors responded, "'She,' sir? Didn't you know that Gourmet was born a boy? But like all virile young lads, of course, he is very popular with the ladies." While the tone is joking, the gendering was serious. *Gourmet* was originally conceived and publicized as a magazine for men. Although women readers were welcome and necessary, the magazine's editors cultivated the ideal reader as male. Advertisements and articles repeated the conceit consistently through the 1960s and men were well represented among readers' letters published in the magazine.[2]

The maleness of the magazine and its readership were neither accidental nor anomalous, but rather part of a small, but important trend in cookbook publishing that focused on men as cooks.[3] Although *Gourmet* was sold as a men's magazine and letters indicate that men really did read it, the majority of readers were most likely female. The magazine successfully sold itself to women as a magazine for men by dissociating the magazine from the everyday cookery performed by millions of women in millions of kitchens.

The Gourmet

Gourmet was the first American publication to be dedicated to cooking and eating as pastimes and it helped to broaden the American audience for food writing as a genre. Many of the writers who contributed to *Gourmet* also wrote cookbooks, building their own reputations at the same time that they collectively established a new style of writing about American food. Many of them also wrote books and articles about topics other than food. Stephen Longstreet wrote detective novels, Ruth Harkness was a travel writer, Robert P. Tristram Coffin was a poet, Charles Morrow Wilson wrote about folk life and politics. *Gourmet*'s writers had lives outside the kitchen that reflected glory on the work they did at the stove.

Gourmet writers routinely assumed, and frequently argued, that French food and American food were opposites. The model of French cuisine—a set of rules and flavors—was established as the ideal. American food was generally described as offensive but perhaps capable of improvement. In *Serve It Forth*, published in 1937, M. F. K. Fisher made an archetypal statement of this position: "France, today, possesses what is probably the most intelligent collective palate," while. "In America we eat, collectively, with a glum urge for food to fill us. We are ignorant of flavour. We are as a nation taste-blind."[4] In the course of constructing this dichotomy, the cooking of contemporary American women was denigrated at the same time as that of French women and American men was celebrated.

In 1930, Allan Ross MacDougal published *The Gourmet's Almanac*, in which he claimed cooking as a male pastime and also emphasized the experiential aspects of cooking and eating—the journey rather than the arrival on the plate. MacDougal's recipe for scrambled eggs begins: "Talking one day in Steve Greene's place with Charles Sheeler, the artist-photographer, photographer-artist, about cooking and kitchens we came to the subject of eggs and omelettes. He told me that he had made for Brancusi, when he was in New York, a dish of scrambled eggs as follows."[5] The recipe that follows has nothing to do with Brancusi's or Sheeler's work. The two men simply serve to authenticate the recipe as part of a lifestyle that was masculine, artistic, and improvisational, rather than female and quotidian.

MacDougal's book, which went into a second edition in 1933, appears to be the first American cookbook to use the term "gourmet" in its title.[6] During the 1930s, cookbook authors began to use the terms gourmet and epicure in their titles, as well as including mention of wine, in such numbers that it constituted a new trend. MacDougal's book was given a brief review in the *New York Times*, where it was described admiringly as a "combination of glorified recipe book and alleged almanac," and "a unique book whose whimsical but serious purpose of making a fine art of cooking and eating both amuses and edifies."[7] In *Saturday Review*, Helen Buckler set MacDougal's work apart from other cookery books: "Though its author hastens, and only too rightfully, to decry the benighted calory-and-vitamin school," the book "contains between its frivolous orange linen covers more instruction for the happy dining of mankind than ever yet entered into the dull pages of the tome confined in the ordinary oil cloth." The book did not even dress like an "ordinary cookbook," in a practical spill-proof cover.[8]

Another representative member of the gourmet class, Charles Browne, who had been mayor of Princeton, New Jersey, also published a cookbook in 1930 that expressed his cohort's values: "In general this book is dedicated to those who agree that the sense of taste has an aesthetic value; who believe that the proper preparation and presentation of food is no mean art and who know that to honor one's stomach is to humor one's disposition."[9] Browne presented his book in the least effete terms possible, titling it *The Gun Club Cook Book*. It was named for an all-male dining club to which the author belonged. The book was popular enough for the *New York Times* to note when a new and revised edition was published in 1931. The newspaper's obituary of Browne in 1947 mentioned the book as well as referring to him as "a well-known epicure."[10] A reviewer in the *Washington Post*, declared of Browne's book, "A man couldn't have a more palatable and persuasive introduction to cookery."[11] The gendered reader was typical of the gourmet genre.

Perhaps the most famous writer in the gourmet style was M. F. K. Fisher, a Californian woman who had lived in France during the 1920s and who introduced a new kind of food writing in 1937 with *Serve It Forth*. Fisher's writing emphasized the personal voice and food experience over the themes of tradition or progress that had been dominant in writing about food in earlier eras. "M. W." who reviewed *Serve It Forth* in the *New York Times*, described Fisher's style as "erudite and witty and experienced and young." Her book was "no book of practical counsel," including only two recipes, but "really is a book about food . . . filled with odd fact and obscure fantasy, illuminating comment, personal reflection and remembrance."[12] This would be a good description of *Gourmet*'s contents and style too. M. W.'s assessment that Fisher's work was not practical set the author apart from other female cookbook authors of the time and aligned her with male writers like MacDougal.

An American chapter of the English Wine and Food Society began meeting in 1934.[13] Members of this and other similar societies, readers of Browne's book, of Fisher's unsentimental though deeply felt food writing, and of MacDougal's *The Gourmet's Almanac* were the preexisting audience for *Gourmet* when it first appeared. These authors rejected the usual association of the kitchen with mundane women's toil by reframing it as adventurous and male.[14]

Fisher was bitingly clear that she was *not* writing for those she termed "the blind in palate." While some of this category, she explained, cannot help themselves because they are "physically deformed . . . others never taste because they are stupid, or, more often, because they have never been taught to search for differentiations of flavour." Such people "like hot coffee, a fried steak with plenty of salt and pepper and meat sauce upon it, a piece of apple pie and a chunk of cheese." Blatantly American and consistent both with American cookbooks and restaurant menus of the time, Fisher's example damned a nation for enjoying what she deemed unenjoyable.[15]

If we look past Fisher's disdain, however, we can argue that each element in this meal actually does involve differentiation of flavor. The steak is fried rather than broiled, and it is flavored generously with salt and pepper as well as "meat sauce," one of the vinegar-based condiments, like Worcestershire sauce, that were familiar in Anglo-American homes from the late nineteenth century on. The apple pie is served with a piece of cheese, creating an interplay between sweet and savory flavors. The coffee is hot, bringing its own aroma to the combinations of the table. The gourmet, however, understood without being told just why this combination was "stupid."

The term gourmet had been in existence since the early nineteenth century, but was rarely used commercially in America and was still obscure enough that a reader of *Gourmet* wrote in 1942 to ask what the proper pronunciation of the word should be.[16] "Gourmand" had been used to describe someone who indulged in food beyond the ordinary limits of pleasure and "epicure" generally referred to someone who took an unusually intense interest in foodstuffs. Both were comic figures, signifying excess of self-indulgence on the one hand and of fussy pretension on the other. The term gourmet, in contrast, came to stand for the food connoisseur, the person who knew all about food but was also able to enjoy it without going too far either in his particularity or his consumption.

In 1942, Pearl Metzelthin, editor of *Gourmet*, posed the question, "Who is a Gourmet?" Metzelthin argued he was a person who "realizes that the food set before him is not only meat for his bones, but also pleasure for his taste." Metzelthin used "taste" here to refer to something beyond the physiological, reaching into the aesthetic. When the gourmet ate, he did not feed his face; rather he participated in a performance of high culture.

As portrayed in print, the gourmet was an educated male, middle aged, usually a bachelor. He was particularly knowledgeable about wine and had spent time in France. Although postwar tourism and rising standards of living among Americans certainly helped introduce greater numbers of Americans to French food, the crucial dichotomy between French and American food had already been established in print before the war. *Gourmet* itself began publication just as America was entering the Second World War, before American servicemen got a taste of French rations. Thus when they first encountered food in France, many Americans already knew they were now eating "good" food. Because it is so difficult to separate taste from cultural expectations, these first tastes were in a sense already appreciated before the palate came into play.

While condemning most American food, gourmet writers made exceptions for food of cultures identified as "folk," such as the hams and pies of Amish Pennsylvania and the seafood dishes of coastal New England.[17] The food of African Americans, however, was significantly not part of this celebration of folk cuisine. African American cooks were recognized only as producers of the foodways of elite Southern whites, as discussed in Chapter 1. What had first become a convention in cookbooks in the post-Civil War era remained the standard through the 1970s. African American cooks were routinely represented by white authors in ways that characterized their cooking as resulting from primal impulses rather than training, family traditions, or intellectual capacities.

Gourmets also ignored contemporary Latino foodways. Although writers for *Gourmet* often waxed poetic about food in Mexico, they never wrote about visiting Mexican American or any other Spanish-speaking communities in their own country in search of food. Perhaps this was because a version of borderlands food, in the form of tamale pie, chili con carne, and "frijoles," a mixture of pinto beans and cheese, had become mainstream in American middle-class cookbooks by the 1920s.

Native American foodways were occasionally mentioned, but usually only in relation to one foodstuff—wild rice—which already had a high social status in American cooking because it was expensive.

The gourmet perspective, self-consciously allied to "good living," was established through public networks and private performances. Public networks included cookbooks, food and wine societies, and, of course, *Gourmet* magazine.[18] Private performances were the meals and food-related moments that self-identified gourmets experienced and shared with others. There was much overlap of public and private within the pages of *Gourmet* as readers wrote in to relate what they cooked at home and which restaurants they liked.

Reading closely in the cookbooks and food magazines of this period reveals three qualities essential to the American gourmet. The first two, which predate the Second World War and *Gourmet*'s first issue, were love of wine and disdain for nutritional science. After 1945, as postwar prosperity expanded the availability of convenience foods, the gourmet also defined himself in opposition to this trend in American cooking. Writers associated each of these trends with middle-class American women. Thus the attack on American foodways was also an attack on American women's culture; it was essential for *Gourmet* to identify itself as "a boy."

A Love of Wine

The first important influence in the creation of the gourmet was Prohibition and the recognition, following repeal, that the majority of Americans had limited interest in wine. When Prohibition ended in 1933, America had been through thirteen years during which the sale of alcoholic beverages, including wine, was illegal but drinking rates rose. It became clear that the dry years had actually produced a new interest in liquor and in how drinks could enhance eating.

Partly this was because speakeasies often served food as a way to appear to be legal businesses. Italian restaurants gained new popularity during Prohibition, because their owners sometimes offered homemade wine. Mary Grosvenor Ellsworth, author of *Much Depends on Dinner*, published in 1939, recalled, "The Italians who opened up speakeasies by the thousand were our main recourse in time of trial. Whole hordes of Americans thus got exposed regularly and often to Italian food and got a taste for it."[19]

Prohibition and slow sales after repeal provoked a reaction against mainstream American food culture. The fact that Americans could have suffered Prohibition to happen at all seemed to prove that they did not care about wine. As Charles Browne wrote in the *Gun Club Cook Book* in 1930, "Prohibitionists . . . who do not want others to have what they don't like themselves, having no appreciation of the social or traditional value of the products of the vineyard, it is hardly likely that they can comprehend the aesthetic value of food preparation or presentation."[20] Browne argued that disinterest in wine was tantamount to willful ignorance of food as a source of pleasure and actually indicative of a national mindset that resisted pleasure in all forms.

In his introduction to Jeanne Owen's 1940 *Wine Lover's Cook Book*, noted food lover and theatrical producer Richardson Wright blamed Prohibition for the American lack of interest in wine. Disinterest, he reasoned, could only be the result of ignorance. "Amid the spate of cookery books that is pouring from the presses," which Wright saw as "a sure sign of America's gastronomic rebirth," he deemed it "a rare pleasure to find one that dares to look on the wine. . . . All too many of the minor Apicians who pen our kitchen guides necessarily avoid the subject of wine in cooking." The women who wrote the bulk of American cookbooks were "Daughters of the Dark Ages of Prohibition," and thus "their ignorance of wines is so profound as to make the angels weep."[21] In 1934, a writer for the *Washington Post* included books specifically about "wine cooking" in his collection of books "selected for the bachelors," connecting the pro-wine attitude to masculinity and implying that women had no interest in alcohol.[22]

Wright hastened to reassure his readers that Jeanne Owen was not one of *those* women, but rather a "gourmette by birth and practice," and an appreciator of wine from infancy when, "At baptism, having been regenerated by water, her parents then assured the salvation of her palate by touching her infant lips with rare old brandy." She wasn't like other women.[23]

A reviewer in the *New York Herald Tribune* noted that *The Wine Lover's Cookbook* was addressed to a limited audience. It was "a book for gourmets, for those who make of cookery a hobby," or for the ordinary person on a special occasion, "when you are preoccupied with the nuances of food, and the exchequer is not at a low ebb." But for "daily use, I doubt whether many of us would go to the trouble that most of these recipes entail." They were, in a word, "recherché."[24]

Artist and Chicago restaurateur Ric Riccardo posited that Americans were afraid of wine, linking it subtly to national anxieties about gender roles: "We [Americans] suspect the masculinity of anyone who sports a cane and we sometimes question the honesty of those who are interested in wines and *aperitifs*. It is a self-consciousness that is limiting and that may be one of the reasons why many of us are running away each year to soak up the atmosphere and tradition of Capri, Paris, or Majorca." Americans, in other words, were rubes who mistrusted as illegitimate anything that did not fit outworn patterns of behavior. Winelessness was just one tragic symptom of the emptiness of American civilization.[25] Riccardo ended his preface to Morrison Wood's 1949 cookbook *With a Jug of Wine* with the dramatic announcement that "As I am writing this preface I am in the midst of packing my things for a trip to Europe—the main reason for this trip is that I am actually *hungry*." Vast and wealthy though it was, America could not provide edible food for the connoisseur.

Once Prohibition, with its home brews and bathtub gin, ended, Americans once again had access to higher-quality alcoholic beverages. The American wine industry was largely destroyed by Prohibition, but winemakers in California were quick to mobilize a recovery. Beginning in 1934, they became very active in publicizing California wine in ways that had a profound impact on American culture long before their wines became famous or respected in international markets. Because they wanted to increase their market share, California winemakers had to convince middle-class people, especially men, that they could understand and enjoy wine. The wealthy class in America was both too small and too accustomed to importing their wines to be any real help in the restoration and expansion of the American wine industry. The marketing associated with this need to grow did not necessarily succeed in meeting sales goals, but it did help establish a class-within-a-class, the middle-class gourmet consumer. That consumer was male for two reasons: men had more disposable income than women did, and it was not yet considered respectable for women to enter liquor stores.

In order for wine to become an expected part of middle-class meals, however, it also had to become attractive to women as a beverage appropriate to their lifestyles. A writer in the *Chicago Daily Tribune* reviewing Wood's *With a Jug of Wine* argued, "the American housewife, or 99 percent of her, has a closed mind: she will not use wine as a flavoring because her cookbooks were written by prohibitionists, because Mother never cooked that way, because she doesn't know anything about wine, and finally, because the stuff is too expensive." Granting that "on the last count she is right," the author promised that Morrison Wood would nonetheless "lead her into temptation with his numerous recipes."[26] Women had to learn to see men like Wood as partners in the production of a desirable food culture. For men to be able to buy wine for regular meals rather than just for special occasions, women, who did most of the cooking, had to think about food and wine together, so that they could provide the edible portion of the pairing.

Rexford Tugwell, Franklin Roosevelt's secretary of agriculture, was one of the first and most ardent boosters of the American wine industry. In 1934 he told the Women's Democratic Club of Washington, D.C., that wine was not only *not* disreputable, but was a positive force for good in the nation. Looking into a future that he hoped to create through government support of the wine industry, Tugwell claimed, "I foresee the day when the average American home will be able to enjoy good beer and good wine produced in the neighborhood at moderate prices . . . And better still, I foresee that, with this change in the drinking habits of our people, may come a change of temper and temperament . . . I anticipate a calmer and more leisurely type of civilization, in which there will be time for friendly conversation, philosophical speculation, gaiety and substantial happiness."[27] Tugwell's assumption that broad knowledge of and access to wine would naturally lead to love for the beverage and from that to a superior society was a common theme among American wine enthusiasts of the 1930s.[28]

Writers frequently informed readers that Thomas Jefferson—founding father—loved wine, imported wine, and tried to grow wine in Virginia. If we could all agree that one of his passions—representative democracy—was good, why not the other? The Jefferson legend, perfectly true as to the facts, if not logical in its implications, was repeated to reassure Americans that they somehow had a history with wine, a useable past that could be uncorked at will. Most important, it served to disassociate wine with Italian immigrant culture, appropriating it to the national spirit. Food writers continue to tout Jefferson's credentials as a wine-loving gourmet. As recently as 2012, *New York Times* food writer Marian Burros identified him as the nation's "Founding Foodie."[29]

Very soon after Prohibition ended, California winemakers joined together to promote their industry through marketing and advertising. They created the Wine Institute in 1934 as a trade organization and the Wine Advisory Board in 1938 as the promotions department of that organization. The advertisements commissioned by the board and designed by the J. Walter Thompson agency began to appear in 1939.[30] The Wine Advisory Board was a major sponsor, through advertising, of *Gourmet* in its first years and was simultaneously heartily supported by *Gourmet*'s editorial staff. In the very first issue, Peter Greig (publisher of *Wine and Food Newsletter*) encouraged readers to take advantage of the expected wartime shortage of European wines to "to experiment with American wines and see what he or she can find." Greig reasoned that American foods might be best paired with American wines: "Such a magnificent American fish as the pompano surely has just the perfect American wine to enjoy with it, if we will profit by the varieties that are to be found on every side until we find just the right one."[31]

From its very first issue, *Gourmet*'s advertising was dominated by liquor interests, beginning with the first three pages, which featured ads for White Rock mixers, Lord Calvert Whiskey, and Angostura bitters. The magazine was filled with encouragements to readers to try American wines and become comfortable with wine terminology and wine drinking in general.

When *Bon Appétit*, the second American magazine dedicated to food culture, became available in 1956, it was sold only at liquor stores, indicating a persistent connection between marketing wine and marketing the gourmet. The editor's introduction to *Bon Appétit*'s first issue announced that the magazine "wants to share with you . . . The manly—and womanly—appreciation of fine wines and liquors, and their proper service." Selling a recognizably "high-brow" magazine in selected liquor stores also helped the chosen stores to market themselves to middle-class customers who aspired to higher cultural status. Through their exchange of the magazine for money, customers and storeowners assisted each other to gain class.[32]

In its early days, the post-repeal campaign to get Americans to drink their own nation's wine, including products from New York, Ohio, and Virginia, as well as California, was assisted by the outbreak of the Second World War, which, as Greig noted, made it very difficult for Americans to buy the European wines that they typically valued above domestic products. Advertising and food writers emphasized that while European wines were unavailable, American wines could more than compensate the interested drinker. This was an obvious moment for winemakers to push their products. The appearance of *Gourmet* just as America was entering the war was a vital moment in the campaign. Before Prohibition, American wines were commonly sold straight from a barrel, decanted into bottles or jugs brought into the market by customers. In such transactions, it was not possible to really know (or care) what you were drinking. After repeal, producers instead began to sell wine in carefully labeled bottles in what can be seen as an appeal to the middle-class audience and certainly a rejection of poor and working-class consumers, since bottling and labeling raised the prices of wine significantly. Yet bottles and labels, however exclusionary they may have been economically, were democratizing to the extent that they did make it possible for drinkers to acquire the kind of knowledge Greig advocated when he argued that Americans lumped their national wines together when they should instead be "profiting by the varieties which are to be found on so many sides."[33]

As an example of how wine knowledge could help ordinary Americans, Greig iconoclastically attacked the most sacred of American meals, the Thanksgiving dinner. Noting that the centerpiece turkey "can be pretty unattractive meat at the best of times, so often dry and tasteless," Greig argued that matters were often made worse by (what he considered) the disastrous pairing of sauterne with the meal. "Turkey," Greig wrote, "calls aloud for a rich red burgundy or Rhone wine to instill warmth and flavor to the proceedings." The most-beloved American meal needed a red wine accompaniment in order to be edible.[34]

A 1944 advertisement created for the Wine Advisory Board featured a large roasted turkey, in this case associated with Christmas dinner, and instructions to "Baste your Holiday Turkey with Wine." To do so would be to produce "A flavor harmony that . . . adds an extra pleasure to the year's most important dinner." Although the ad suggested that readers drink Greig's dreaded sauterne with the main dish, burgundy was also mentioned, as were port and sherry, which were to be served with "sweet cookies, crackers, or cake."[35]

Wine advertising emphasized the concept of relaxation, repeatedly using the words "mellow" and "moderate." Illustrations showed small groups, almost always featuring mature men and women, always in private homes, usually seated and always with food accompanying the wine, which was served in small glasses. The message of the advertisements was subtle but strong: drinking wine will not turn you into a drunk. Sometimes recipes were given as part of the text of the advertisement, focusing on the entire event of the evening, rather than the one commodity actually being advertised. Wine was presented as part of a whole package of gentility, not an end in itself. MacDougal gleefully quoted wine expert William Bird who promised that, "The genial exhilaration that accompanies the reasonable consumption of wine is an intoxication more nearly akin to that produced by music than to that produced by distilled liquors."[36] Wine drunkenness was as respectable as music appreciation. In an archetypal 1942 advertisement, a small family group is gathered around a dinner table in a modest middle-class home to celebrate the birthday of an elderly woman.

The text of the 1944 Wine Advisory Board ad gently encouraged readers to try the product. "Some time soon," it suggested, "share some wine with people you are fond of." If you do, "you will make a discovery" that "wine is for friendship" and "made on purpose for relaxation of the moderate kind most of us prefer now." Making veiled reference to the wilder days of Prohi-

FIGURE 6. California Wine Council Advertisement, *Collier's*,
December 23, 1944, 52. Collection of the author.

bition, the advertisement insisted that the reckless style of drinking was outdated. Instead of making people raucous and perhaps abusive—one of the
temperance movement's arguments against liquor—wine actually helped
people to "be good companions." It had a "friendly nature" and could be
served "simply—as tea and coffee are served." Equating wine with tea and
coffee was an attempt to make it approachable in case readers were afraid
that drinking wine required special knowledge. It also helped to naturalize
wine, which Americans might think of as part of foreign cultures. Perhaps
most importantly, it suggested daily consumption rather than just special
occasion use. This was an economically important point to push, as was the
ad's final suggestion, added casually: "it's worth knowing that judges find
California wines excellent by any standard in the world."[37] If the advertisement had convinced readers that wine was a friend, it was now vital to the
industry that they look locally, rather than globally, for that friend.

In an obvious attempt to associate wine with high culture, opera singer
Beverly Sills appeared in what was probably one of the first television ads
for wine, signaling to the audience that American wine was a legitimate
drink of the nation's elite. Dressed opulently and seated at a lavishly decorated dinner table, Sills drew on her experience as an international star to
endorse a local product, explaining, "Of all the wines I've tasted, here or
abroad, I prefer this excellent Gallo Sauterne." Just in case viewers were still
nervous about wine as an intoxicant, Sills assured them that Gallo sauterne
"enhances any meal," defining wine's role as part of the meal, not the party
in itself.[38]

Cora, Rose, and Bob Brown, a prolific family cookbook-writing team,
also coaxed their readers to take American wine seriously. Publishing their
Wine Cook Book at the first possible moment after Prohibition's repeal, they
noted, "We were just getting a start towards producing some pretty fine
wines of our own when something happened." But now that Prohibition was
over, "there is no reason why our own Scuppernongs, Catawbas, and Cali-
fornias should not be produced so perfectly that even Frenchmen will cry
for them . . . California can now produce enough wine to supply each and
every one of us with a gallon a year." In other words, demand, not supply

A birthday wish together—over good food and Wine

Wine is for times when those we care for draw close and enjoy each other

Some time soon, share wine with people you are fond of. When you do, you will make a discovery.

You'll find a deeper value to wine than its glowing, lordly color in your glass... or the interesting experience its taste and bouquet bring you.

You'll discover wine is for friendship. Made on purpose for relaxation of the moderate kind most of us prefer now. When you serve wine you help everybody to ease up from the strains of the day, and be good companions.

That seems to be the chief reason why more and more people are coming to prefer wine.

The friendly nature of wine suggests you serve it simply — as tea and coffee are served. If you'd like a new booklet about wine serving, it's free — just write to the Wine Advisory Board, 85 Second Street, San Francisco. The Board represents all the wine growers in California.

When you come to select wines, it's worth knowing that judges find California wines excellent by any standard in the world. Let your dealer help you choose from among the good wines of California.

FOR VICTORY BUY UNITED STATES BONDS AND STAMPS

A red table wine like Burgundy or Claret brings to perfection the natural goodness of roast beef or any "red" meat. With chicken or sea food, set out white table wine like Dry Sauterne. For evenings at home, refreshment wines such as Port or Muscatel are justly famous. And as an appetizer — Sherry!

FIGURE 7. Wine Advisory Board Advertisement, _Collier's_,
April 25, 1942, 47. Collection of the author.

was the problem. Americans just needed to need wine.[39] Selling them on French foodways would be a good start toward creating that need. American foodways, however, were headed in other directions.

Disdaining Nutritional Science

The 1920s era of Prohibition was also when Americans first learned about nutritional science. Vitamins were discovered in the 1910s, but the information did not become part of popular consciousness very quickly. Researchers were still figuring out the basic workings of vitamins in the 1920s. Writers in the popular press picked up the story of vitamins as part of the larger story of technological advance that seemed to set the twentieth century apart. The idea that there could be heroes and villains among foodstuffs made for exciting reading. For example, a *New York Times* article published in 1921 announced "Vitamic Discovery to Aid Humanity."[40] Many Americans, however, were hostile to assimilating nutritional knowledge into how they thought about food. Where nutritionists sought, like other scientists, to make their findings accessible to an audience that might benefit from them, their work was frequently rejected as prescriptive rather than informative.

For gourmets, the new thinking about food as fuel and chemistry seemed to go hand-in-hand with the joylessness of food without wine. Food, they argued, was to be experienced sensually, not rationally. As early as 1930, Browne, author of the *Gun Club Cook Book*, claimed that nutritional knowledge was the enemy of pleasure: "While we have tried to suggest well-balanced meals we care nothing at all about calories or even vitamins nor have we any interest in 'diet kitchens.'" Browne was reacting in part to new knowledge about nutrition and in part to the recent reducing diet fads of the 1920s.

Ellsworth, author of *Much Depends upon Dinner*, also dismissed nutrition as antithetical to enjoyment: "I can't and don't pretend to domestic science. My ambition is domestic art. If I can develop the cunning, the perception necessary to produce a perfectly balanced sauce, I shall never care about its calories, vitamins, or mineral content."[41] The gourmet prized emotional ways of knowing—cleverness and perception—and saw cooking as an art in opposition to science.

In an ad for *Gourmet* published in October 1941, the magazine's editors also presented nutritional knowledge and culinary pleasure as opposites, announcing, "Right at the pop of the gun we want to tell you that *Gourmet* is a man's magazine on food that men enjoy. No vitamins, no calories. Just good food—yes, and good drinks." The association of women with food science and nutrition and the construction of these branches of knowledge as being in opposition to alcohol and pleasure led to the rejection of women's abilities as cooks.[42]

Writer and founder of the "great books" movement in American education, John Erskine, contributed to the mythology of the joyless nutritionist in an article in *Gourmet* in 1943: "The hopelessness of the elders is demonstrated, in my opinion, not only by the domestic science cooking that they support and pay for, not only by their contentment with their own inadequate cooking, but by the newspaper and magazine departments, which dispense advice as to how to cook in the home. These departments or columns wouldn't be maintained if they hadn't a pathetically large number of readers."[43] For Erskine, the problem was a failure in American culture, particularly the female culture of cooking schools and the women's pages of newspapers where readers actually demanded instructions for what he judged "inadequate cooking." Not only was the food bad, Erskine argued, it was also very popular!

Like Fisher, Erskine wrote in reaction to the trend toward rationalization in cooking that had occurred in the previous generation and become mainstream, but gourmet writers often conflated the trend toward systemization with the science of nutrition. Indeed, the emergence of food writing as a genre separate from instruction can be seen as a determined departure from the stereotyped approach to food as necessity and also in reaction to the new scientific approach to food characteristics by nutritionists and dieticians. As one of the first Americans who could be identified as a food writer, Fisher shifted attention away from cooking and eating as a matter of daily preparation toward food as singular experience. In staking a claim to this new literary territory, she brushed aside the most respected names in American cookbooks, rejecting their approach to food, cooking, and consumption.

MacDougal, author of *The Gourmet's Almanac*, also portrayed the nutritionist as a villain when he wrote in 1930, "It is all very well for domestic science cook-books to marshal and measure their ingredients down to the ultimate pennyweight; but if the cook is a sluggard and has no taste at his or her tongue's tip, how shall the meat be succulently roasted or the sauce be seasoned to a nicety, except by one of God's own miracles?" Where popular cookbooks written by cooking school teachers sought to take the mystery out of cooking for the millions who did it to feed their own or their employers' families, MacDougal argued that in fact intangible inspiration was the key to culinary success.

The Cursed Cuisine of Convenience

As early as 1930, MacDougal hesitated to give a recipe for pot-au-feu, a classic French stew of beef and vegetables, because he was "afraid that in these days of whirl and rush no one will ever find the time in America to let a soup simmer by the side of the fire during six or seven hours."[44] This sense of haste created markets for new, easy-to-use time savers and, the gourmet argued, sapped all pleasure from food. Browne warned that his cookbook was "not for the blushing bride—if such there be nowadays—fuming in a kitchenette. To cook needs time and room and concentration."[45] Gourmets did not reject mainstream American foodways only for what they lacked—wine—but also for what they included. Rather than focusing on any single ingredients as distasteful, the gourmet criticized what he saw as the spirit of American cuisine, innovation in the service of speed.

By the 1930s technological development had changed the kitchen, pantry, and market. Progress was a desirable ingredient. This could mean something as simple as adding canned fruit to a salad, or it might mean using a gas range and oven to prepare in one hour a meal that previously would have taken twice as long. During cooking, one might also enjoy the strange new privilege of peeking into the oven without opening its door and, further (if the new clear glass product, Pyrex, was used), into the dish itself to see the transformational act of cooking in progress.[46]

Safe commercial canning processes, refrigeration, gas and electric stoves, refrigerated rail cars, and frozen food; together these innovations were not just individual changes, but a generational shift in thinking about the world of food as a world of progress. Even as Ellsworth declared frozen foods "modern magic," she cautioned, "unless we know their limitations we may be courting disappointment. For they have their limitations, of course."[47]

Technological developments existed in a cultural context, too, which might imbue a new product with added social value. Frozen meals, for example, were not immediately embraced by families, but were quickly adopted by the airline industry and railroad dining cars. Because these two forms of transportation were associated with luxury, frozen meals acquired reflected glory in the consumer market. Airlines and railroads favored frozen meals because they could be stored easily for long periods and in situations where demand could not always be predicted accurately. Because frozen meals served the logistical needs of high-speed transportation, they acquired an incidental aura of glamour in addition to their reputation as labor-savers.[48]

Despite the social significance of convenience foods and domestic appliances, a small but vocal group rejected the new cuisine, arguing that convenience and taste were virtually irreconcilable elements. This rejection grew slowly, as convenience became central to American foodways. The first issue of *Gourmet* offered subtle opposition, presenting the new magazine as celebrating "a time when [the diner] completely dissociates himself, if only temporarily, from the discordance of the world . . . when, for a brief moment, we recapture the mellow moods and manners of a bygone day."[49]

Samuel Chamberlain's "Burgundy at a Snail's Pace" appeared in the magazine's first issue. This tale of "a leisurely trip" focused on eating and drinking. *Gourmet*'s first cooking column, by professional chef Louis P. De Gouy, was devoted to game cookery, the antithesis of the cuisine of convenience. Far from instructing readers to combine the contents of cans, De

Gouy suggested they shoulder their rifles and hunt their own dinners in the wilderness.[50]

Gourmet frequently featured stories like De Gouy's that celebrated the long way to the table; clambakes or multiday barbecues. Many of the events depicted in the magazine employed preindustrial cooking methods in an early celebration of what is now termed "slow food."[51] An article published in the magazine in 1942, for example, celebrated preindustrial production methods for cornmeal: The real Marylander "knows that the cheapness of 'store' flour and meal is the result of cutting corners—fast, hot grinding, sacrificing rare, fresh goodness to speed."[52] Obviously, stoneground corn meal was more expensive than the usual factory-milled kind and much harder to come by, but *Gourmet* and gourmet food writers consistently repeated the message that it was worth paying more for an authentic product. For these writers, authenticity appeared to be bound tightly to leisurely modes of life.

By rejecting convenience cuisine, *Gourmet* set itself apart from other magazines with recipes in a way that readers often noted and sometimes complained of. Writing to *Gourmet* in 1952, Mrs. Marvin Hirschberg of Cincinnati asked for "some quick and easy recipes with the Gourmet touch." The magazine answered evasively, noting that a spaghetti sauce recipe she had shared with them showed, "You've already found one solution to the problem [:] A good dash of imagination, a generous amount of ingenuity." Progress must come from within the cook, not from the nearest supermarket aisle.[53]

In 1952 one reader of *Gourmet* railed against convenience and nutritional science. She lamented, "Gone are the days (or at least I fear so) when women exercised art and patience [in daily cooking]. The prevalent idea is to prepare a meal with as little effort as possible, with as many prepared products as possible, and to supplement a faulty diet with vitamin pills." She liked *Gourmet* so much, she explained, because "you don't encourage laziness."[54]

Gourmet's editors responded enthusiastically, sharing her grief over what was perceived as a decline in distinction: "We are trying to . . . renew interest in cooking and eating as an art, not a penance. We in this country have been enslaved for so long to the ritual of vitamins, calories, cook it quick, get it on the table, get it down, take a pill, that we have lost sight of the obvious fact that it is perfectly simple—cook willing—to plan and prepare a meal that is nutritious and delicious."[55] Convenience and nutritional science were commonly vilified together in this way in critiques of modern American foodways.

The rejection of American foodways and concomitant elevation of French cuisine often focused on the salad. In *Clementine in the Kitchen*, which was the seminal text for the American gourmet of the 1940s, Samuel Chamberlain used salad as his definitive dish. Chamberlain had taken his wife and two children to live in France for several years. There they had all grown to love French food, as prepared by their family's Burgundian cooks.[56] Chamberlain defined his family's essential (though adopted) French-ness through their approach to salads. "We would rather," he explained, "have a few crisp leaves of lettuce, properly seasoned with olive oil and wine vinegar, salt, pepper, and a sprinkling of chopped chives, than the exotic salads which are the delight of wise-cracking columnists in American papers."[57] Chamberlain identified the simple salad in the French style as "proper" in contrast to the "exotic" salad of American food writing. American food was at best a stunt, at worst stunted and certainly not a cuisine, with all the complexity and dignity that the term contained.[58]

Other writers of the era shared Chamberlain's assessment of the fresh green salad as the apotheosis of all that made French food different from American. In her 1939 cookbook, Ellsworth had noted, "American salads as a class have spent the last fifty years under the concentrated odium of all Continentals. It seems we do everything wrong. First and worst, too many of our salads are sweet. Second, we make them look like boudoir ornaments instead of food. Third, we have absolutely no respect for dressings." While claiming a "renaissance" for "the classic salad" in America, she unquestioningly accepted that the French model was correct.[59]

An interview with Georges Auguste Escoffier provided an example of the continental "odium," Ellsworth detected. Escoffier was one of the founding fathers of the gourmet genre, a chef and restaurateur whose *Guide Culinaire* did much to codify French cuisine. In the interview, journalist Ernest Lorsy asked Escoffier to compare French and American cuisine. Escoffier claimed generally that, "The use a nation makes of its natural wealth of herbs for salads is a touchstone of its taste." What he termed being "salad-conscious" was a mark of civilization. When Lorsy pressed him to apply this formula to American food, "A shadow clouded Escoffier's pale forehead," and the master delivered his judgment: "I am afraid that although individual Americans may occasionally be so, America as a whole is not [salad conscious]." Judged by its salads, America was "a kind of gastronomic futurist. In painting, futurism is a thing of the past, but it seems to me that this saddest aberration of our epoch found a sanctuary in the American salad bowl."[60] Escoffier rejected what he identified as overimaginative cookery in favor of idealized tradition.

Chamberlain's tale of Clementine and her food gave a personal face to that tradition for Americans. When Ellsworth reviewed *Clementine in the Kitchen* for the *New York Times*, she noted that in reading Chamberlain's book, "We become aware that in the gentlest possible way [anecdotes of Clementine's cooking] enable the author to point up the differences between two approaches to food." Chamberlain's "moral is the superb consequences of maintaining a stern French respect for sound ingredients and devout preparation in all matters pertaining to food." Chamberlain's "scorn is reserved for the spurious, the characterless, the merely time-saving which take up such a large share of food merchants' shelves" in America." Ellsworth signaled her agreement with Chamberlain's perspective in this description, while the *New York Times* indicated the cultural importance of the book by dedicating a full review to it in 1943.[61]

The author of Esquire's *Handbook for Hosts*, a boldly masculine cookbook, similarly rejected American salads, damning them further by associating them with women's food:

Hostesses and tearooms . . . marry pineapples to cream cheese, nuts to marshmallow, mayonnaise to onions, and so on. American women go berserk when it comes to salads; they try so hard to be unique that in their zeal they really confuse things. A purist in gastronomy acclaims only one category of salads; green leaves . . . well washed and dried, seasoned with salt, pepper, oil, vinegar and mustard.[62]

Trumpeting the gourmet's cardinal virtue of "simplicity," the *Esquire* writer condemned as not fitting the category and thus not *really* salad all that diverged from his one, French model. That simplicity was identified with tradition is worth noting. While the French food that gourmets admired might not actually be quick and easy to prepare, it was always identified as simple or "honest" in its character, as if simplicity were a temporal rather than structural matter. That which had stayed the same for many years was simple, that which developed and evolved was not.[63] Salads were particularly potent as a symbol of all the gourmet rejected in American foodways precisely because they represented both the stylized cuisine of American middle-class women and also this cohort's embrace of innovation, using, as they frequently did, canned and packaged ingredients.

The salads that the *Esquire* writer condemned had first become fashionable in the late nineteenth century. As Fannie Farmer noted in 1896, "Salads, which constitute a course in almost every dinner, but a few years since seldom appeared on the table." Farmer explained that salads "are now made in an endless variety of ways, and are composed of meat, fish, vegetables (alone or in combination) or fruits, with the addition of a dressing."[64] The "endless variety" was a feature of the great number of ingredients, both fresh and canned, that Americans could now find on their market shelves.

The Hawaiian Pineapple Company, now the Dole Food Company first started offering canned pineapples in 1901, and mass-produced marshmallows appeared in markets at the end of the nineteenth century. Both these items had once been luxuries because fresh pineapples were difficult to transport and marshmallows were time-consuming to make by hand. The availability of commercial gelatin and commercial mayonnaise made it possible to assemble items more picturesquely than in the past, when cold meats were simply eaten sliced or warmed in a hash. The popularization of iceboxes—precursors to modern refrigerators—also supported the fashion for salads, as delicate greens and complex constructions could be kept fresh in these cool spaces.

Gendering the Gourmet

In another attack on women as corrupters of food, Walter Buehr, writing in *Gourmet* in 1941, dismissed "The 'Tea Shoppe,' with its inevitable tiny tables, candles, and lace-paper doilies, [which] serves tiny portions of dainty creamy dishes" to women "and sometimes manages to throw in a free palm reading with the regular luncheon." This kind of food, he suggested, was just as unreal and frivolous as the fortunes told at the tables. Tearooms, Buehr wrote, "Make the red-blooded extravert with the convex front acutely uncomfortable; he's much happier behind a red and white checked table cloth at a barbecue or a rotisserie, watching" as the meat is roasted and sliced.[65]

The connection between masculinity and "real" food was crucial to the gourmet identity. In order to get men into the kitchen, even if only symbolically, as arbiters of taste, women's longstanding dominance had to be overturned. In an act of synecdoche, gourmet writers used a part—upper-middle-class ladies' lunchtime food—to stand for the whole—the everyday cuisine of American homes. In the process they rejected all mainstream American cooking as "women's food." The argument against American food turned neatly round on itself: Americans ate food cooked by women. Women did not like real food; therefore the food Americans ate was not real.

Gourmet writer Eric Howard claimed, "Women are good cooks, but it is axiomatic that men are better. Women are inclined to follow recipes too closely. They may be adept at complicated desserts, tricky salads . . . but much of their cooking is fussy and finicky . . . women do not cook, generally, with the fine careless rapture of the male."[66] Apparently, women had technical knowledge, but no soul. The author of Esquire's *Handbook for Hosts* explained the difference: "A bride takes up cooking because she must, whether she's an eat-to-live gal or just medium-bored with the whole idea." Women had no passion for the work society told them they must perform. A man, on the other hand, "takes to the stove because he is interested in cooking . . . and therefore starts six lengths in front of the average female."[67]

At least one woman agreed with this assessment. A reader wrote to *Gourmet* in 1945, "With the risk of being branded a traitor to my own sex, I strongly insist that men are better cooks than women." The traitor, Winnie Meeks, argued, "In addition to their possessing an innate talent for concocting delectable dishes, men are usually more efficient and more dependable than members of the weaker sex." To support her argument she turned to evidence that was used again and again in this era: "If the consensus of opinion does not support my belief, why do all the large hotels employ male chefs?" Impervious to the history of gender hierarchy in the Western World, these writers used discrimination as proof of the inferiority of those discriminated against.[68]

William Irwin Wallace, author of *The Garrulous Gourmet*, argued that women's inadequacy went beyond their work in the kitchen and extended to their use of the pen; men were also better at writing about food than women were. Although the outlook in American food writing was "far from brilliant," he claimed, "There exists today in the United States a small (but growing) group of men who not only can really appreciate fine food and drink, but who are beginning to write about it in the lyric manner that such a subject demands." Typical women writers on food topics, meanwhile, "know nothing of the potentialities of the English vocabulary, and even less of food as a fine art." After studying a selection of recipes written by American women (sent to him in Paris by an American friend), Wallace determined that newspaper and magazine recipe writers were not merely stupid, but probably malicious: "A psychologist, after reading the recipes, many of which are excellent, might go so far as to draw the conclusion that the authors of some either had no sense of taste or occasionally indulged in the sadistic pleasure of seeing what they could put across on their innocent readers in the way of vile and unheard of gustatory combinations."[69]

Clementine Paddleford, who was a food columnist for several New York newspapers, reiterated the dichotomy between the fussy female and the authentic male in a list of suggested New Years' resolutions for women, published in *Gourmet* in 1946:

> Cook for flavor, not for the sole effect upon the bathroom scales.
> Don't cook to astonish other women or just to please yourself. Cook
> to delight your man. Forget about landscaping the salad—men hate
> such creations and it's bad taste, anyhow. Don't forget all men like
> gravy. Don't tilt your nose at ground beef . . . Present it with elegance
> and with cheer for the palate. Experiment with the use of wines and
> herbs and spices.

Paddleford rejected as illegitimate any pleasure that women might take in cooking unless it supported masculinity. Although she wrote about a great variety of foods, Paddleford herself was reputedly only adept at making steak, a stereotypically masculine dish.[70]

Journalist and regular *Gourmet* columnist Iles Brody wrote a column entitled "Manning the Kitchenette" for *Esquire* magazine, which began publication in 1933. Joining the attack on female foodways, he urged, "you should not rely too much on the usual recipes published and on the monstrosities of tea-room experts."[71] Instead, the way to cook was to "Use your imagination together with some knowledge of modern dietetics." Although he was willing to concede that nutritionists might have some sense, ultimately the art of cooking "calls for an adventurous spirit and often for disregard of precedent. The kitchen becomes really exciting when it is realized that rigid recipes are for bureaucrats and dullards, and that recipes were expressly invented so they could be tempered and experimented with—naturally by persons with an *esprit*."[72] That "esprit" was also the essential ingredient in Fisher's essay "Gourmets Are Made—Not Born."[73]

Fisher reassured readers that "It does not matter how much money or time a person spends on a fine dinner, if he cannot sense what is in good taste and what is merely stylish or showy or impressive."[74] Not having money was no obstacle to being a gourmet. The gourmet simply had an "instinctive feeling that simplicity is best."[75] This would allow him to perform gracefully in any circumstance. For her example she posited a man who had to serve dinner to three "world conference delegates," knowing that each had different dietary requirements. In this sticky situation, perhaps even ominous in the Cold War era in which she wrote, the gourmet's instinct would "come to his aid," and reasoning "that his guests have endured countless, lengthy state banquets . . . will help justify his seemingly rather lazy decision to serve a light simple supper to them, most probably built around fish and not too definite in flavor."[76] Only the man who had no fear for his social position could dare serve something simple to important guests.

In the spirit of improvisation as the manly approach to the kitchen, the real-life version of Fisher's imagined gourmet, diplomat and journalist Nicholas Roosevelt titled his book about food *Creative Cooking*. Providing his credentials as both a member of the elite and a manly cook, Roosevelt noted, "My earliest recollection of enjoying food goes back to camping trips with former President Theodore Roosevelt in my boyhood, when he fried steaks and chickens in bacon grease." Although "More mature judgment suggests that T.R. was a better President than cook," the former president's cousin valued the unfussy spirit of his famous relative's cookery. Nicholas Roosevelt provided no actual instructions in his cookbook, offering instead a work in which "Emphasis throughout is on the 'how' and the 'good,' rather than on recipes . . . no art can be learned by slavishly following rigid rules."[77] The theme of breaking rules gave encouragement to men by making them believe that they would not really have to work to become food connoisseurs—it was simply in their nature.

To help men claim their space in the kitchen in a simple but very meaningful way, *Gourmet* carried advertisements for the "British Butcher's Apron," featuring a mature man in a long, flounce-free apron. It was "man sized" and "tailored of heavy navy denim striped in white," not a flower upon it. Long "the distinctive uniform of butchers at London's Smithfield Market," those blood-spattered warriors of the marketplace, it now "becomes the perfect gift for the American 'Gentleman-in-the-Kitchen.'"[78]

Popular portrayals of men with compromised masculinity frequently featured frilled aprons tied over male frames. One well-known example of

FIGURE 8. British Butcher Apron Advertisement, *Gourmet* 16, 6 (July 1956): 52. Image courtesy of New York Public Library.

this was the disempowered father figure played by Jim Backus in the 1955 film, *Rebel Without a Cause*. The butcher's apron allowed men to enter the kitchen in their own stereotyped costume—the professional dismemberer. It also reminded men that their gender did have a history with food, just as De Gouy's article on game cookery had reminded readers that hunters were food providers. Rather than losing manhood in the donning of an apron, a man could actually enhance his masculinity by becoming the British Butcher.

To claim her own space as a food writer who was not one of the finicky, fussy, fantastical women, Fisher emphasized at every opportunity, that she was not like other women. In *The Art of Eating* Fisher began with an essay on the development of the palate, titled "When a Man Is Small," in which she wrote about the physical development of a man, but gave an example from her own life. Writing that young men have a period of food bravado when they drink hard liquor and black coffee and eat chili and rare beef, she offered the example of her own machismo in taking male dates to a place called Henry's in Los Angeles. At Henry's she took on the traditionally male role of ordering for the table, always choosing a dish—the German pancake—that created a spectacle of attendance by staff and overconsumption by diners. Fisher did not comment on her own crossing of the boundaries of gender expectations; she simply used her own behavior as an example of the way a young man acts. Although the German pancake was a sweet dish, it was served in a restaurant at night instead of a tearoom in the afternoon and Fisher ate it with a man, all details that set it apart from female cuisine. The story helped to establish Fisher's credentials as serious about *food*, not the despised fluff of women's cookery for women.[79]

In case readers did not believe her own assertion of masculinity, Fisher brought as character witness the most stereotypically masculine figure she could conjure, Caesar, a womanizing French butcher from a small seaside town where Fisher and her first husband once lived. Except to fulfill his sexual desires, Caesar associated only with men, coaxing local husbands and fathers into evenings of drinking and gambling. One evening, Fisher and her husband invited Caesar to dinner. At first the evening went poorly due to Caesar's lack of experience socializing with women, but then Fisher's masculinity rose to the rescue. Fisher had cooked a piece of meat brought by her guest that she remembered was "the best I have ever tasted." In response to Fisher's own obvious enjoyment of the meat, "Cesar put down his knife and fork. 'She likes it, she likes good food!' he said, wonderingly, to Al. 'She cannot be a real woman!' After that things were very pleasant." Fisher won Caesar's approval not as a cook, a traditionally female role, but rather as an eater in masculine style.[80]

As an alternative to the female world of recipe swapping and church suppers, *Gourmet's* letter section was full of letters from military men of high rank, sharing and critiquing each other's recipes. These men demonstrated the ability to be both masculine and culinary at the same time. The portrayal of men as culinary connoisseurs was part of a larger postwar redefinition of manhood in popular culture that encouraged men to think of themselves as creatures of pleasure rather than creatures of labor and service, the dominant models during the Depression and the war. The creature of leisure spent money, of course, on wine, on steaks, on lunch at the Playboy club, on barbecue kettles and skewers. Producers of domestic goods had been marketing their wares to women for a long time, although men often made the large purchases for a family because they managed family bank accounts.[81] Advertisements had previously addressed men as consumers in matters that directly affected their performance as members of society, such as appearance and hygiene, matters usefully categorized as "character." Postwar advertisers began to focus closely on men's personal fulfillment or expression of personality.[82]

Combating challenges to masculinity during the Depression, when many men were unable to fulfill the traditional role of provider, and the trauma of the war that followed after the Depression, marketing and advertising writers urged men to think of themselves as powerful, passionate, and in control of a world that had too long controlled them. The new masculinity was itself a product of consumer culture.[83]

Literature and popular culture in this era often focused on a tension between men who wanted to freely choose their own destinies and women who wanted to tie them to traditional conformity. It had its roots in the masculinist writing of the 1920s and 1930s, as practiced by writers like Ernest Hemingway, Henry Miller, and Raymond Chandler who emphasized a gender division in society that did not necessarily exist, or at least not with the starkness that they used to portray it. Indeed, *Esquire*, the magazine most dedicated to the modern masculinity, published a Hemingway story in its very first issue.[84] Popular fiction and nonfiction such as *The Man in the Gray Flannel Suit* and *The Organization Man* brought this tension into the world of postwar prosperity while movies like *The Wild Bunch* and *Rebel Without a Cause* made male escape from social expectations a heroic act.

*   *   *

By the time Julia Child arrived on American TV in 1963, the position of the gourmet was well established in American culture. Child fit this persona well. Although female, she was not feminine and indeed behaved toward food in a way that was exuberantly rough, grasping wet lobsters, playing games with chicken carcasses. She offered American women the chance to become *masters* of an art, rather than mistresses of their own kitchens. Her masculinity, apparent in her slapdash treatment of foodstuffs and familiarity with foreign terms and a cuisine associated with higher earning powers, allowed a generation of American women the chance to depart from their mothers' culture.

Just before the second wave of the women's movement made it possible for middle-class women to enter the workforce as professionals, Julia Child enabled them briefly to achieve the cultural status of maleness simply by flipping a crepe. Most important, she gave them permission to make mistakes—to let the crepe fall to the floor on the first try, for example—without losing their honor. She gave women access to the "careless rapture" of the idealized male cook.

Child's television persona popularized the gourmet as a way of being, an identity formed around a particular approach to food. This was a new phenomenon in American culture. In the nineteenth century, a small number of Americans had identified as vegetarians and had struggled against popular perceptions to define this persona as healthy and virile, but since that time there had been no popular character in American culture defined by his approach to food.[85] The gourmet became a fixture in American culture. *Gourmet* magazine remained popular until it ceased print publication in 2009 and marketing and advertising professionals picked up on the term's power to raise expectations for a product, justifying higher prices. Amazon, the nation's largest online retailer, for example, lists food for sale as "grocery and gourmet food." Between 1941 and 2014, the Library of Congress listed 852 titles found with the search terms "gourmet" and "cooking." In many of these titles, the term gourmet is paired with another food trend or concern. For example, readers can choose from *Gluten Free Gourmet Recipes* and *Guilt-Free Gourmet* recipes, or consider *Artisan Vegan Cheese: From Everyday to Gourmet*. The term gourmet signals that despite dietary restrictions, pleasure will not be sacrificed.

The word's broad success at denoting connoisseurship and sophistication made it problematic. Angelo Pellegrini, a food writer active in the 1950s and 1960s, described people who aspired to the identity as "not true gourmets." He explained, "their interest in food is superficial and inchoate; it is not ingrained in a clear realization of the significance of food and drink in the good life." They knew good food when they tasted it, he said, but "their gastronomic self has remained immature out of sheer neglect."[86]

In the twenty-first century, the term "foodie" displaced "gourmet" as a way to signify someone serious about the enjoyment of food. And in the same way that gourmet lost its power to denote distinction, foodie too became suspect.

In June 2014, *New York Times* food writer Mark Bittman attempted to reclaim the word from those he saw as dilettantes. For Bittman, the term was too often used by "new-style epicures" who care only about their own connoisseurship and not enough about the extended food chain. Faux foodies could be found "doing 'anything' to get a table at the trendy restaurant, scouring the web for single-estate farro, or devoting oneself to finding the best food truck." The true foodie, in Bittman's terms, was the "conscious foodie," who looked beyond his own pleasure to embrace ethics of sustain-ability and fair trade. If only everyone who was interested in food could be-come activist about it, then Bittman believed he could stop cringing when he heard the "demeaning-sounding word." Looking back at the construction of the gourmet in American culture, we can see Bittman's plea as another chapter in the history of American culinary identities. We are not just what we eat or how we eat it, we are what other people think of the way we eat.[87]

CHAPTER 4

MASTERING THE ART
OF AMERICAN COOKING

JULIA CHILD AND AMERICAN COOKBOOKS

IN 1961, JULIA CHILD published *Mastering the Art of French Cooking,* an event that has frequently been described as a watershed in the history of American cooking.[1] According to legend, after reading the book, Americans set aside their bland palates and mass-produced foodstuffs to joyously embrace the rich glories of French cuisine. But even apart from the misrepresentation of American foodways this scenario relies on, the story of Child's first book is as significant a story of continuity as of change. In many ways the book was not remarkable in its genre. The New York Public Library catalog lists almost the same number of books—approximately fifteen—about French cooking for American kitchens in the ten years before *Mastering the Art of French Cooking* was published as for the ten years after the event. Many of those were from major publishers, including two from Knopf, the press that published *Mastering* in 1961.

While the book changed the cooking habits of a particular cohort of American women, as will be discussed below, it did not have much effect on content in the American publishing industry. This absence of transformation is intriguing because it runs counter to popular assumptions about how the industry works as well as our ideas about Child's importance as a cook-book writer. Because *Mastering the Art of French Cooking* was such a success, we might expect to find a slew of imitators in its wake, lots of books about French cooking, or lots of books illustrated with line drawings. Instead we find a diverse field of books that continued to develop themes in play well before Child's book was published, including an almost perversely growing interest in American food history, the very flavors and techniques Child was supposed to have freed Americans from.

Considering how Child's book fit into a preexisting discourse as well as observing trends in cookbook publishing after her initial success provides a more balanced picture of the place of *Mastering the Art of French Cooking* in American cookbook history.

In the decade before *Mastering the Art of French Cooking*, writers had great success with cookbooks that embraced foodways of convenience and industrial processing despite or perhaps *to* spite the generation of gourmets who had tried to lure them out of the freezer section and into the herb gar-den. *Betty Crocker's Picture Cook Book* was a bestseller while M. F. K. Fisher's passionate musings were not. Betty Crocker was not even real, of course, but a corporate identity, while Fisher was adamantly sui generis. Americans ap-parently even preferred their cookbook authors prepackaged.[2]

The gourmet movement had made its mark on American foodways, how-ever, and even those who wrote in opposition to its values acknowledged their power. Both direct rejection of and more subtle developments of gourmet themes showed the impact of the movement. Food writer Angelo Pellegrini, for example, launched a sustained attack on gourmet writers with his first book in 1948 and continued his impassioned critique in the 1960s. While Pel-legrini objected to what he saw as pretension in the movement, other writ-ers, Peg Bracken (author of *The I Hate to Cook Book*) most notable among them, attacked the gourmets for their willful impracticality and launched a proto-feminist assault on the idea that cooking was a fulfilling activity.[3] As will be discussed below, Julia Child entered this conversation in opposition to Bracken but not entirely sympathetic to Pellegrini, who begged Americans to create their own superior cuisine rather than borrow from foreign kitchens.

Bracken, Pellegrini, and others who challenged gourmet foodways, produced cookbooks as a form of social critique, a use first pioneered by the gourmets themselves. Child's book, in contrast, though it has been credited with starting a revolution, was radical in neither tone nor technique. Devoted to one version of French cooking celebrated for its endurance across time, *Mastering the Art of French Cooking* was a much more conservative book than the most popular American cookbooks of the decade before it. These books presented a distinctly modern American cuisine—foodways of the moment that blended tradition with novelty and multicultural elements with regional and national foodways.

Betty Crocker's America

In terms of sales figures, the most popular cookbooks of the postwar era were corporate cookbooks that celebrated mass-produced foods, but they also presented home-cooked food as both a central part of American history and part of the social lives of middle-class families. This was a new way to think about food, brought about by changes in the postwar economy. Middle-class suburbanization and the growth of the white-collar workforce combined to establish the home as entertainment center where social status could be bolstered or undermined. The many TV show episodes that revolved around the boss coming to dinner reflected a culture in which private homes and women's home cooking were used to support men's corporate ambitions.[4]

Where past generations of women might have been blamed obliquely for a hired cook's bad meal, the housewife of the 1950s had to take all the responsibility for an interesting and tasty meal on herself. Interest, rather than expense, was the focus as the meal became the evening's entertainment. Cookbooks of this era reflect this expectation with their many suggestions for party meals to suit all age groups and gender configurations. The *General Foods Kitchen Cookbook*, published in 1959, for example, offered the reader menu plans for events titled, "the seated dinner," "come watch the big TV show," "strictly for the boys," and "your teenager entertains," as well as a whirl of other social occasions.⁵ For each of these, an ordinary middle-class woman needed to prepare both her kitchen and herself.

While lists of such events may appear overwhelming in isolation, cookbooks strove to make the work seem like fun. The cook/hostess was not only setting the stage for others to have a good time, she was enjoying the process herself. Simple, whimsical illustrations brightened the pages of most books and a playful conversational tone seemed designed to give the reader confidence. Meals with themes offered the opportunity for fantasy travel, as the *General Foods Kitchen Cookbook* suggested with its menu, "Build your own castle in Spain." To introduce the menu of gazpacho, paella, tossed greens, mocha pecan pudding, and coffee, the book's editors declared, "The hot sun of Spain, reflected in the drama of the bullfight and the fire of flamenco dancing, flickers in its food as well." Furthermore, it was easy to make: "Any American cook can turn out a [Spanish] dish that will make her famous."⁶ Julia Child's *Mastering the Art of French Cooking* would soon offer women accustomed to this kind of invitation a passport to France, although she wouldn't promise them it would be easy to get there.

As a corporate cookbook, the *General Foods Kitchens Cookbook* represented the triumph of the genre, in which a few large companies had switched focus from a single product to an entire lifestyle. The most commercially successful cookbooks of the 1950s and 1960s were corporate cookbooks that presented themselves as complete household manuals. Taking the role of domestic guide one step farther than the progressives, these cookbooks strategically identified specific branded products in their ingredients list to "help" the home cook prepare her recipe correctly. Perhaps the recipe would work just as well with the rival company's baking soda, but should she risk it?

Betty Crocker's Picture Cook Book was consistently one of the most popular cookbooks through the 1950s and into the 1960s, first appearing on the *Publishers Weekly* nonfiction bestseller list in 1950.⁷ General Mills, the major food processing company that published *Betty Crocker's Picture Cook Book*, had obvious reasons for including endorsements of their own products, such as Gold Medal Flour, Bisquick, and Wheaties. The editors also emphasized the collective aspect of their book in their greeting to the reader, "This book seems like a dream come true for us. And we hope it will be for the thousands of you who have requested a cook book full of our tested recipes." Those recipes had been tried out both at General Mills and in the kitchens of "representative homes across the country," to ensure that the book suited its target audience. General Mills here borrowed the ethos of a community cookbook to promote corporate food writing.[8]

Yet for all its encouragement to try new products and new methods, *Betty Crocker's Picture Cookbook* recognized the pleasures of hands-on cooking. In a section about yeast breads, editors commented, "Handling yeast dough is more fun than any other 'cooking.' Members of our staff always feel this."[9] In the "Cakes" chapter, two types of recipes are given, one using the conventional method, which requires creaming the butter (using the back of a spoon to smash it into a paste), and another "modern" and "double-quick method" in which fats are added to dry ingredients without creaming. Because the second method is less labor intensive, offering both methods, side by side, acknowledged home cooks' attachment to old habits, even when new ones could save time. It also offered the reader a chance to choose, an interesting feature in a genre that was typically prescriptive. Cooking could be about the journey as much as the arrival, a message Julia Child would deliver a decade later in her unusually long recipes and in her television show, *The French Chef*.

Betty Crocker's Picture Cook Book used several different media to keep the reader engaged with the text: step-by-step black-and-white photo essays about how to prepare many of the recipes; pen-and-ink style illustrations of family life and anthropomorphized foods (a cucumber, radish, and celery stalk dancing together), and large color photographs of prepared meals. These illustrations represented different aspects of the cooking experience—the practical, the beautiful, and the fun. The book's three-ring binder format also made it practical for everyday use, assuring it would stay out on the countertop rather than gather dust on a shelf.

Further emphasizing the social aspects of cooking and perhaps to arm the hostess with entertaining trivia for cocktail party chat, the editors included brief sections about American food history. These sections added a new element to the comprehensive cookbook by connecting the everyday activities of the kitchen to a national, even global narrative. Readers could learn, for example, that "appetizers are comparative newcomers in our American cuisine," that had originated in Ancient Greece in the form of chicory or endive, "munched on . . . to excite hunger." Even if a woman did not trot out this historical tidbit to impress her guests, by setting it beside a recipe General Mills subtly elevated kitchen work into the realm of the academic, another way of selling women on this work that would in turn produce more sales for the company. This kind of supplementary material was the result of *Gourmet*'s success in establishing food as a sophisticated topic. Where previous generations of middle-class Americans had shown their cosmopolitanism through what they ate, their contemporary counterparts showed it also in what they could say about food.[10]

Gourmet writing clearly influenced particular features of *Betty Crocker's Picture Cookbook*, such as the "dictionary of special and foreign terms" that tutored readers in a new culinary vocabulary, much of it French. Terms such as brioche, croustade, and pâté de foie gras as well as grits, gumbo, and tamale, were considered appropriate to the mainstream American kitchen. An illustration shows a woman smiling while a cloud of French culinary terms rises from her open volume of *Betty Crocker's Picture Cook Book*. Ten years before Julia Child, whose book also included a chapter of culinary terms, General Mills encouraged home cooks to see an expanded vocabulary as a happy side effect of good cooking.

The household magazine *Better Homes and Gardens* published many of the bestselling cookbooks of this era. These books functioned in the usual way of corporate cookbooks to tie the home kitchen to a commercial product, in this case a magazine. *Better Homes and Gardens* also strategically published books on single topics—dieting in 1955, barbecue in 1956, and salads in 1958—that became bestsellers. This pattern fit the magazine's model of offering new material with each issue. It also provided a steady market for new books when new topics, such as microwave cooking, became popular. This model both drove and supported an American market for novelty in culinary matters.

The *Better Homes and Gardens New Cook Book*, a comprehensive volume that was a bestseller in 1954, opened with many of the elements of cooking that gourmets opposed. Its first chapter was dedicated to nutrition and meal planning, beginning with the declaration that "The meals you plan should be easy on the cook, kind to your budget, and full of the nutrients that keep your family in tiptop health."[11] Gourmets believed that ease and nutrition were the last elements to worry about when entering the kitchen.

Accompanying photographs portrayed lavish servings in artfully de-signed settings. Meals had multiple elements—a meat dish, a "starchy dish," a vegetable dish, salad, dessert, and other items classified as "nice to serve." A sample menu to be served with flank steak, for example, included celery stuffing or baked sweet potatoes and succotash or brussels sprouts, followed by ambrosia salad or cranberry Waldorf salad and finished up with a nut-meg feather cake or apple dumplings. It would be "nice to serve" butterhorn rolls or sauerkraut juice with this meal. Sauerkraut juice would have served as an appetizer in the same style as tomato juice, both considered "cocktails" in this era.[12] As with *Betty Crocker's Picture Cook Book*, readers were given both structure and choices.

A chapter on appetizers and beverages affirmed the world of postwar domestic sociability in which food was central. Both the "Oahu frappe," an orange and pineapple sorbet, and a shrimp cocktail were designed to "tanta-lize the appetite before a meal," and could be made "long before your guests are due."[13] Julia Child's later success depended on this new culture of home entertaining in which middle-class women cooked to impress their friends.

As the General Foods Spanish menu and the Oahu frappe suggest, cor-porate cookbook writers went beyond internationalism into the realm of what would come to be called "fusion." Since the first of the genre was pub-lished at the end of the eighteenth century, American cookbooks had typi-cally included recipes from other nations, but the habit took on particular life in the 1950s as themed meals allowed home cooks to create cosmopoli-tan experiences for their guests. French and Spanish were only two of many common themes. *Betty Crocker's Picture Cook Book* suggested "Curries from the Far East," "Hot Tamale Pie, Picturesque Dish from Old Mexico," "Ital-ian Macaroni" with chicken livers, and "Sub Gum," a Chinese-style rice dish. The book also featured proto-fusion dishes like "Spaghetti Oriental," "Chow Mein Loaf," and what the editors called "Kaedjere, American Indian version of a fish-and-rice dish from faraway India." These dishes may test contemporary taste biases, but can more usefully be seen as representative of the continuing force of innovation as a theme in American food writing as well as openness to blend new flavors, textures, and techniques with more established materials and methods and to borrow from the global kitchen.

Perhaps the international journey-by-dinner plate served as a counterbalance to the potential claustrophobia of suburban life, or perhaps American home cooks enjoyed the sense of their nation as preeminent among others, able to borrow whatever elements pleased them as older empires had once done. This trend would be taken up by the Time Life Corporation soon after Julia Child's success, as the Foods of the World Series, discussed below, offered American cooks the world's cuisines in one lavishly illustrated set.

The appropriation and reinvention of international foodways as a form of entertainment was a notable feature of postwar American cookbooks. Even in "foreign" menus, cookbook writers mixed origins and reinterpreted dishes. The mocha pecan pudding mentioned above as part of a Spanish menu, for instance, is a riff on the typical Spanish dessert of flan that uses a distinctly American nut and would probably have seemed quite unusual to anyone from Spain.

This spirit of playful adaptation also inspired the writing of James Beard, one of the most important voices in American food in the postwar period. Beard, born into a restaurant family in Oregon, first became known in New York culinary scenes as a successful caterer for wealthy customers. Although he spent time in France and appreciated French food, he never presented American food as the opposite of French, defying one of the gourmet's guiding principles.

James Beard and American Cooking

In his first successful book, *The Fireside Cookbook*, published in 1949, Beard declared, "More than other countries with longer histories or narrower traditions in food . . . America has the opportunity, as well as the resources, to create for herself a truly national cuisine that will incorporate all that is best in the traditions of the many peoples who have crossed the seas to form our new, still-young nation."[14] Beard agreed with gourmet critic Pellegrini that America had not yet achieved its culinary promise and identified immigrant contributions as the key to future greatness.

Pellegrini, an Italian immigrant who became a professor of English literature at the University of Washington, praised American produce—Kansas steaks, the mushrooms he foraged near Seattle, the Cougar Gold cheddar cheese his own university produced. He railed against Americans who turned to France for culinary sophistication. In this spirit, he once set up an elaborate dinner to trick a local gourmet club into admitting they preferred some California wines to French vintages. But Pellegrini also decried American tastes for commercial goods, claiming "America's gastronomic coming of age will be heralded by a national uprising against tinned spaghetti."[15] Neither blindly aping French cooking nor mindlessly heating up cans, "The ultimate goal" for American cooking "should be the perfection of a native cuisine, varied and enriched by the culinary ideas brought to us by our immigrants from the four corners of the world."[16]

Also like Pellegrini, James Beard went on to decry Americans' attempts to imitate other national cuisines as a divergence from its own best qualities, which Beard identified as, "straightforward, honest, and delicious as the fish that swim off its shores or the cornmeal dishes that were the mainstays of its earliest settlers."[17]

Beard found another fault in contemporary American cooking, however, that no gourmet would have noticed: Americans were not cooking their *own* food skillfully. Beard called attention to "the sins that are daily committed in scores of public dining rooms—and private ones, for that matter—in the name of Southern fried chicken." His mission as a cooking-school teacher, caterer, and cookbook writer was to teach the nation's cooks to honor their own traditions. In the service of this goal, Beard also rejected the gourmet's fear of innovation, encouraging readers to "take advantage of new developments in the growing, shipping, preserving, and cooking of food." Like the fictional Betty Crocker, Beard reminded readers to "Take time both to cherish the old and to investigate the new" in American foodways.[18]

Beard's confidence in his own taste helped those who might otherwise be skeptical about American food to bring it to their own tables. Beard was, for example, an early adopter of the barbecue craze that swept America in the 1950s, publishing *Cook It Outdoors* in 1941, following this with several other outdoor cookbooks through the 1950s and becoming the preeminent expert on grilling.[19] Beard's books about outdoor cooking, as well as those about entertaining and hors d'oeuvres, bridged middle-class sociability and the more economically privileged social set to whom Beard had (professionally) catered in New York. Food was no longer a matter merely of display; it had become a form of play in adult life.[20]

In many ways, Beard helped to establish the market Julia Child would later tap into by letting his own enthusiastic personality become indelibly associated with enjoyable food. Through the 1970s Beard's publishers could profitably use his name as their main draw—*Beard on Bread*, *Beard on Birds*, *James Beard's New American Cooking*. Beard has been identified as the first food celebrity (although a failure at television cooking) because his personality rose above the vagaries of food fashions. As we'll see in Chapter 6, Beard was the hero of the generation of American restaurateurs—Larry Forgione, Jeremiah Tower—who are more commonly identified as the first celebrity chefs. In the 1950s, Beard served as a friendly guide for men and women ready to cook for their own entertainment as much as for that of their guests.

The widespread expectation, wholeheartedly endorsed by the corporations, that middle-class women were responsible for using food to entertain an extended social network, drew critics even as these corporate cookbooks were most popular among readers. By the early 1950s, writers were challenging stereotypes of women as stay-at-home cooks to address a cohort of readers who wanted to entertain as if they had spent the day at home cooking, but who didn't have any interest in actually staying home.

Anti-Gourmet Cookbooks

In 1951, Poppy Cannon noted that women were now likely to be "frying as well as bringing home the bacon." Partly this double shift, which she did not critique, was the result of the gourmet movement. Cannon wrote that even in this era of increased job opportunities for women, "It is no longer considered chic, charming, or 'intellectual' to be ignorant in the kitchen." Women

should be proud of "preparing and serving interesting meals" for their families.[21] The idea that the family would take an interest in what was on their
plates before they ate it reflected the new role of food in social life. It was because of this persistent theme that Julia Child would be able to presume that
multipage recipes would not frighten off any reader who opened her book.

Although Cannon endorsed the interesting meal, she admitted, "there
is always the problem of time."[22] To deal with this problem, Cannon sought
help from the gourmet's arch-nemesis, the processed food industry. She
claimed that the can opener, which had once been the "badge of shame," indicating a woman's inability to cook, had become "a magic wand" enabling
her to prepare impressive meals with very little labor. The trick, Cannon suggested, was to see yourself as a professional, not a housewife: "The modern
cook looks at it this way: other people have the responsibility for the selection of my raw materials, the cleaning and preliminary preparation." All the
prep work could be outsourced, leaving the cook to "move onto the scene
the way a chef comes in after a corps of kitchen helpers has done the scullery
chores . . . armed with a can opener, I become the artist-cook, the master,
the creative chef."[23] Prepackaged goods enabled the busy woman to take on
the characteristics of a high status male who earned credit for his genius,
not the grunt work. Cannon's ideal harkened back to Frigidaire's promise to
make women feel like guests in their own homes.

To demonstrate the process, Cannon began with canned stews, noting,
"Although such stews are notoriously under-seasoned to appeal to the *average palate*," the gourmet-with-a-can-opener could rise above national culinary limitations by adding French ingredients: "they can be transformed
with a rinse of red wine, a clove of garlic, parsley, half a bay leaf, and a flicker
of mixed herbs to make something delightfully akin to Le Boeuf en Daube
as served in France." No one would know the difference.[24]

For Cannon, wine was an essential tool in the gourmetization of packaged foods. Wine of all kinds was "employed frequently" in the recipes and
she urged readers not to forget "rum and brandy for the glorious and ever-
so-easy and dramatic trick of serving food flambé (afire)."[25] A reviewer in
Life named Cannon "the high priestess of things practical," and declared her
"able to turn tinned grub into gastronomic delight in 30 minutes or less."[26]

Cannon followed up with other cookbooks of this kind, including, in 1961, *The Electric Epicure's Cookbook*, which contained both a dedication to her friend and famous gourmet, Alice B. Toklas, and thanks to the appliance manufacturers who had given her their goods to experiment with.[27]

If Cannon tried to use convenience foods to achieve gourmet status, Peg Bracken preached open rebellion against the tyranny of the epicure. Bracken had an abiding dread of the kitchen. Bracken's *The I Hate to Cook Book* was published in 1961 and eventually sold more than three million copies.[28] It began with mordant humor: "Some women, it is said, like to cook. This book is not for them."[29]

Bracken's intended audience were women who, in total defiance of stereotypes of feminine domesticity, "want to fold our big dish-water hands around a dry martini instead of a wet flounder come the end of the day." She was writing for women who wanted to live like men.[30]

While she advertised all her recipes as easy, Peg Bracken noted that one particular chapter offered "really jet-propelled recipes." Using the language of the space program, Bracken allied her foodways to modernity. By contrast, Child's *Mastering the Art of French Cooking*, published one year later, suggested time-honored practices of the artisan and apprentice. "Mastering" is a process that takes time; jet propulsion does not. That Child and Bracken became famous in the same moment suggests that the theme of time-on-task was a bone of contention among cooks and writers. The publishing industry seems to have successfully played both sides of the debate simultaneously, helping to create a market of partisans. Bracken wrote in reaction to books like Child's that celebrated the slow and complicated, while Child wrote as a corrective to the slapdash style and prepackaged foodstuffs Bracken celebrated.

Bracken was avowedly in favor of corporate cuisine but warned readers that cultural expectations could make it difficult for a modern woman to benefit from all of the technological progress that had been made in foodways. Addressing her cuisine-phobic reader, she summed up the situation: "You buy frozen things and ready-mix things, as well as pizza from the pizza man and chicken pies from the chicken pie lady." Modern foodways made it easier to feed a family without cooking.[31] However, the outmoded expecta-

tions of "the basic male," complicated the picture. Husbands not only expected but actually "want[ed] to see you knead that bread and tote that bale,
before you go down cellar to make soap."[32]

Bracken's answer to this was not to educate husbands, perhaps even encourage them to put on a British butcher's apron and get into the kitchen,
but instead to lie to them. As long as husbands did not see frozen rolls going
into the oven, wives could dissemble and claim to have baking skills. Brack-
en's cuisine was based in the art of deception.

The *I Hate to Cook Book* recipe for Honest John's Clam Chowder was
one of these ruses. It began, "As a matter of fact, this isn't exactly honest." It
wasn't "honest" because it didn't include salt pork, a traditional ingredient
in many chowders. Rather than apologizing, Bracken asked, "Who has salt
pork around these days besides butchers?" The question mocked the stereotypical gourmet cookbook's call for hard-to-find ingredients. Not content to
confess only to the lack of salt pork, she added, "The clams are canned, too,
instead of fresh. But it tastes honest." In direct rejection of gourmet connoisseurship and authenticity Bracken implied that "honesty" was just a matter
of presentation.[33]

Bracken hoped her book would free women from the competitive entertaining that had become a social norm for the middle class: "Do you know
the really basic trouble here? It is your guilt complex. . . .We live in a cooking-happy age. You watch your friends redoing their kitchens and hoarding
their pennies for glamorous cooking equipment and new cookbooks called
Eggplant Comes to the Party or *Let's Waltz into the Kitchen*, and presently
you begin to feel un-American."[34] It was ironic to suggest that to be authenti-
cally American in 1960 one had to adopt the gourmet foodways that were
rooted in idealized French cuisine.[35]

Similarly exasperated with the time-intensive methods of the gourmet,
convenience cookbook writer Jo Coudert described her own first attempt to
make beef stroganoff using the sort of cookbook that was "intended for people with time to cook—and surprisingly often, for people who already know
how to cook." After "painstakingly adding one ingredient after another and
stirring constantly over a low flame," Coudert recalled, "I suddenly said to
myself, 'Oh, my goodness, it's beef gravy. Why didn't they say so in the first

place?' Now I buy a can of beef gravy and make Stroganoff that is unfailingly delicious in something less than one-quarter the time."[36] Coudert's approach blithely ignored the gourmet's emphasis on the value of process and the experience of cooking. Her anecdote, like Bracken's many critical comments, suggested there was something fundamentally dishonest about the gourmet. In the spirit of culinary debunking and demystification, her book was titled, *The I Never Cooked Before Cook Book.*

Bracken had the most withering putdown for those who celebrated cooking as a creative pleasure: "We [who hate to cook] don't get our creative kicks from adding an egg [to a recipe]," instead, they found satisfaction in artistic expression, professional work, motherhood, or "engaging in some interesting type of psycho-neuro-chemical research like seeing if, perhaps, we can replace colloids with sulphates." In other words, cooking was a waste of the modern woman's time. If you claimed to like it, you were probably just not smart enough to do something more meaningful with your time.[37]

Pellegrini agreed with Bracken that overemphasis on process and ingredients could drive women out of the kitchen:

> The American housewife has been convinced by these culinary
> fakirs that cooking is an art, and since she is at the moment in full
> revolt against the thesis that woman's place is in the home, she is
> quite willing to admit that her cooking isn't worth a damn. . . . She is
> in no mood to achieve distinction in the kitchen if to do so she must
> go snouting for truffles in the oak groves of Piedmont and preying
> upon snails in the vineyards of Burgundy.[38]

Italian though he was, Pellegrini could understand why a woman might not want eggplant to come to dinner.

Agreeing with Bracken that there were better places for women to be than the kitchen, Lynn Dallin offered *The Stay Out of the Kitchen Cook Book*, published in 1968, most likely in response to Child's first success. Dallin explained that her own inspiration to find culinary shortcuts came when she was a young wife in a university town. Her husband was a composer and professor and she worked in the university public relations office: "In these capacities we met distinguished educators, lecturers, political figures, and performing artists." Dallin invited these exciting visitors to her home, and "Drudging in the kitchen was unthinkable with such fascinating personalities in the living room. I was determined to *stay out of the kitchen*."[39] To that end, she offered a few simple recipes with many variations.

The grand-sounding Lecadre Queen Cake Francais is an example of Dallin's technique, made with store-bought lady-fingers and apricot jam, sprinkled with rum, and chilled overnight in the refrigerator. The same cake could be made with sherry or port instead of rum, layers of almond paste, cherry jam, or pineapple chunks instead of apricot jam, and vanilla ice cream.[40] Like Poppy Cannon, Dallin advocated the "generous" use of wine and liquor to give processed foods enhanced flavor: "These are the secret ingredients of flavor-conscious cooks and professional chefs."[41]

Dallin was concerned with how food tasted and appeared, not just in getting it onto the table. Cannon had also offered guidance on presentation. For middle-class women of their generation, meals, especially those for company, posed a tremendous problem. Although they had jobs of their own and no household help, Dallin and Cannon and Bracken (with her arts of deception), all knew that cultural expectations did not take the new reality into consideration: women were still responsible for "meals of elegance and distinction," as Dallin put it.[42] The celebration of the "cooking-happy" lifestyle, convenient as it was to hierarchical gender norms, might make it hard for women to escape KP duty. Child's contribution was to argue, as gourmets and corporate cookbook writers had argued before her, that drudgery was only in the mind and that cooking really was as intellectually stimulating as a conversation with academics over cocktails. Her solution to Dallin's dilemma was to make the kitchen, rather than the living room, the place to be.

Mastering the Art of French Cooking

Like Bracken, Child and her coauthors, Simone Beck and Louisette Bertholle directly identified their audience: "This is a book for the servantless American cook who can be unconcerned on occasion with budgets, waistlines, time schedules, children's meals, the parent-chauffeur-den-mother syndrome." All these stereotypical trappings of middle-class American womanhood could, Child explained, "interfere with the enjoyment of producing something wonderful to eat." The book was for people who already loved cooking but it did not claim to be for everyday use—the phrase "on occasion," set Child's menus apart from the daily grind.

The first paragraph of *Mastering the Art of French Cooking* was both welcoming and defensive, situating the book in the market by justifying elements that were likely to come under attack. The authors acknowledged that their recipes would seem longer than what readers usually found in a cookbook, but explained that this was because they were so full of useful instructions. The book's title might scare off cooks who were afraid they would be told to buy lots of hard-to-find ingredients, so Child and her coauthors assured them the book might just as well have been called "French Cooking from the American Supermarket." If readers were worried that French food was just too fancy for their own lifestyle, Child reassured them that the gourmet approach was all nonsense and "romantic interludes" that put French cooking "into a never-never land" instead of appetizingly on the American table.

Child's awareness of her audience's preconceptions and anxieties showed that she was in tune with the contemporary discourse of American domestic life and enabled her to address the reader in very reassuring tones. She promised, for example, that the recipes provided everything one needed to know "in the sweep of an eye," and that there was really nothing difficult about cooking. She and her coauthors acknowledged not only the novice but also the more educated reader who might wonder why the book left out recipes she expected to find, such as "*pâté feuilletée*" (a type of pastry). The reference flattered the reader who already considered herself a gourmet.[43]

While acknowledging limitations to what the book could cover, Child, Beck, and Bertholle also made some subtle statements about American food. They blamed "pseudo-French cooking," which they claimed all their readers would be familiar with, on corner-cutting and substitutions. Approaching cooking with the attitude that it would be "'Too much trouble,' 'Too expensive,' or 'Who will know the difference'" if one used premade ingredients was fatal to good eating. This oblique reference to Cannon's genre of shortcut gourmet cooking encouraged readers to think of *Mastering*'s time-consuming methods as more authentic. This was exactly the kind of claim Bracken fought with her Honest John's Clam Chowder.

The American interest in visual novelty and transcultural foodways was also implied as a contrast to the French, who are "seldom interested in unusual combinations or surprise presentations." French people preferred familiar foods cooked well to anything new. This culinary conservatism was not small-minded, the authors argued, because the French had so many good dishes in their repertoire to choose from. For the American reader, however, as the book's first two chapters indicated, mastering the art of French cooking would depend on willingness to assimilate not only a whole new collection of kitchen tools, but also a new vocabulary. As we have already seen in *Betty Crocker's Picture Cook Book*, this would not have surprised the average American cookbook reader, steeped as she was in a culinary culture of adaptations and internationalism.

Child, Beck, and Bertholle noted differences between American and French foodways throughout the book, so that it served not only as a guide to French cooking but also as a mirror for American cooks. The point at which French and American food customs diverged "most radically," according to the authors, was in the treatment of vegetables. The difference was that "The French are interested in vegetables as food rather than as purely nutrient objects valuable for their vitamins and minerals." Stereotyping American cooks as blinkered by their trust in nutritional science was a familiar trope from the gourmet era and one unsupported by the evidence in cookbooks, which provided diverse ways to cook and enjoy vegetables that had nothing to do with their vitamin content. Child and her coauthors, however, also poked fun at Americans who spoke with "trembling nostalgia" of the French way with vegetables. Neither the dietician nor the gourmet escaped their gentle scorn. Picking up these preexisting themes in their book allowed Child, Beck, and Bertholle to situate their work in a broader context of what the reader already knew and expected from food writing.

Two of Child's American readers who became writers, Mary Cantwell and Betty Fussell, recalled the impact of Child on their own lives in memoirs. Cantwell experienced Child as one in a line of culinary gurus who helped her cohort perform their social roles. In her memoir *Manhattan When I*

Was Young, she recalled her own evolution as a cook in the 1950s and 1960s: "My dinner parties grew ever grander," she writes, "culminating in the evening I served beef Wellington. 'Gourmet's,' I said, when asked. That was how one answered culinary questions then. Another guest, usually a woman, would raise an inquisitive eyebrow, and the hostess would say 'Gourmet's' or 'Dione's,' and later . . . 'Julia's.'"[44] Cantwell and her friends established their credentials through whose words they consumed as much as through the food they made consumable. To inquire "Gourmet's?" and be told "Campbell's" would have been a shocking, an even unappetizing disappointment.

For Fussell, who became an important American food writer, Julia Child was the first guide into the world of cooking as high culture. Fussell, who was a member of a university community, recalled, "Overnight [Julia] turned our amateur bouts into professional matches." Having enjoyed adventures in postwar Europe, Fussell's crowd had come to believe that "to cook French . . . was to become versant in the civilized tongues of Europe as opposed to America's barbaric yawp."[45] In their attempts to re-create French cuisine in American kitchens, Fussell argued, she and her peers were doing more than cooking.

The unemployed wives of male professionals, they were attempting to elevate their own status: "The trick was to be a lady in the dining room, yet an amateur-pro in the kitchen." This trend had been clear since the early 1950s, in corporate cookbooks like *Betty Crocker's Picture Cook Book*. Americans were not learning to cook like French people, but like Americans—for entertainment and semi-competitively. And like the male gourmets who shunned the frills of traditional domesticity, Fussell "never wore an apron . . . partly to ease the oscillation between hostess and cook, but also to refuse the badge of household drudge."[46]

When Child's book came out, the work of the amateur-pro had a new guide. "Julia choreographed the production [of party meals], plotting the time of preparation for each stage of each dish. . . . We each felt we had Julia in our corner, and if your keenest rival led with a buffet of baked ham and roast turkey, you knew how to counter with a *jambon persille*, pre-sliced and molded into a beautiful green-flecked mountain, or a boned turkey stuffed with veal forcemeat larded with truffles."[47] Child enabled women to outclass each other in what for Fussell was the competitive realm of social entertaining.

Despite Fussell's feeling that Child's contribution was new, however, American authors before her had included menus and timing, and books like the *General Foods Kitchen Cookbook* were nothing if not guides to out-shine one's neighbors at entertaining. Child's own Smith College classmate Charlotte Turgeon had published *Time to Entertain* as a friendly guide to kitchen timing and dedicated it to "Fellow gourmets in Amherst Massachu-setts" in 1954.[48]

What made Child important, then, was not her message or her recipes, but her moment and her media. The people who became Child's acolytes in the early 1960s were a generation who had come of age during and just after the Second World War. They were not the children of the fifties who would soon turn against American mass culture, nor were they these chil-dren's parents—the squares to be rejected. Many of the men were veterans and their wives had risen with them on the wave of postwar prosperity that brought new cohorts from the working class and ethnic Americans into the universities and professions. Pioneers in the middle class, they possessed a sense of potential, but not always of confidence.

For Americans in this cohort, Child offered sophistication without stuff-iness, acceptance into high-class culture through kitchen work. Women of this generation were those caught on the cusp of feminism, more likely to work outside the home than their mothers but still not welcomed in the pro-fessions and simultaneously encouraged by popular culture to devote them-selves to domesticity. The moment for Child's debut, 1961, was a moment of restlessness for a particular cohort of women, and her message—cook dif-ficult food for fun!—strangely resonated with them.

The media in which Child delivered this message made all the differ-ence. It is likely that had she only appeared in print, she would have been a much more modest success. Her book was encouraging in tone, but this was not a new approach, and neither was the idea of helping American women cook French food. In 1959, for example, John Marshall published *Classic Cooking*, which employed a charming, conversational tone and promised readers that although his recipes were long this was only so that he could provide all needed instruction.[49] He spoke directly to American women using American markets—his located specifically in New York—and gallantly demystified while also celebrating French home cooking. Marshall's book even included a section like Child's *batterie de cuisine* titled "The Kitchen," illustrated with simple ink drawings.

There was unsurprising overlap between Child's recipes and those that made up Marshall's thirty recommended menus, although Marshall also included some American dishes (Lobster Newburg) that one could argue might even have made his book more appealing than Child's devoutly French volume. Marshall and Myra Waldo, who published *The Complete Book of Gourmet Cooking for the American Kitchen* in 1960, both dedicated their books to their grown-up daughters—the very generation who would be most impressed by Julia Child.[50] As Evan Jones, husband of Child's editor Judith Jones, reflected in 1975, by 1961, "Food had become a central factor in living well, in pursuing a stylish life. Mastering the art of the cuisine had become more than a fad." So Child's book publication had been "fatefully timed" and her television show persuaded "thousands that the ability to turn out epicurean dinners could be achieved by all who were seriously intent upon cooking well."[51] That cooking well meant cooking French was a long-established concept among the gourmet set.

Working against it in a market full of insouciant and bright cookbooks, *Mastering the Art of French Cooking* was dense and illustrated only with instructional black and white drawings. But on television, the medium newly available to the middle class and short on programming, Child's book came alive through her own charm.[52] Had she published her book ten years earlier, there would have been no WGBH willing to take a chance on a local character; ten years later, she might have been drowned out by vastly more diverse programming. Because WGBH was a public station thus far dedicated to programming for the erudite—the Boston Symphony Orchestra and famous theater critics—Child's cooking received an extra imprimatur of high culture that made watching a woman cook on TV part of a cosmopolitan lifestyle. In this moment, too, the medium of television was not yet entirely associated with a stereotyped emptiness of popular culture, as it would be in the generation to come.[53]

On her television show Child particularly emphasized the notion of fun in the kitchen. Her book and TV show implicitly advocated for the kitchen as activity center. Here the experience of cooking took precedence over the responsibility of serving. Just as architects of the 1950s and 1960s physically opened the kitchen to the rest of the home, Child strove to make it a place where people would want to be, where what had once bluntly been called work could now be celebrated as action. She had, after all, made her own private kitchen into the set of a TV show, opening it up to the entire viewing public.

Child clearly tapped into Fussell's and Cantwell's yearning to know how to perform their roles as cosmopolitan middle-class American women correctly. Where American food was famously indefinable, Child gave them a weighty but finite set of rules. As Fussell said, she was in their corner. While Child won many individual converts to her style of cooking, however, we know that American cookbook publishing did not suddenly turn Francophile. Instead, it shifted toward an eclectic collection of styles and approaches that exploited the market for cooking-as-entertainment. Moving beyond the usual chapters titled "foreign foods," publishers began to offer more books dedicated to non-U.S. foodways, presupposing a hungry market for readers who wanted to master the arts of many other kinds of cooking. At the same time, the number of books about American food increased, but these books, in mimicking the structure of travelogues, also offered the cookbook as a journey of discovery. The most important event in cookbook publishing after Child's debut was publisher Time-Life Books's attempt to corner all markets for culinary explorers with their Foods of the World Series.

Time-Life Foods of the World Series

In 1968, Time-Life Books published the first in its Foods of the World Series. Commitment to an entire series strongly suggests that executives at the major media company considered the time right to make a profit in cookbooks. Time-Life Books sales director Joan Manley noted, "There are thousands of people in America buying cookbooks who have never bought another book."[54] One writer described the series as having "the grandest budget in cookbookdom."[55]

The Time-Life series included books about Japan, Latin America, Germany, Italy, and one by Fisher about provincial French cooking. It also included books about American regional and national cooking. Attempting (successfully) to cash in on growing national interest in cookbooks, Time-Life gambled that Americans were as interested in their own national foodways as they were in foreign cuisines. The publisher dedicated a test-kitchen in corporate headquarters to their cookbook series and hired well-known writers, many of them veterans of *Gourmet*, to write about national or regional cuisines. Titles in the series about the United States presented foods of "The Great West," Creole and Acadian cultures, the Northwest, the "Eastern Heartland, New England, the "Melting Pot," and foods in "Southern Style." The culinary nation was divided not only into regions, but also into "native" and "foreign" foodways with the inclusion of the melting pot theme.

The books can be seen as providing another version of the educational voyeurism popularized in *National Geographic*. They are also consistent with their parent company's other publications—*Time* and *Life*—which both offered American readers the world—in words and large pictures—as a consumer good.[56]

The first American book in the Time-Life series, Dale Brown's 1968 *American Cooking*, opened with a chapter titled "From a Cookery to a Cuisine," which employed the popular idea of American food as a work in progress. Brown claimed that American foodways had been decent but bland until recent waves of immigration began to introduce diversity. The book also employed the theme of America as cornucopia, with chapter titles "America the Plentiful" and "Dairy Riches and a Mountain of Snacks." James Beard provided the introduction for Brown's book, setting the tone early by offering an appreciation of American culinary heritage and a refusal to apologize for its dissimilarities to French cuisine. Beard proudly proclaimed, "We are an amazingly versatile nation, producing everything from good caviar to good salted peanuts."[57]

Brown took a personal approach to American food, dedicating his first chapter to his family's farm in Chenango County, New York, and including photographs of it. Brown's descriptions did not glamorize the farm, with its linoleum floor that "contains black islands of wear and is tacked to the wooden floor." His relatives, too, are portrayed unsentimentally as prim and hard working. Remembering one meal from his childhood he recalled, "I watched the old people break bread and drop the jagged pieces into bowls of milk to make one of the most basic and the oldest of farmhouse suppers." Readers were unlikely to seek out recipes for this kind of food.

When Brown's grandmother and her sister died, many of their recipes "died with them." And although there are "some we may try to revive," others will be allowed to fade away because "We of the younger generation are cooking differently, and we drink wine at our tables when the occasion calls for it."[58] Like Child, Brown recognized the internal structures of a particular people's foodways, but unlike Child, he didn't pass this on to his readers.

Brown also acknowledged the contributions of immigrant groups to national foodways: "Chinese, stir-frying the Chinese way, opened restaurants that tempted millions with their combination plates." He gave most credit for change in the American diet, however, to developments in his own era. Postwar prosperity and "the revolution in communications brought American cooks a profusion of magazines, cookbooks and television programs loaded with enticing recipes and culinary aids." Julia Child was clearly referenced here and Brown himself had been part of the revolution.[59]

Time-Life's *American Cooking: The Melting Pot* took the theme of multicultural national foodways as its organizing principle, for the most part focusing on "ancient traditions . . . redolent of dishes that originated across the sea."[60] In his introduction to the book, James P. Shenton, a historian of immigration, argued that the cuisines of Northern and Western Europe had become part of mainstream American cooking through earlier waves of immigration. Since the 1880s, however, the flavor of immigration had changed with the influx of Eastern Europeans, Italians, and people from "the old Ottoman Empire." While the regional books in the series would include the influences of earlier immigrant groups, this volume would concentrate on the newer groups. Pellegrini contributed to this volume, telling his own story of migration from poverty-stricken Italy to what he deemed "a little paradise" for the food lover in rural Washington state.[61]

The book was organized around what would be termed ethnic enclaves, places in which a majority of people identified themselves with a place beyond the U.S. borders. The list of chapter titles reveals a subtle shift in thinking about American ethnicities. Alongside the expected Italians and "The Lusty Foods of Central Europe," are "A Cook's Tour of Six Communities" that included Armenians in Central California, Greeks in Florida, and Basques in Idaho as well as the more familiar Germans in Texas and Portuguese in San Francisco. In direct contrast to the contemporary suburbanization of American culture, it included a chapter titled "A Moveable Feast of the Caribbean" that celebrated the foodways of Puerto Ricans in New York City.

The author of this chapter, Peter Wood, was a journalist who explained that he lived near, though not in, Manhattan's Puerto Rican Barrio. Wood identified Puerto Ricans as new immigrants, replacing the older settlements of Jewish migrants on the Lower East Side of New York, suggesting that "if you had a parent, grandparent, or great-grandparent who came to this country in steerage, and if you would like to see what his first years in an American city were like, visit El Barrio or the Lower East Side." Although Puerto Ricans had been in America and indeed been American citizens since the early twentieth century, their presence seemed new to Wood.[62] The delight he took in Puerto Rican cooking signaled the emergence of multiculturalism in American culture, a movement to embrace cultural diversity as national heritage.

The at least partial acceptance of America as a multiracial society, as well as multicultural, was also reflected in Eugene Walter's *American Cooking: Southern Style*. Although Walter began his book with the usual celebration of lost cause rhetoric, titling his first chapter, "The Southland I Remember," he did also include a chapter about soul food. Soul food was, "a basic element of 'soul'—black life-style that disdains the hide-bound puritanical Anglo-Saxon culture and instead emphasizes directness, spontaneity and uninhibited feeling." As in earlier writing about African American foodways, the notion of instinct is privileged over practice and technique.[63] Walter also challenges the old clichés, however, with the argument that Africans who first cooked in America had "ingenuity" and "resourcefulness," to create new foodways in difficult circumstances.

To represent contemporary African American foodways, Walter turned to a friend and fellow expat-in-Rome, opera singer Leontyne Price. When he arrived at her home bearing some sprigs of herbs she had requested, "she was regally dressed in a Dior hostess gown and seated at the oval table in her dining room overlooking a court with a gently plashing fountain." Her setting signaled cosmopolitanism rather than the Southern regionalism typically associated with African American cooking. Walter celebrated the ways in which Price was a global citizen while also retaining culinary ties to her cultural roots: "The coffeepot was beside her, the score of *Salome* was propped up before her—and she was sorting turnip greens." Walter's celebration of the mixture of high and low culture—opera and turnip greens—acknowledged that African Americans lived complex lives beyond the older stereotypes of their work in Master's kitchen.[64]

The Time-Life series on American cooking used photo essays, personal essays, and local color reporting to portray American foodways. This combination of approaches was much more descriptive than prescriptive. The company also republished each book's recipes in a smaller, spiral bound format that lacked the commentary and illustrations, a move that recognized readers would, and perhaps also encouraged them to, accept the illustrated books in the series as entertainment rather than direct guidance.

While it might seem a smart business decision to separately monetize these two aspects of food writing—the inspirational and the practical—this model did not become popular. Instead, decorative illustrations became ubiquitous while practical elements like ring-bindings became less so. Readers seemed to want the fantasy elements of the pictorial without necessarily being dragged back into the kitchen by useable recipes. That fantasy cooking now included the local—the family farm, one's urban neighbors—signaled the popular appeal of American foodways. No longer merely the foil against which French food was admired, American cooking was deemed worthy of study on its own terms.

Americana Cookbooks

Sensing a market in curiosity about American foodways, publishers brought out an increasing number of cookbooks about America beginning in the 1950s. These semihistorical cookbooks were in tune with two new trends: an interest in Americana, which emerged in the 1950s, and the historic preservation movement. The preservation movement was first organized on a national scale in 1949 with the founding of the National Trust for Historic Preservation and picked up momentum later in the 1960s with the wide-scale mourning for the 1964 demolition of Pennsylvania Station in New York.

The Americana trend, which can also be seen in the colonial revival architecture of much of 1950s housing and furniture design, was loosely based in the culture of the Cold War and in postwar domestic tourism. Defining nationhood in opposition to vague stereotypes of communist Russia, American culture-makers turned to their own history and landscapes for sources of pride. Historically, the postwar years were an era of intensely politicized patriotism, in which the question of what was American and what was anti-American became highly charged.[65] The publishing industry's confidence in a market for historical writing about American food also suggests that these books might have been intended to serve as alternatives to the Eurocentrism of the dominant gourmet perspective.

Many of the new Americana cookbooks used a travelogue format to represent American food, dividing recipes by region and opening each regional section with a brief sketch of the history and culture of the area. That this format was more suited to the coffee table than to the kitchen suggests that publishers posited a market for material about American foodways that was not solely practical. The physical books could serve as objects of Americana on display in private homes, linking their owners to the contemporary fashion.

Linda Wolfe's 1962 *Literary Gourmet*, for example, was lavishly decorated with historical paintings of food, cooking, and eating. Typically, cookbook illustrations had given readers a guide as to what a dish was supposed to look like or illustrated the process of preparation. The illustrations in Wolfe's book, however, were drawn from the canon of fine art and were thus texts in themselves, part of the anthology rather than decorations. Wolfe established the place of food in intellectual life by anthologizing diverse texts about food primarily from the Western literary tradition. Excerpts from Horace, the Bible, the *Arabian Nights*, Tolstoy, Melville, and many other great works were set alongside recipes they had inspired. The whole project was given a final stamp of elite culture with the note that the recipes had been tested in the kitchen of the Four Seasons, one of the nation's most famous rarified restaurants.

Wolfe's chapter about American food was fraught with tension over realities and perceptions of national foods. She made the usual claim that America had some great ingredients but no real culinary artistry and fretted, "what is so confusing about American cuisine" is that no one can answer the question "what is it? Does it exist at all? Actually no one yet knows." It certainly wasn't in the public eating places that Wolfe thought produced boring fare, even "singularly bad" meals.

Ultimately, Wolfe mused, "If America can be honored with possessing a national cuisine at all, its components are: for wine, a coke; for dessert, a blueberry glue-pie more glue than berries; for the piece de resistance, a charcoal-broiled hamburger." Using French categories as benchmarks made it difficult for American food to live up to the standard.[66] Yet Wolfe found American food writing and art about food worth collecting and publishing, perhaps reflecting the influence of Beard, who helped Americans to see their food on its own terms.

Most Americana cookbooks did not engage in Wolfe's kind of soul searching, concentrating instead on the more distant past to establish a common narrative of national foodways. Almost all took the story of the Plymouth Colony Puritan settlers as the American origin story, naturally preferring the 1620 settlers with their roast geese and cranberry relish to Jamestown's 1607 settlers who ate rats, boiled shoe leather, and their dead comrades' bones.[67]

San Francisco was always represented by cioppino, while a chapter on Alaska could be counted on to offer a recipe for sourdough bread or pancakes. Regions were identified with eating styles that built on stereotypes. Jean Hewitt, for example, wrote in the *New York Times Heritage Cookbook*

that, "The Midwest is meat 'n' taters country," while "Southern-style hospitality and some of the country's most gracious hostesses," mark the South.
The Southwest had "infinite variety to shock and please the palate." Collectively, the recipes from each region were America's culinary heritage. Lest
the author be accused of wallowing in nostalgia, she claimed a kind of advocacy for the book, that it would "bring honesty back into cooking." Peg
Bracken, she of the not-so-honest John's chowder, would have cringed.[68]

Cookbooks also persisted in portraying Native Americans as kindly
benefactors who essentially ceased to exist soon after the arrival of English-
men.[69] Authors of the 1957 *Famous American Recipes* cookbook, John and
Marie Roberson, for example, wrote of cranberries, "The Indians learned
how to preserve and cook with these tart little red berries and taught this
art to the white men."[70] Anglo-American recipes using cranberries then followed and the book contained no Native American recipes either contemporary or historical.

Native Americans reappeared in the modern era when books included
recipes with wild rice. Because wild rice was a highly valued, "gourmet"
product but also indigenous to North America, it was a favorite of writers
who wanted to claim a noble American food past. The previously mentioned
"kaedjere," for example, used wild rice. As Charlotte Turgeon noted in the
heritage-themed *Saturday Evening Post All-American Cookbook*, "Wild rice
is a luxury . . . [and is] the product of perennial wild grass that the Indians
knew long before the arrival of the white man."[71]

Dale Brown's Time-Life *American Cooking* included a full page photograph of wild rice harvesters and the observation that, "with a retail price of
up to $10 a pound, wild rice may be the most expensive grain in the world."
Acknowledging that "traditional harvesting methods are still used," but
showing no interest in traditional preparations, Brown wrote, "After being
parched, winnowed and threshed, the grain is ready for the epicurean market."[72] Apart from these superficial kinds of excursions into Native American foodways, the travelogue cookbooks assumed that American food was
the food made by descendants of European immigrants to North America.

American Heritage, a popular history magazine, published *The American Heritage Cookbook and Illustrated History* in 1964, a collection of essays

on themes of American food history with recipes designed by a historical food consultant, presumably a rather new career field.[73] The historical food consultant was Helen Duprey Bullock, who had, much earlier in her career, assembled the nostalgic *Williamsburg Arts of Cookery*, which was sold at the historic site in Virginia.[74]

The American Heritage Cookbook and Illustrated History included recipes only up to 1890, the era of famous American businessman and glutton Diamond Jim Brady, who the book celebrated as a great American eater, leaving most of the era of industrialization out of the nation's heritage. It treated the usual themes of Pilgrims, Indians, and immigration, but offered a more nuanced presentation of Southern cookery than was usually found in such books. Of Thomas Jefferson, so often praised as the nation's first gourmet, essayist Marshall Fishwick noted, "Jefferson's leisure was made possible by three generations of slaves." He could not have been such an epicure had he needed to plough his own fields.[75]

Even the ur-gourmet Chamberlain family got into the Americana act, publishing *The Chamberlain Sampler of American Cooking* in 1961. Just as the rest of the world was discovering French cuisine with Julia Child's help, the family of *Clementine in the Kitchen* finally found something to eat in America. While Samuel Chamberlain, *Clementine*'s author, provided some of the photographs, his wife Narcissa and daughter Narcisse Chamberlain wrote the text. Narcisse had been an editor at *Gourmet* and was editor at Hastings House, the book's publisher. Rather than making a claim to encyclopedic coverage, the Chamberlains breezily informed readers, "This sampler of American recipes represents the authors' personal idea of good food in America today; we have given the book room only for our preferences. We've been equally personal about our bird's-eye view of the national scene, which includes only photographs of America as we prefer to look at it."[76]

There was much of America, the Chamberlains admitted, that they did not want to look at: "It is a pleasure to give photographs of Georgian architecture precedence over those of industry, to let New England valleys outnumber skyscrapers, to have the picturesque override the portrait of mass civilization which might have been more representative of the facts." The facts, she reminded readers, "are, also, that ready-mix cakes have come to

outnumber real ones. So why go into all of that?"[77] Eliding "all of that" was
a way to give American food the French treatment in which a cuisine was
praised for being homogeneous and unchanging.

The Chamberlains found much to praise if one focused on "the sensible,
well-made recipes referred to as plain American food." Dishes like "Texas
chili, boiled beef, steak and kidney pie, cheese blintzes, butterfly shrimp, or
beef Stroganoff" represented the best America had to offer. Her choices reflected the increasing popularity of both Tex-Mex and Chinese food as well
as the postwar mainstreaming of Jewish culture in American life.[78]

Chamberlain promised that American food was making progress, such
that she begged, "Let no one say that American food is limited. At worst
it has only fallen on occasional unhappy days." In particular, she regretted,
"the years between the two wars when the percentage of uninspired cooks is
supposed to have reached an all-time high." Although she did not cite any
authority for the supposition, her version of food history was clearly rooted
in the gourmet perspective, as she asserted, "Prohibition and marshmallows
in the salad both date from these curious times; maybe there is some sinister
connection."[79] The implication was that the old stereotype, that wine-hating,
pleasure-averse women had ruined American cooking, though perhaps not
permanently.

Authors of Americana cookbooks sometimes offered their work as a
last stand against what they saw as increasing conformity in the American
diet. Jean Hewitt, editor of the 1972 *New York Times Heritage Cookbook*,
mused, "It is unfortunate that a foreign visitor can travel on our superhigh-
ways from coast to coast, Maine to Florida, and go away with the impression
that Americans subsist largely on a diet of hot dogs, hamburgers and soggy
French fries." For those who lived in America, too, there was little variety:
"Even a tour of a large supermarket in any one of the fifty states would reveal
similar packaged convenience foods, suggesting a uniformity of eating patterns in homes across the land."[80]

Hewitt argued that although advances in the technologies of production and distribution had brought welcome variety to the American diet and
made it possible to eat foods out of season, "a growing uniformity in the

American diet has created a serious threat to our nation's fine heritage of regional cooking." A determined search of "homes, grange halls, festivals and fellowship rooms"—spaces associated with tradition and the elderly rather than innovation and youth—could turn up something more interesting. Among the recipes one editor rescued from obscurity were "wild persimmon pudding in Mitchell Indiana, kolache in Oklahoma and Wisconsin, lambs quarters and sour dough pancakes in California and Wyoming and enchiladas in a pink adobe house in New Mexico." Giving each food a geographic location, the writer tied the picturesque to the palate.[81]

Natural History magazine's food writer, Raymond Sokolov, searched out regional specialties for his food columns. He titled a collection of these columns, published in 1979, *Fading Feast*. Sokolov claimed to have spent two years searching out the "last, authentic exponents of regional foods, learning their recipes and recording the food wisdom of our past before it fades completely from view." He too blamed industrial food processing for the "radical loss of diversity" in American foodways and for the disappearances that made his chronicle seem necessary.[82] While Sokolov sought to record his fading feasts, a few intrepid curators saw value in foregrounding foods at historic sites.

Two historic sites, Old Sturbridge Village in Massachusetts and Colonial Williamsburg in Virginia, both published cookbooks (in 1963 and 1971 respectively) inspired by the growing interest in American culture and the expansion of domestic tourism. The books served as fundraisers and also appealed to fans of Americana, making more people aware of these sites.[83] Representing what are erroneously understood in popular history as the two origins of American society—Colonial Virginia and Puritan New England—these books cultivated an interest in the past through food by providing recipes that fed nostalgia but were mostly adapted to modern kitchens.[84]

Jane Whitehill, who edited the Sturbridge Village cookbook *Food, Drink, and Recipes of Early New England*, took a practical approach to nostalgia— the past was nice to know about but you wouldn't want to dine there. She wrote confidently that "We who do not plant peas or beans by the light of the new moon, or carrots by the old one, we who live in heated houses with running water, cooking packaged foods on gas or electric stoves—we cannot return to the earlier times. Nor do we wish to, really." Echoing the *Betty Crocker's Picture Cook Book*, she asked, "Who wants to carry water, save yeast, or strike fire with flint and tinder?" Happy in our modern lives, we might, just for the sake of fun, cook up a few of the dishes that fed the first English settlers in North America.[85] Whitehill's book offered a counterbalance to Julia Child's by celebrating change in cuisine where Child argued that the appeal of French food was in its timelessness—it had already been perfected.

Letha Booth, who compiled the cookbook for Colonial Williamsburg, focused on the historic site's three "colonial taverns" as tourist attractions, promising that the décor was in the colonial style and that servers dressed in period attire. The food, however, was more modern than strictly colonial. Contemporary kitchen technology in the form of "modern cookstoves, refrigerators, and cooking utensils" might be hidden "behind the scenes," for the sake of appearances, but she was happy to assure readers and visitors that it was all there.[86]

The 1971 *Williamsburg Cookbook*, like *The Food, Drink, and Recipes of Early New England*, sought a usable past. Elevating palatability over historical accuracy mattered a great deal when real meals were part of the scenery. When Queen Elizabeth and Prince Phillip visited the Colonial Williamsburg Foundation's hotel, the Williamsburg Inn for the 350th anniversary of the founding of Jamestown, they were served Virginia ham, baby green beans almandine, avocado slices, Veuve Cliquot, and strawberry mousse, a meal less historical but more appetizing than the dogs, cats, mice, rats, and boots eaten by the first English settlers in Virginia.[87] Booth wrote primarily as a way to raise interest and funds for the historic site, but she also wrote for the same audience who watched *French Chef* on WGBH, the generation who expected to entertain and be entertained through food.

In 1976, Judith Jones, who had brought Julia Child's first book to the American public, had her second big editorial success in cookbook publishing with a book, *The Taste of Country Cooking*, which successfully brought together the themes of culinary preservation and contemporary entertaining. Grounded in a vanishing past, but replicable at home, the book secured its author Edna Lewis's own future as a culinary authority. It also ushered in a new era of cookbook writing that was driven by personalities and vignette, a style that is still one of the driving forces of the industry.[88]

Edna Lewis and African American Culinary Heritage

When Lewis published *The Taste of Country Cooking* in 1976, she was already known to the New York food world as the chef of Café Nicholson, a fashionable restaurant. That her first cookbook, *The Edna Lewis Cookbook,* included her name in its title suggests that her fame as a chef was already great enough that her publisher could assume the name would sell books, although in the end it did not turn out to be a great success.[89] In her second book she stepped back from her celebrity to reconnect her cooking to sources beyond her own ingenuity. *The Taste of Country Cooking* was a memoir of collective foodways of a bygone era. Lewis's portrait of her community's cuisine, especially because it was published in the bicentennial year, 1976, established the American-ness of African American cooking and the cultural origins of her own unique style in the kitchen.[90] Lewis's book was unlike other African American cookbooks of this era in that it did not take the confrontational and at times countercultural tone of other African American writers but rather quietly insisted on her ancestors' food as national cuisine.

Because Lewis and Child shared an editor, indeed shared the editor one writer referred to as "the queen bee of cookbook publishing," comparing the two books reveals changing emphases and values in the field.[91] Where Child had served as liaison between her readers and a distant and revered cuisine, Lewis's book was intensely local and personal. Both women played the role of guide, one as former novice, the other as native. Child's television success had established the importance of a personality to lead readers through a cookbook while the growing interest in American cooking since 1961 made it possible for Jones to bet on Lewis's success. Jones herself had helped to build this market when she collaborated with her husband Evan, author of

American Food: The Gastronomic Story, just a year earlier in 1975. While the Joneses could offer the tour-guide view of American cooking, Lewis had a marketably authentic insider's voice.

The food Lewis had identified with herself in her first cookbook was a combination of gourmet and American dishes, similar to James Beard's. A menu that leaned toward the French, for example, included "Cold poached lobster with special sauce; roast rack of spring lamb with herb butter; asparagus with browned bread crumbs; sautéed potato balls; lettuce and watercress salad with French dressing; French bread, assorted cheeses; baba au rhum with whipped cream and strawberries."[92] A deeply American Lewis menu actually offered up the very foods that Linda Wolfe had stereotyped as terrible American food in her *Literary Gourmet*: charcoal-grilled steak marinated in grated onion; baked Virginia ham; shrimp salad on lettuce bed garnished with cherry tomatoes, hard-cooked eggs, and Russian dressing; salad of summer greens; blueberry pie; watermelon slices and coffee. Lewis combined the gourmet's most loved and hated foodways into one elite-pleasing cuisine.

When Lewis was introduced to Judith Jones, the two began to work on a new cookbook. At first, Lewis continued in the style that had established her reputation at Café Nicholson, blending folk and high cultures. Jones, however, sensed a market for something different. Reading Lewis's first drafts, Jones was disappointed and attempted to steer Lewis in a new direction: "This isn't you, Edna," she explained "gently [,] 'It isn't the voice I heard when you were talking to me.'" Sensing that Lewis was "uneasy about going it alone," Jones set out "to help Edna recover that voice." She encouraged Lewis to write down what had until then only been spoken memories of the food of her childhood. The book that these instructions produced is a collection of intricately food-focused vignettes of country life, focused on the past, not the contemporary foodways that were Lewis's professional forte.[93]

Like other Southern cookbooks, Lewis's looks back to a precious lost moment. In explaining her reasons for writing the book, she noted, "Since we are the last of the original families, with no children to remember and carry on, I decided that I wanted to write down just exactly how we did things when I was growing up in Freetown that seemed to make life so re-warding." Referring to the "original families," could have great resonance in the bicentennial year. It also echoed the contemporary trend in Americana cookbooks to capture what Sokolov had termed the "fading feasts." In Lew-is's case, the original families were the formerly enslaved men and women who established Freetown after the end of the Civil War, a conflict some-times referred to as the second American Revolution. Especially fitting was the inclusion of a menu for the celebration of Emancipation Day, a second American Independence Day.

Organized by season rather than dish or material, Lewis's evocative book is rich with nostalgia and a little disappointment in modern foods as when she complained that "The fur has been bred out of peaches today, as well as most of the flavor," and that "Everyone seems to have forgotten how de-licious blackberries were—if they ever knew." Celebrating rural Virginian foodways, Lewis also told a story of African American recovery and success after the trauma of war. A corrective to prevalent images of black poverty and hardship, *The Taste of Country Cooking* is a chronicle of joy and bounty.

Lewis's book also presents a distinct version of African American food as gourmet fare. Lewis, for example, remembers that the spring surplus of milk resulted in one of her favorites, blancmange, a dish typically consid-ered part of middle-class white foodways, usually prepared by kitchen staff. Suspecting that the reader might be surprised to find blancmange on a Free-town farm, Lewis assured them that "I hadn't thought of blancmange as be-ing a fancy or unusual name . . . It was just a delicious dessert."[94]

Wild mushrooms and asparagus, two of the totemic foods of the Ameri-can gourmet, were also frequent treats in Freetown. Foraged by her mother in Lewis's childhood, the mushrooms "have a superior flavor to that of the hothouse variety. They are most delicious and are an elegant accompani-ment to any sauce." In describing their place in her family's cuisine, Lewis momentarily allowed her cosmopolitan self to enter the idyllic past, assur-ing readers that "If it is impossible to go picking wild mushrooms, all isn't lost. Many fine food departments, such as that in Bloomingdale's, carry wild varieties."[95]

This moment of bridging folk and gourmet foodways, while in some ways specific to Lewis's persona, was also attuned to a new way of thinking about food that was emerging simultaneous to her own rise among food writers. The fashion for finding food at its source began with the surprisingly popular work Euell Gibbons's *Stalking the Wild Asparagus*, a manual for foragers first published in 1962 and discussed later in this book. As Lewis recalled, her family had stalked plenty of wild asparagus in their time.

While there was nothing of the whole-food maven about Lewis, there was also nothing of the corporate kitchen to her foodways. The beloved food of her childhood memories was foraged, homegrown, and home processed even to the level that the children watched hog butchering and were delighted to be given pigs' bladders to turn into balloons.[96] This consciousness of the natural state of food became an important theme of American cookbooks in the 1970s. The discomfort with modern foods that Lewis only hinted at—that peaches had lost their fur—became a central issue for cookbook writers who began to draw attention to what they saw as the unnatural in contemporary foodways.

Writers like Sokolov and Lewis, who hurried to preserve folk food cultures that seemed to be disappearing, offered a critique of modern consumer society and whatever new foodways were emerging. This nostalgia created a new kind of exclusive connoisseurship about American foods that spoke to the Julia Child generation who had been trained to revere culinary conservatism.

*   *   *

In 2001, Julia Child's kitchen went on display at the Smithsonian Museum of American History. The exhibit, originally intended to be temporary, was a tremendous success and has remained open for viewers ever since. The exhibit has become a kind of shrine to which people (including this writer) make pilgrimages of tribute. This is a testament to Child the TV personality whose real kitchen became a model for her viewers. As much as this exhibit might seem uniquely of its moment, the early twenty-first century, era of the Food Network and the foodie, it echoes an exhibit that opened to the public in 1950 in General Mills' headquarters.

Betty Crocker's Picture Cook Book included a photo essay about what the company identified as a colonial era American kitchen. This room was both the tasting room for recipes tested onsite and the most popular room for groups touring the facilities. Most visitors, the book's anonymous authors reported, "seem to like this room best of all. They come back to gaze at the wide old fireplace [,] the mellow pine paneling from a New England house of 1750." In looking into the past, guests could see that "Some of the early cooking utensils [,] the heavy iron kettles, and spiders and long handled waffle iron around the fireplace . . . are evidence of the heavy labor that went into cooking in early days." Looking into the past could implicitly make guests and readers more thankful for the convenience of the supplies General Mills provided.

Guests' interest in the room also indicated an interest in kitchens as historical spaces. This curiosity about how the culinary past shapes the present and also fits into more well-known narratives inspired the market for Americana cookbooks. While these books at first seem to have nothing to do with Julia Child, looking at how Child's audience received her at the time as well as how she has been memorialized in contemporary American culture reminds us that she helped spread the idea that cooking was intellectual work. The gourmets of the 1930s first propagated this notion and even their nemeses, the corporate cookbooks, had adopted it in small doses by the 1950s. The designers of General Mills' colonial kitchen assumed an interest in outdated cooking technologies for their intrinsic value as historical objects, not merely as foils to make contemporary life look good. That they chose 1750 rather than any other moment in U.S. history reflects the more widespread colonial revivals of the era. From that initial trend, cookbook writers quickly moved on to a more comprehensive fascination with America's edible past.

Edna Lewis's *The Taste of Country Cooking* was a watershed book in the genre because it brought together so many trends as well as inaugurating something new. Lewis's book blended Americana with a gourmet sensibility and added to this an oblique connection to countercultural Black Power cookbooks. She and her editor Judith Jones packaged this combination with a unique and appealing personality. Child's success as a lovable eccentric on TV as well as James Beard's success as an arbiter of taste had paved the way for this last element—the cookbook as personal statement.

By the postwar period, publishers of all kinds, literary as well as corporate, recognized that cookbooks were a lasting and lively market. The gourmet's insistence on food appreciation as high culture had helped to promote diversification in cookbooks as lifestyle manuals and as elements within that lifestyle. The two major trends of the 1970s, the health food movement and New American Cuisine, maintained the idea that food mattered as a marker of cultural politics as well as social status. Just as Peg Bracken boldly rejected the gourmet celebration of cooking as repressive, counterculture cookbook writers of the 1970s rejected Bracken's foodways as both conformist and complicit in the over-industrialization of contemporary life. The chefs of the New American cuisine blended Angelo Pellegrini's pride in American produce with the Time-Life approach to American foodways as they sought out and updated American traditional fare in a statement of culinary nationalism.

CHAPTER 5

OPPOSITIONAL APPETITES

COOKBOOKS AND THE COUNTERCULTURE
IN THE 1960S AND 1970S

A NEW TONE OF DREAD appeared in American cookbooks in the Cold War years. Gourmets had once despaired that Americans lacked taste, but food writers now worried that their countrymen were literally eating poison. Those who had derided the maraschino cherry for its perceived tackiness now dreaded its industrial dyes.[1] Foodways seemed to become a matter of life and death.

In 1962, Adelle Davis prefaced the revised edition of her 1947 *Let's Cook It Right* with this ominous note: "During the past fifteen years, chemicals by the thousands have been poured into our foods." Davis warned more specifically that among these chemicals were "a large variety of preservatives and bleaches; artificial sweeteners, flavorings, and dyes; texture modifiers, softeners, agers, and fresheners; emulsifiers, fumigators, anti-foaming and anti-sprouting agents, and paraffin sprays." Not only were foods chemically treated in processing, Davis added, packaging also contributed to their potential poisoning as "contaminants" leached from "lacquers, enamels, and plastics used in canning, packaging, and shipping." While "No fewer than 75,000 processing plants are now putting chemical additives into our foods," there were at times a dozen added chemicals in a single item.[2] Although she did not offer substantive evidence that any of these chemicals were actually harmful to humans, the implication was that no additives could possibly be good.

Davis's book was an early example of an important shift in American food writing. Leaving behind the triumphalism of the travelogue and the pleasure-focused experiential writing of the gourmet, a new cohort of food writers took up the tragic mode. Instead of basing the distinction between "good" and "bad" food in culture, these writers drew the line between the poisoned and the pure.[3]

The first edition of *Let's Cook It Right* won praise from Lois Palmer, a regular cookbook reviewer in the *New York Times*, who wrote, "No cook can help taking a greater interest in each dish that she prepares after reading *Let's Cook It Right*. Guidance toward the best in cooking is given through friendly, firm, often amusing advice."[4] By the early 1970s, Davis's books had been so successful that she was featured in *Life* magazine as "Earth Mother to the foodists."[5]

Confirming this characterization, her books were recommended in the pages of feminist journal *Off Our Backs* alongside the invitation to "keep our money away from the food corporations until they give us something worthwhile to spend it on . . . let's keep the crap out of the kitchen."[6] Critics of industrial food production approved of Davis's message. The collective authors of *Eat, Fast, Feast*, a book produced by the True Light Beaver commune also recommended using Davis's *Let's Eat Right to Keep Fit* as a guide to nutrition.[7] While participating in the new critique of industrial foodways, the Beavers also echoed older gourmet ideas when they recommended readers "keep in mind that eating should always be a sensual, pleasurable experience."[8] The True Light Beavers made these suggestions as part of their broader invitation to join a new, communal way of living.

Health Food Lifestyles

The distinction between "bad" food as chemically treated and good as "natural" was part of a radical change in lifestyle in which not only ingredients, nor even just kitchens, but entire households shifted from an individualistic to a communitarian model. The communal living movement began in Northern California in the late 1960s, with the opening of Morningstar Ranch in 1966 and its neighbor, Wheeler Ranch in 1967. The movement spread east with high density in New Mexico and smaller numbers in the colder climates of the Northeast. It is difficult to know exactly how many communes, in which members shared rent and household responsibilities but otherwise participated in the life of the city around them, existed in the late 1960s and early 1970s because while some were well known and written about in mainstream media, others were much less visible, especially in urban areas. One sociologist who studied the movement estimated that there were three thousand communes in 1970, while the *New York Times* was able to identify only two thousand the same year.[9]

Communal living was a notable phenomenon in the Vietnam War era, largely practiced by young middle-class European Americans, usually college graduates. Scholars of the movement saw it as a rejection of middle-class consumerist culture but also consistently noted the diversity of communal living styles, which made it hard to generalize about the trend. The element of food commonly prepared and consumed, however, appears in most accounts of commune life.[10]

One contemporary commentator described the communal phenomenon in relation to food: "All over the West, boys whose fathers worked in air-conditioned twenty-story office buildings were discovering how to grow wheat," getting in touch with the food chain. Meanwhile, "Girls whose mothers never dreamed of baking bread were finding mystical joy in learning to knead and to bake." Commune-dwellers were farming and baking together and for each other rather than relying on the industrial food system.[11]

This altered approach to food was at once wary and hopeful; food might be poisoned but, if produced and processed mindfully, food might be health-giving. When leaders of the Morningstar and Wheeler Ranch communes attempted to create a new religious faith to unite their members, they included a prohibition against "Self poisoning—eating poisoned food, breathing poisoned air." The oath reflected widespread beliefs that commercially processed foods were harmful to human health as well as the less widespread commitment to social reform.[12]

Agnes Toms, author of several popular natural foods books, including, in 1963, *Eat, Drink and Be Healthy*, spoke to this new audience in her introduction: "This book is not for the empty-calory and can-opener cuisine type homemaker but rather an avant-garde approach to better living through recipes that are enhanced by unrefined foods, properly prepared and appetizingly served." Although most of her recipes were for familiar dishes such as hamburgers and baked beans, Toms also provided instruction in making bran broth, soy flour, and carob powder. These foods were substitutes for items—beef broth, white flour, and chocolate—that were more familiar in the American repertoire but had been deemed unhealthy.[13]

Toms admitted that finding these substitutes could be difficult: "I know it is a real problem for many people to find the food products mentioned in this book." Instead of giving up or substituting when one of her arcane ingredients was recommended, Toms urged readers to work harder to find their ingredients. They were advised not only to "Search the shelves of your local market for unsulphured molasses, spray-dried milk, unflavored gelatin, honey, herbs, spices, nuts, vegetable oils," but also to go beyond the conventional, seeking out local grain mills, hatcheries, and dairy farms.[14]

Toms encouraged her reader to demand access to the points of production. She told readers to "Scour the neighborhood for some one who has a flock of chickens on the ground," an unlikely neighbor in contemporary suburban life. Building on older models of female activism around consumer issues, and also perhaps tapping into the emergent second wave of the women's movement, Toms suggested group action: "Get the health-minded women in your neighborhood together and demand that the local dairy produce raw certified milk."[15] Where an earlier generation of progressive women had joined to promote the pasteurization of milk for the sake of public safety, Toms's imagined activists sought a return to the "natural," defined in opposition to the processes associated with modern production.[16] These processes increasingly came under scrutiny during the 1960s.

In 1962, biologist Rachel Carson published *Silent Spring*, one of the most influential books of the twentieth century. The book sparked the modern ecology movement and also had a major impact on food writing because it encouraged readers to distrust mainstream American agriculture and to advocate for pure foods. Carson's central argument was that the unexamined use of pesticides was harmful to living creatures and must be stopped. Although her message was shockingly new to many readers, there were some, like Adelle Davis, who already distrusted the use of chemicals in food manufacture.

A university-trained nutritionist and biochemist, Davis became well known as a public speaker on issues related to diet. While some of her material was in line with contemporary understandings of nutritionists, other recommendations were of her own invention. Her importance to the history of cookbooks is not in her quackery, a persistent strain in American food writing, but in the connections she made between the natural environment and family meals by warning that both were in crisis. Her alarmist tone found a responsive audience: the *Life* magazine profile of Davis reported that four million copies of her four books had sold by 1971.[17]

This new approach to food borrowed from the findings of nutritionists but was also flavored with the apocalyptic dread that was common to much cultural expression in the nuclear era. Educational films showed fallout shelters in the single-family housing developments that were a mark of postwar suburbs, not in cities where shelters were shared communal spaces. In such films, each family had its own shelter, just as each suburban family had its own home, and each housewife had the responsibility for stocking the underground shelves for her own family's survival. This collective experience of anxiety that focused on the single-family home resonates in the cookbooks of the era.[18]

Davis, for example, noted that she had revised her cookbook to include more calcium-rich recipes because "radioactive fallout appears to be particularly dangerous to persons whose calcium intake is inadequate." Where previous writers had defined food as an expression of connoisseurship and others had emphasized ongoing health benefits, Davis presented food's most important role as a prophylactic against the nuclear disaster that seemed imminent.[19]

The U.S. Department of Defense issued a bulletin for civilian education in 1961 titled *Fallout Protection*, which included guidance about food safety after the explosion of a nuclear bomb. Alongside the reassurance that the family refrigerator could protect anything inside it from contamination was the sobering observation that "milk from cows that have grazed on contaminated pastures would be radioactive, but in the absence of other food in an emergency it could be used."[20] Davis's warnings joined a growing body of writing linking the Cold War and food safety.

Davis's ability to blend mainstream American foodways with the new safe food movement helped to make her book appealing. Mary Ann Cronin, in her endorsement of Davis's books in *Off Our Backs*, noted that Davis's recipes for "custards, pancakes, cookies and soups and main dishes [are] so delicious . . . that you won't even know you're on a health diet and neither will your kids."[21] Davis did not advocate a vegetarian diet, because she did not believe it could provide enough protein for health. Instead, she favored fortification of foods with powdered milk and the substitution of whole wheat for white flour. Acknowledging that Americans were unfamiliar with yogurt, she advocated adding it, and another health food favorite, wheat germ, slowly. But she also included recipes for old dessert favorites such as Bavarian cream, gingerbread, and marshmallows.

Davis's writing had a wide-reaching impact on what became the health food movement of the 1970s. Her ideas, as expressed in the 1947 first edition of *Let's Eat Right* even had an important impact on the 1951 edition of the mainstream standard, *The Joy of Cooking*.[22] Marion Rombauer Becker, daughter and later coauthor of the book's original writer, Irma Rombauer, had read Davis and absorbed her ideas about food and health. One example of this effect was that Rombauer removed references to salting water when boiling vegetables because Davis advised against it.[23]

In Albuquerque, New Mexico, a group of men and women who called themselves the Natural Food Associates of Albuquerque credited Davis as an authority and inspiration in their 1961 collective cookbook, *Tempting and Nutritious Recipes for the Avant-Garde Homemaker and Hostess*. The book had been published in four editions by 1971.[24] It is particularly interesting in that it represented the thinking of a group of people rather than one author. The Natural Food Associates of Albuquerque borrowed ideas from Davis but also advocated their own quasi-mystical approach to food. One member, for example, claimed, "Food saved my life," a statement that had nothing to do with rescue from starvation. It was the story of a young man suffering from cancer, given up on by doctors and nursed back to health by "an old German" who simply told him what to eat. No details were given of the diet prescribed, but the implication was that the "old German" emphasized "traditional" foods not processed by the modern food industry.[25]

This kind of story connected the Albuquerque group's book with an older tradition of eccentric cookbooks, like those published by Christian vegetarians or raw food enthusiasts, which periodically appeared in print to suggest radically alternative foodways. An example of this kind of book was Bernard Jensen's 1952 *Vital Foods for Total Health*, which advocated a mostly raw and mainly vegetable diet. Jensen argued, "The foods we eat must be as natural or as nearly like that which God provides for us as possible. It is only natural foods that contain the life-giving forces. In this way perfect bodies may be built, free from disease and pain."[26]

Tempting and Nutritious Recipes was also ahead of its time, however, in its advocacy of organic farming, raw milk, and frequent use of the chickpea spread, hummus, a substance little known in America at the time but later to become central to health food cuisine and recently so naturalized in American foodways that it is available in supermarkets nationwide.[27]

Although quite outside the mainstream in its ingredients, including carob and kelp, the Albuquerque cookbook attempted to align these new foodways with contemporary American social life, suggesting that raisins mixed with orange juice and rolled into balls coated with dried coconut were the perfect "TV Snacks." Although TV-viewing was criticized as having "become a nationally absorbing pastime," during which "the commercials (so artfully designed to brainwash all viewers into thinking that Ultima Thule lies in an over-processed, sugar-saturated food or a pill made necessary by over-processed food," the Natural Food Associates suggested making the best of a bad thing by ignoring the commercials and using the time between programming to shell walnuts instead.

The Natural Food Associates advocated learning new foodways to protect families from the "Unholy Alliance of food processors (interested, of course, in profit not health) and a clique of professional men (who, for some reason, have chosen to align themselves with these commercial interests)." This alliance, according to the group, branded as a "food faddist" anyone who criticized contemporary food systems and sought control over their own nutrition. The term implied an uninformed approach to food and a tendency to be swayed by fashion instead of reason.

That the group should have felt besieged is an important indicator of how widespread resistance to modern food processing and delivery systems was already becoming, despite the very few cookbooks that expressed an oppositional viewpoint during this period. If anyone should be shamed with the name of "faddist," one writer in the group declared, it was not the advocates of whole grains and organic meats, but "those who so cold-bloodedly recommend feeding our population on what, research has conclusively proved are 'crippled and crippling foods,' actually not foods, just imitations."[28]

This construction of American food as *not* food echoed but also differed from the gourmet critique. For gourmets, American food was not food because it lacked the qualities of taste that were valued by that group. For the natural food enthusiasts, it was not food because it was inauthentic in its chemistry not just in its cultural affiliations. Gourmets dismissed processed American foods as tasteless and sought alternatives in France; natural food advocates rejected them as poisonous and sought alternatives in organic farming. In 1962, a new book urged Americans to look to the fields and forests for their chemical-free sustenance.

In 1962, when Davis published her updated *Let's Eat Right*, signaling expectations of a new audience for her message, Euell Gibbons published *Stalking the Wild Asparagus*, which become a bible of oppositional eating.[29] Born in 1911, Gibbons had learned from his mother how to feed himself with wild plants, a skill the family put to use during the Great Depression. In a life of much travel and many careers, Gibbons retained his appetite for wild foods and finally published his guide to this specialized cuisine in 1962.[30]

Reviewing the book in the *New York Times*, Craig Claiborne assured readers that Gibbons was "a most temperate and conservative gentleman," rather than a "dilettante or food faddist bent on bending the public diet to his own free will." Claiborne found the book fascinating and, after eating a foraged lunch with the author, declared Gibbons "a first rate cook [who] creates and improvises with authority and imagination." Claiborne included a few of Gibbons's recipes in his review, tempting readers with pickled walnuts, tempura fried fish, and "old fashioned huckleberry pie."[31] A writer for the *Saturday Evening Post* who foraged and lunched with Gibbons in 1964 referred to him as "the weed eater," but also praised his ingenuity and cooking skills.[32]

Gibbons opened his book with a critique of modern American food culture and subversively offered a way around the "Unholy Alliance's" dominance. He attempted to frighten his readers out of the supermarket by claiming the fruits and vegetables there were not only "devitalized and days-old" but also "raised in ordinary dirt, manured with God-knows-what, and sprayed with poisons." If this wasn't scary enough, he also noted that, "They were harvested by migrant workers who could be suffering from any number of obnoxious diseases, handled by processors and salespeople and picked over by hordes of customers before you bought them." As an alternative, readers should know that "wild food grows in the clean, uncultivated fields and woods, and has never been touched by human hands until you come along to claim it." The same claim—"untouched by human hands"—that had helped generations of food processors sell their products was here used to endorse the right to forage. Nature, once avoided as a source of contamination, was here redefined as the source of purity. Gibbons's neopastoralism helped lay the emotional groundwork for the countercultural return to "the land" in the 1970s.[33]

Appealing to potential gourmets, Gibbons also promised, "Adventurous epicures can expect to find flavors and textures in wild foods that can't be obtained elsewhere. Here are new gustatory thrills that can't be purchased at a restaurant or food market." The invitation fit well with existing themes common to the gourmet perspective, which celebrated such activities as mushrooming (for morels or truffles), game hunting, and wild delicacies such as *fraises de bois*, which, because rare and thus expensive, also served as status markers. The connoisseur need not fear this extreme version of the natural diet, indeed it shared many of the flavors he already idealized—sharp greens, wild meats, and fruits. Gibbons followed up the success of his first book with *Stalking the Blue Eyed Scallop* (1964) about foraging in coastal areas, and a *Field Guide* edition of *Stalking the Wild Asparagus* to help readers put into practice the lifestyle advocated in the original text.[34]

Identifying himself as one of "the growing army of neoprimitive food gatherers who are finding new fascination and meaning in America's great outdoors," Gibbons related his movement to two separate cultural trends of the era, the rise of a counterculture that rejected modern values, and the much more mainstream growth of domestic tourism.[35]

Fed by postwar prosperity and highway construction, a major tourism industry had emerged in America for Americans, providing access to "nature" in the public spaces of national parks and trailer camps. This same prosperity was also supporting access to academic and intellectual life for a broader range of Americans. Attendance at colleges and the growth of graduate programs produced a larger class of cultural scholars and critics. No longer just breeding critics from the "top," American society began to experience critiques from within, as, famously, children reared in relative affluence emerged dissatisfied with what they saw as their culture's conformist values. Gibbons's neoprimitivism, though very much limited to food sourcing, appealed to young people looking for ways to create a new authenticity outside the norms of their parents' cultures.[36]

Stalking the Wild Asparagus also potentially assuaged broader fears about the future of the planet. Publishing at the dawn of the modern ecology movement and in sympathy with its most powerful voice, Rachel Carson, Gibbons could offer a more reassuring perspective on the pollution of everyday life than Carson provided. The earth, Gibbons promised, was still bountiful, still able to feed its people, and offered an easy escape from the industrialized food scene.

While Gibbons's approach to food was certainly far from mainstream, he did not present himself as a countercultural figure in any other way, which may well have helped increase his readership. Aside from his critique of contemporary food systems, Gibbons made no political statements and offered no other critique of modern society. He even insisted that suburbs were wonderful places in which to forage.[37]

Indeed, very few avowedly countercultural cookbooks were produced before the 1970s. By this time alternative lifestyles, while never widespread, were much more common. Cookbooks do not seem to have provoked communal lifestyles but instead to have served as affirmations of those already established. As a new genre of commune cookbooks were published in the early 1970s, the number of "whole foods" and "natural foods" cookbooks also increased. Between 1940 and 1970, approximately fifteen books in the category of natural foods cooking were published in America; between 1970 and 1980, the number was more than three hundred.[38] A writer for the *Chicago Tribune*, whose column "Natural Foods" had run every week for five years, quit in 1981 because she believed that the trend, in food writing as well as in products, had been so well established it no longer needed her advocacy.[39]

This bounty gave readers who were still committed to single-family dwelling an opportunity to resist what seemed unhealthy tendencies in their culture without joining the "freaks" who rejected the mainstays of middle-class culture in their embrace of drugs, free love, and communal living. The speed with which industrial food producers absorbed new ideas about food, though not necessarily acting on them in good faith, made it very easy to eat counterculturally without manifesting any other signs of dissent.[40]

Freak Cookbooks

Although freak cookbooks were a rare genre during the 1960s, they can help us see the ways in which the more numerous natural food and health food cookbooks of the 1970s, even when associated with alternative lifestyles, actually represented continuity more than change in American food writing.

In *The Beat Generation Cook Book*, published in 1961, editors Carl Larsen and James Singer offered a humorous portrait of beatnik cuisine that normalized drug use and willing alienation from mainstream culture. Mocking the tone of women's magazines and simultaneously skewering popular culture stereotypes of beatnik lifestyles, the book began with the question, "When the old man drags in after a rough night at the coffee house, and bugs you about what's for breakfast, do you glare at him and yell, 'Chicken Pox!'?" The authors promised inspiration for meals that will "tempt him into Togetherness, and bring light into your pad."[41]

The first recipe served to separate the squares from the heads. A yogurt concoction called Kerouac Kocktail was recommended, "If you are supporting a monkey and still have to eat occasionally," if, in other words, the reader was a heroin addict. Similarly, the Subterranean Spudniks were invented by a "young Beat doll who is also the mother of three Beatlets," who advised that the dish is "a handy place to stash The Junk in case the Fuzz drop in at mealtime."[42]

The actual recipes combined mainstream American ingredients in unorthodox ways. One example was the recipe for Mulligan Stew, which borrowed its name from a traditional American camp dish. In *The Beat Generation Cook Book*, this involved a can of cream of tomato soup, a can of pea soup, molasses, milk, Worcestershire sauce, and sherry and was attributed to a "temporarily reformed Jazz&Opium addict from New York's Lower East Side Smart Set." The recipes served as a way to jest about American culture, in which contemporary cookbooks encouraged new mixtures of packaged goods. There was no identifiable cuisine at work aside from the haphazard, playing on the notion of the beatnik as improvisational. The beatnik scrounged his dinner from the supplies of mainstream culture instead of critiquing its palate or systems.[43]

Another poet, Ira Cohen, writing under the pen name Panama Rose, published *The Hashish Cookbook* in 1966, also largely as a celebration of drug culture.[44] The book was illustrated with black and white photographs of Moroccan scenes featuring half-clad female figures and with the author's pen and ink drawings. Cohen lived in Morocco, but as recipes suggest, he had strong connections to the foods of New York City.

Recipes featured hashish in combinations with Moroccan, Indian, and American ingredients. Cohen's recipe for "Farouk's Dick," for example, seemed to have its origin in a New York City kitchen. It began, "Fry six 2 inch baby bananas from a Puerto Rican grocery in a little butter along with

SUBTERRANEAN SPUDNIKS

This bit was supplied by a young Beat doll who is also the mother of three Beatlets. She claims it's a handy place to stash The Junk in case the Fuzz drop in at mealtime. We have preserved it in its original j u i c e, as her vernacular b e a t s her verse.

Method for Untouchables:
    "Dig 3 cups raw potatoes. Shave their hungry little i's off. Chop them up and brown them in 3 tablespoons of fat (bacon, lamb, or moose). Best to pull this off in a skillet. Add a cup and a half of Half & Half (or Seagram's), and cook slowly until they are loving (but not mushy). Keep mixture creamy by adding more Half & Half. Then add a can of corn, salt, pepper, paprika, and give it some thyme. When moved by an inner light, turn off the heat, and sprinkle the whole bit with bacon crumbs. Serves 4 or 5 Beats, 8 or 10 Squares."

FIGURE 9. Subterranean Spudniks, Carl Larsen and James Singer, eds., *The Beat Generation Cook Book* (New York: 7 Poets Press, 1961), no page numbers. Image courtesy of New York Public Library.

6 slices of bacon." The resulting dish was dusted with hashish before it was eaten. Similarly reflecting Cohen's roots in mainstream American foodways, the "Seed Fritters," which he promised would provide "a weird breakfast," were made with buckwheat pancake mix, available on the average American supermarket shelf. Less ordinary was the recipe for Black Sabbath salve, to be applied to the outside of the body and begun with the melting of "100 grams human fat." Cohen allowed chicken fat as an alternative.

The playfulness of both *The Beat Generation Cook Book* and *The Hashish Cookbook*, neither of which claimed relevance to the routines of daily cooking, expressed how little food was part of the alternative cultures of the 1960s. The authors of these books, like those written for men in the postwar period, rejected the notion of family cooking as a meaningful exercise, designating food as an item solely for play. Unlike the soignée bachelors of the postwar cookbooks, however, these three authors, also all male, primarily played with food as a vehicle for or adjunct to the culture of drug use.

Drug culture was at the time extending beyond small subcultures, to a broader range of participants and a broader audience. More Americans both used drugs and became aware of drugs during the 1960s, thus mainstreaming them in the popular imagination. Both *The Beat Generation Cook Book* and the *Hashish Cookbook* addressed themselves subtly to an audience outside that drug culture simply by appearing in print. To publish, even on the small scale, was to declare the authors' comfortable defiance of the law as it related to drugs. Food was not the point in these cookbooks, serving merely as a gimmick to establish an outlaw culture.[45]

Alice Brock's *Alice's Restaurant Cook Book* represents a transition from these purely playful volumes into a new kind of countercultural cookbook. Written by the woman made famous in Arlo Guthrie's song, "Alice's Restaurant Massacree," Brock's book is also an early example of the celebrity cookbook. Brock ran a restaurant, but her ability to publish her book came from her pop culture fame, not her culinary reputation. Publisher Random House gave the book what one industry insider described as "a publicity-promotion treatment a la Ringling Brothers or Sunset Boulevard," which included radio and TV performances for the author, cooking demonstrations, "an initial printing of 40,000 copies," and "eventual tie-ins with Miss Brock's planned chain" of restaurants. In addition, radio DJs received singles of Arlo Guthrie singing a recipe for "'My Grandma's Beet Jam.'"[46]

As with the *Hashish Cookbook*, the food in Brock's book was mostly beside the point. What mattered was the cook's attitude. Brock advised, "There is no **one way** to get what you want unless it is to remain open. Keep guessing. There are as many ways as you can think of" (boldface in original). Even the most basic cooking could be reimagined: "No one has ever fried an egg without turning on the gas, but maybe this time if you look that egg straight in the eye and say 'FRY!,' it will." And if that egg should fry, "a whole new world will open up and that's a gas." The fried egg was not an end in itself but just something that happened on the way to having a gas.[47]

Happily admitting that she spoke to her food and pots while she was cooking, Brock demanded the reader "Stay Loose," warning, "If your kitchen is purely 'functional,' chances are your cooking will be, too." For Brock, staying loose meant using whatever the markets provided. Americans of her generation and cohort prized looseness as an alternative to what they termed the uptight world of authority figures. Relaxing into the flow of the moment rather than worrying, planning, or following rules offered escape from what seemed oppressive lifestyles. Brock's work advocated practicing this kind of relaxation-as-enlightenment in the kitchen.[48]

Brock's contemporary, Ita Jones, also advocated communion with food, advising, "When cooking, if you leave yourself fairly open to suggestion, the foods themselves will let you know when they want this bit of cheese, that drop of wine." Verta Mae Smart-Grosvenor, another countercultural cookbook author, similarly advocated self-discovery in the kitchen, advising, "When I cook, I never measure or weigh anything. I cook by vibration. I can tell by the look and smell of it . . . I just do it by vibration. Different strokes for different folks. Do your thing your way." Even recommending specific amounts of seasoning could be repressive: "The amount of salt and pepper you want to use is your business. I don't like to get in people's business."[49]

Smart-Grosvenor advocated self-determination at least in part as a political process, encouraging her African American readers to reject white
culinary culture: "*What kind of pots are you using?* Throw out all of them except the black ones." Brock, by contrast, was much more comfortable adapt-
ing elements of mainstream foodways to her own ends.[50]

Instead of buying dishes, Brock advocated washing and reusing cans
and plastic containers, including "empty TV-dinner plates [and] the tins of
ready-to-eat rolls," two items not usually associated with the countercultural
lifestyle. Smart-Grosvenor, for example, wrote, "I can't understand how a
woman can feed her man TV dinners." Brock's instructions for how to acquire tableware mimicked nineteenth-century household manuals in which
settings were treated with as much attention as was food itself. Brock's aesthetic, however, turned the conventions of middle-class dining accoutre-
ments upside down, turning to the trash bin instead of to Wedgwood or
Royal Doulton.[51]

Brock actually celebrated industrialized food as long as the cook added a
personal touch. Echoing Poppy Cannon, she wrote, "You don't really have to
know how to cook at all these days. All you have to know is how to operate
a can opener." Amazing but true, "There are even Western omelets that slip
out of their plastic pouches into your electric toaster." Instead of criticizing
this kind of food for its standardized flavors or its preservatives, Brock complained it was "boring." In opening the Western omelet's pouch, she asked,
"where are you—where's your touch—where's your personality?" The answer
was not to go back to the stove and make your own omelet from scratch; instead Brock encouraged readers to play with prepackaged goods. When she
wanted a pudding, Brock explained, "I buy a mix and mess with it." Food
was part of a lifestyle of improvisation, the perpetual search for "a gas," holding no inherent social significance or political meaning.[52]

Counterculture Cuisine

Alicia Bay Laurel's *Living on the Earth* was the first countercultural cookbook
in which the food truly mattered.[53] Laurel, a young resident of the Wheeler's
Ranch commune in Sonoma County, California, hand wrote and illustrated a

guide to life outside the mainstream, providing instructions for how to build a house, plant a garden, make clothes, shoes, soap, toys, musical instruments, pottery, and food, as well as how to give birth and cure common ailments with herbal medicines. Laurel even offered advice on "How to Die in the Forrest," by teaching readers how to build their own funeral pyre.

Illustrated with words and images that wandered the page, the design of *Living on the Earth* exemplified trends in publishing during this era. Elevating the amateur, this fashion for loose layout challenged the authority of professionals and "the establishment" more broadly.[54] Laurel's book was also an example of how quickly major publishing houses picked up on the marketability of this style. First published by an independent Northern California press, Bookworks, *Living on the Earth* was picked up one year later by Random House for a wider distribution.[55] With its new publisher, the book sold more than three hundred thousand copies.[56]

The mostly naked figures who served as illustrations in Laurel's book also challenged social conventions as they fed themselves on homemade tofu, whole wheat bread, and wild game. Her audience were those who "would rather chop wood than work behind a desk." Laurel's readers were ready to give up "industrially produced consumer goods," so that they could "discover the serenity of living with the rhythms of the earth" and "cease oppressing one another."[57] Essential to this lifestyle was a cuisine of personal connection to the earth.

Laurel provided "a list of good things you can pick yourself," following Gibbons's example to discover the edible environment. She assumed a countercultural reader who could identify with the nudes in her illustrations and who was interested in learning both how to grow marijuana and how to make fruit balls with it. As isolationist as Laurel's guide was in its encouragement to readers to drop out of society and live beyond its laws, she also assumed an interest in world cultures. The book included recipes from multiple foodways and attempted to familiarize readers with new foods through cross-cultural comparison such as the interesting, if not necessarily accurate statement that "Felafel [*sic.*] are the Arabic taco."[58]

The food Laurel included in her book reflected her values in that nothing was pre-packaged and that all made the most of local natural resources.

Yet it also carried reminders of the mainstream foodways presumably left behind in the world beyond the commune. While her book included recipes for soy milk and tahini, for example, it also taught readers how to make coffeecake, mayonnaise, doughnuts, and Monte Cristo sandwiches. The resulting foodways, syncretic as are all cuisines, represented a distinctly American counterculture in that it both included and resisted mainstream American cooking.

A similar act of synthesis was also probably responsible for the surprising popularity of two cookbooks produced in 1970 and 1973 by an American-born Buddhist monk from California, the *Tassajara Bread Book* and *Tassjara Cooking*.[59] Author Edward Espe Brown had, by his own account, wandered into Buddhism while working as a cook at what was at the time the Tassajara resort in Northern California. As the resort changed into a Buddhist monastery and retreat, Brown changed, too, learning to practice Zen meditation and then becoming a food writer when fans of his cooking demanded the recipes. Brown later explained that he wrote the *Tassajara Bread Book* as a way to "repay my tremendous feeling of gratitude" to the monastery and that "maybe a book about making bread would earn money for the Zen center and be a nice thing to do for people." In this way, the book was like both the community cookbooks of the early twentieth century and the historic site cookbooks of the Cold War era.[60]

The Tassajara resort's shift from a place for leisure to a site for self-improvement through meditation was part of a growing interest in what were loosely termed Eastern spiritual practices. This interest was first popularized through Beat culture, which had its homeland in San Francisco, just up the coast from Monterey County, where Tassajara was located. Expanding consciousness, whether through drugs or meditation, was first a Beat and then more broadly a countercultural pursuit. Brown brought this increasingly fashionable notion of higher consciousness into the kitchen.[61]

The Tassajara books, bound in what looked like homemade brown paper and illustrated with Japanese style ink drawings, offered recipes for both the food served to the center's monks-in-training and that served to its less committed short-term visitors. In Tassajara kitchens, "Milk, cheese, eggs, occasional meat, and a monkish enthusiasm for good taste make the guest diet more suited to American tastes than brown rice, miso soup, and garden greens." The culinary Buddhism of Tassajara was adaptable to American kitchens because the monks themselves possessed the quality of "good taste," which Brown did not define.[62]

What this "good taste" meant in terms of actual recipes was that readers did not have to give up old favorites in order to reach enlightenment. The book's focus on bread signaled a "return" to basics, in tune with contemporary countercultural trends, but the inclusion of familiar sweets made the work seem as much a return home as an adventure into a new lifestyle. For all the liberationist spirituality that Brown claimed for bread-making, the actual palate of his cookbook diverged very little from flavors and textures familiar to a mainstream audience. Like Laurel, Brown made coffee cake. This particular snack food was resolutely bourgeois in its associations. Neither sustenance for the worker nor decadent indulgence of the economic elite, coffee cake was the food of middle-class leisure time.

Coffee cake was by no means the only flavor of the mainstream in Brown's book. In fact, most of his recipes would have been perfectly at home in a community cookbook of the 1910s. They were only about sixty years out of date in American kitchens, the food of grandmothers, or more accurately of grandmothers' hired cooks. Cinnamon rolls, popovers, "flakey biscuits," and date nut bread all appeared alongside the more contemporary and countercultural raw fruit candy and sesame tofu. This winning combination of nostalgic familiarity, alternative spirituality, and implicit critique of convenience foodways made the *Tassajara Bread Book* and the *Tassajara Cookbook* standard on commune kitchen book shelves and in the collections of those who only made it back to the land in their hearts.[63]

Reminiscing in 2003 about her own experience with the *Tassajara Bread Book*, Ann Hodgman described it as "a perfect fit for its times," noting that "one fan wrote that learning to make his own bread liberated him from corporate America." Hodgman had been excited by the book because Brown's approach made readers feel they could escape the inexpertly made whole wheat breads her generation produced as a protest against white bread. Noting that her parents' generation's books, like *Joy of Cooking*, did have bread recipes, but "with their primly efficient format and their teeny industrial illustrations they were too much like something you'd use in Home Economics classes."[64]

In pronounced contrast to the typical cook-focused cookbook, Brown's work portrayed foodstuffs as the actors and humans as the facilitators of a natural process. His first words to readers were, "Bread makes itself, by your kindness, with your help." Where other books promised to make the reader a successful artist through special training, whether in the mysteries of French cuisine or the tricks of can-mixing, the *Tassajara Bread Book* assured them that they already had the secret: "You already know. So please cook, love, feel create." Bringing together the material ingredients was a simple task: "your life, your love, will bring these words into full creation." Furthermore, the wisdom "cannot be taught," only lived.[65]

Brown's message was self-empowering but also potentially daunting, as the process of cooking became a process of personal transformation in which ego was abandoned to the service of the material. Food was "asking this of you: / make full use, / take loving care / of me."[66] If each loaf of bread was an act of "the deepest love all the time," the kitchen became a space of new seriousness.[67] This approach removed cooking from the archetypes of domesticity. The kitchen was now a place for monks' home cooking, food on a higher plane of meaning than Mom's apple pie.

Brown's elevation of bread-making to spiritual encounter was part of a larger cultural shift in which bread became emblematic of alternative lifestyles. Books that featured recipes for whole grain breads could offer themselves as tickets to a new culture, in which time was no longer controlled by impersonal systems of mass production but by "natural" rhythms like the long rising time of whole grain yeast breads.[68]

If bread was the staff of life, thousands of young people disillusioned with their parent's version of modernity chose to be supported by something they perceived as sturdier than Wonder Bread. By the time that the reaction against white bread and white flour in general had grown to significant force, in the late 1960s, there were very few alternatives on the market. Indeed, part of what "freaks" rejected was the ubiquity of this

YEASTED BREAD

This is the recipe with variations for the bread which pleases almost all of the visitors to Tassajara, Zen Mountain Center. They purchase hundreds of loaves each summer to take home with them. Now you can make it yourself and invent your own variations. There is nothing difficult about this recipe, for there is a wide margin for error, experimentation, and adaptation. Don't give up.

The most delicious food is made by someone who really cares about what they're doing. If you've never made bread, your first batch is going to be better than nothing. After that, no comparison! Each batch is unique and full of your sincere effort. Offer it forth.

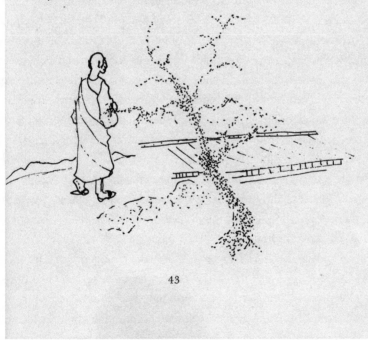

43

FIGURE 10. Freehand illustration and contemplative text by Edward Espe Brown in the *Tassajara Bread Book*. From *Tassajara Bread Book*, by Edward Espe Brown, 43, © 1970 Chief Priest, Zen Center, San Francisco. Reprinted by arrangement with The Permissions Company, Inc., on behalf of Shambhala Publications Inc., Boulder, Colorado, www.shambhala.com.

substance. White bread came to serve as a derogatory term for what was mainstream.

Cookbook writer Lucy Horton described white bread as a dangerously addictive substance. One summer when she worked as a cook at a summer camp, the kitchen ran out of bread and "two of the kids rummaged desperately through the kitchen until they found some stale hamburger rolls." These two "sugar junkies," were led to their disturbing act through family conditioning: "Without white bread on the side, they could barely have choked down their dinner." Horton's language turned the tables on mainstream media's fascination with drug culture by linking the substances designated most pure and wholesome in mainstream society with depravity.[69]

In order to get away from Wonder Bread, the rebel had to make his own bread. In 1972, a scholar of communes noted that the Twin Oaks Community in Richmond, Virginia, "may be the only commune which buys ordinary commercial white bread." The choice was one of economic efficiency, but it was notably anomalous to the scene.[70] Lucy Horton noted that, even beyond rejecting packaged bread, "communes usually grind their own flour," so as not to be dependent on commercial varieties. Commune cooks, too, might liberate themselves from mainstream forms in their baking, as Horton found at the Foundation for Centering, a Massachusetts commune. There she "walked into the kitchen to find Doug making twenty loaves of bread," for sale to a local health food restaurant. He advised Horton to "say in your book that people should form their loaves in fancy shapes . . . I made one that looked like a fetus one time." Bread-baking could be rebirth.[71]

Bread had also served a talismanic role in the emergence of the gourmet, as the difference between the classic French baguette and the loaf of packaged white bread symbolized all that was right with France and wrong with America. Julia Child's recipe for a baguette became the magic key into the kingdom of "good" food. As food writer Molly O'Neil argued, "Julia Child did not become a household name by creating trembling towers of impossible-to-find ingredients . . . she taught Americans how to make a decent baguette."[72] For countercultural cooks, however, the ideal was not the *ba-*

guette, but the wholegrain loaf, sometimes fortified with raisins, sometimes made of rye. This preference perfectly reversed the centuries-old hierarchy of bread by elevating the peasant's dense dark loaf above the aristocrat's fine white "upper crust." Pounding his or her own dark dough, the Tassajara bread maker was free of old status hang-ups. Sharing it with her commune made her even freer.

Commune Cookbooks

In 1971, when Horton made an epic visit to forty-three rural communes in America and Canada, she found that what a friend in San Francisco had told her was true: "'Out in the country, food is what's happening.'" Kitchens, as Horton portrayed the scene, were the centers of communal living. Members wandered through all day long to "respond to the cooking smells with half-closed eyes and moans of pleasure." Indeed, Horton saw the desire for a new cuisine as the impetus for communal living, writing that the "surge of interest" in food that she witnessed, "is no coincidence. Desire for a purer diet is one of the main reasons why so many continue to get it together and split for the country." When the famous Drop City commune experienced a crisis of overcrowding, one member defined the problem in culinary terms: "the kitchen was filthy, the food tasted shitty."[73]

If you were one of those people who believed in the importance of eating organically grown foods and lived in the early 1970s, Horton reasoned, "You almost have to grow your own. "Perhaps biased by her own perspective, as a "food person" who "likes to talk about food the way bikers like to talk about motorcycles or astrology freaks about rising signs," Horton saw that "The garden itself is all the raison d'être a commune needs."[74]

Because she had visited so many communes, Horton was able to generalize the palate of the North American commune, thus giving readers a taste of the counterculture. The "*sine qua non* of commune cooking," Horton declared, "is tamari soy sauce, an unspeakably delicious" substance. Lest readers rush to the local grocery for a bottle of soy sauce, Horton warned that true tamari was not the same as soy sauce and could only be found in health food stores. A footnote went on to explain that while Kikkoman, a widely available brand, tasted like tamari, it also contained preservatives, the shibboleth of natural foods shoppers. This rhetorical distancing of the reader from the desirable cuisine had long been a common trope in gourmet cookbooks, works that also sought to establish a superior taste culture. Where William Wallace Irwin had once sprinkled his book of culinary advice with the pitying refrain, "but then you do not live in Paris," Horton might have intoned just as pityingly, "but then, you are not a freak."[75]

Countercultural food, as Horton witnessed it, was also like gourmet cuisine in that it had its roots beyond America. Horton found, for example, that "Chinese stir-frying is by far the preferred method of preparing vegetable dishes" locating the techniques of this new foodways outside the national borders. Other central flavors and materials were garlic, "cider vinegar, lemon juice, sea and sesame salt, sesame and sunflower seeds, herbs, spices, honey instead of sugar, oil instead of solid fats, whole wheat flour instead of white."[76] Commune cuisine was piquant but also earthy and mixed ethnic traditions freely.

Horton found a recipe for Mexican-Italian goulash, an archetypal recipe of this cuisine, unattributed and tucked among more familiar cookbooks such as the *Joy of Cooking* and *Fannie Farmer Cookbook* on one commune shelf. Recipes like this suggest that in trying to secede from American culinary culture, commune cooks approached world foodways as both broadly accessible and available for disassembly and reconfiguration. For one New Mexico commune, however, experimentation became unwelcome and the group passed a rule that all recipes for communal meals had to come from cookbooks.[77]

Horton gamely admitted that the work of revision could sometimes fail. In her section on soups, she noted, "I was served enough bland vegetarian pea soups to conclude that underseasoned pea soup, along with rancid oil, was a major commune problem." She also admitted ruefully that in reviewing her vegetable section, "Commune people may detect a false note" because "an embarrassing percentage [of the recipes] call for cheese, which is actually a luxury on many communes." She reminded her potential critics,

"You gave me the recipes, brothers and sisters." The use of cheese to supplement what seemed unsatisfying fare served to tie commune cuisine back to the protein-rich middle-class diets on which many commune dwellers had been raised.[78]

Horton's anecdotes suggested specific sources for the multicultural nature of commune foodways. She included a recipe for falafel from a woman who had lived on a kibbutz. Another recipe, for a cucumber and mint salad, came from a commune-dweller who had served in the Peace Corps in Turkey. Horton met enough Jewish commune members that she could add a note to one recipe that although "Matzo meal might sound like an exotic ingredient . . . mothers sometimes send it to their children at the commune for the Passover season." A writer in the True Light Beaver commune's cookbook confirmed that many of the parents of commune members "were of the Jewish persuasion."[79] Connections between old world and freak cuisine existed also in many recipes, especially those for breads that borrowed from Eastern European traditions.[80]

Like the cooks profiled by Lucy Horton, the fancifully self-named Crescent Dragonwagon based her foodways in her lifestyle. One of the founding members of a Brooklyn commune while still in her teens, Dragonwagon earnestly put into print in 1972 the kinds of food she had learned to cook and love. She described the process of her own education, beginning when she moved into the commune: "I was ready to change, ready to be affected . . . ready to be turned on to healthy food." Although previously introduced to this vaguely defined substance, she had "either reacted against it or just ignored it." However, three other members of her commune began to influence her: "They didn't push it. They just kind of quietly did it. On their nights they cooked healthy food. On my night I cooked unhealthy food. But somehow, what they were doing rubbed off on me. It made sense. I began to read about it and do it." Her cookbook served as a bildungsroman.[81]

In reading and cooking, the young high-school dropout developed an ardent new political engagement in which she saw all problems of inequality rooted in the issue of ecology. Highly critical of the dominant culture's preference for "perfection" in its foods, she was pessimistic that the industrial food complex could be changed. She worried, too, as Angelo Pellegrini had, that working women were suffering a false sense of liberation from toil when they bought pre-packaged goods, and that "women who are forced to cook will not be interested enough in cooking to investigate healthy versus unhealthy food; often they will just buy instant, prepared, ready-to-use pre-packaged shit, thinking they are buying freedom." Real freedom came, she argued, in knowing your food and taking responsibility for your own health. Like Edward Espe Brown, Dragonwagon located moral value in food preparation. If it was nutritionally healthier to eat brown bread than white, it was also spiritually healthier to make the bread oneself.[82]

Seeking, as the Natural Food Associates had done before her, to avoid the label of food faddist, Dragonwagon differentiated between "health food" and "healthy food." The latter was what she advocated: "Healthy food (as opposed to Health Food, which in my mind has an entirely different connotation) is delicious." The point was not to eat a set of foods identified as health foods but instead to eat healthily of a wide variety of foods that were not bad for one's body. Even this transition, she admitted, could be hard for some. Stereotyping the American diet, Dragonwagon mused, "It *is* true that if all you have been eating is Wonder Bread and marshmallows, [healthy food] will initially taste funny. But you'll get used to it, as I did, in about a month, and then, you'll never be able to go back." Dragonwagon acknowledged the effect of ideas on the palate.[83]

The difficulty of palate alteration was a common theme in the new "natural," and "health food "cookbooks. Horton had noted, "We all know about soybeans. Unless they're cooked imaginatively, they taste vile." The transition to whole wheat flour, the holy grain of commune living, could also be difficult, especially when it came to desserts. Horton admitted, "The results are inevitably heavier than good old shit cake, but a hearty wholesomeness is imparted that makes the changes taste as worthwhile as they are." A whole wheat pudding's proof of virtue was in its density.[84]

Writer Frances Moore Lappé also acknowledged a learning curve in her enormously influential *Diet for a Small Planet*, published in 1971. Having introduced her somewhat arcane ideas about balancing proteins in the diet,

Lappé positioned the reader as skeptic: "By now many of you may well fear that my appeal for a more rational use of our earth will only take the pleasure out of eating and make of it a terrible complicated, even dull, affair." Not at all, she promised, encouraging readers to "Experiment a little and both your palate and your creative sense will likely tell you the opposite." Although confident that nutritionally good food could also be palate pleasing, she did not promise love at first bite.[85]

For Lappé, "The notion of suddenly changing lifelong habits of any kind on the basis of new understanding does not strike me as very realistic or even desirable." In her own family, transition toward a vegetarian diet had moved slowly. Never "did we swear off meat," she claimed. Instead, "The more we learned about the 'costliness' of meat on so many grounds and the more we discovered the delicious possibilities of foods we had always neglected, the less important meat became, and eventually the less attractive." Intellectual knowledge could drive sensual experience so that beans seemed more appetizing just as meat was beginning to lose its appeal.[86]

Mollie Katzen, in her introduction to the 1977 *Moosewood Cookbook*, which became a classic among vegetarian American cookbooks, looked both globally and to the past for inspiration. Katzen explicitly honored the grandparental generation. Explaining that Moosewood restaurant, a collectively run enterprise in Ithaca, New York, was "the focal point to which each cook has brought her or his personal culinary heritage from family and friends," Katzen noted, "Many grandmothers' recipes are featured." Since the grandparents' generation had lived in an era when vegetarianism was rare, Katzen and her cohort had presumably needed to make some adjustments to recipes. Supplementing foods of the golden age of grandmother's kitchen, "we also go to the library often, to read about the foods of other countries." The culinary result, Katzen explained, "is an eclectic cuisine, with vegetarian, international emphases, using the freshest ingredients available." Recipes were sometimes given jokey names—zuccanoes (stuffed zucchini), Soy Gevult, Hippee Style Stuffed Eggplant—tapping into the valorization of play that marked the American counterculture. Tamari was featured, as were tortillas, hummus, and curry, all familiar to commune kitchens of the era.[87]

Although food journalist Nancy Harmon Jenkins has called Moosewood, a "restaurant of ideas and ideals," and food historian Warren Belasco notes it as an example of "hip commerce" in the counterculture food world, there is not much in the way of philosophy in the *Moosewood Cookbook*.[88] Indeed, Katzen avers that "There is no specific dogma attached to the Moosewood cuisine." Instead the collective's cuisine is rooted in "wholesomeness, and tries to present itself artfully." The sole note of evangelism was Katzen's explanation that "we also want to spread the notion that protein and aesthetics need not be sacrificed when you leave meat out of a meal." Like Edward Espe Brown's tasteful monks, the Moosewood collective believed virtue and pleasure could exist on the same plate.[89]

Also in the spirit of play, Dragonwagon declared, "No cookbook for and about groups of us living together would be complete without some mention of the scarfies, alternately called the munchies . . . or the hungry grundies: that strange desire occurring anywhere from immediately to an hour or two after smoking dope; that desire that sneaks up behind you and hits you over the head and says *Food*." Preparing food in such situations could be a challenge, she warned. There was inertia to overcome and then time itself would be an altered substance: "It might take you longer to fix something: you'll get hung up on the way the eggplant feels, or stare for a few minutes at the cut inside a red cabbage."[90]

These complications could be dealt with, however, and the reader was encouraged to "Remember: If it's good when you're straight, it's probably better when you're stoned." Examples, or, as Dragonwagon phrased it, "a few specific rushes" for this moment were "a piece of icy cold watermelon, seeds and all; fresh fruit, chilled deeply, with soft cheese at room temperature; a soup with all kinds of surprising things in it, an Oriental dish with crispy bits of this and that, a slice of warm pie with a glass of cold milk." The range of possibilities reflected the internationality of commune cuisine's palate, encompassing here French, Asian, and American cultures as well as two dishes—soup and fresh fruit—that could have universal corollaries.

The True Light Beavers included a section in their communal cookbook titled "Stonies," which were dishes made with drugs, not food to be eaten when on drugs. Stonies suggested a familiarity, or at least a kinship with Cohen's *Hashish Cookbook* as they included a recipe for "marjoome" made with dates, almonds, mashed chickpeas, and "poor quality hash."[91]

Although the commune lifestyle might have seemed exotic to readers, perhaps titillatingly so, both Dragonwagon's and the True Light Beavers' cookbooks were produced by major New York publishers. In Dragonwagon's case, this might have had something to do with the author's having been the child of two successful writers, but it also seems to reflect a broad interest in both hippie culture and "natural" foods that had reached beyond the "freaks" by the end of the 1960s.[92] A humorous refrain in Horton's multicommune cookbook was that everywhere she went, commune members were working on cookbooks themselves, some already under contract with publishers, and thus were reluctant to share their recipes with her. Like her own publisher, Simon and Shuster, these commune cooks hoped to profit off the growing interest in health food.[93]

Health Food

Responding to the growing interest in the broadly conceived category of health food, in the 1970s, successful publishing companies produced many cookbooks devoted to "natural" and "health" and "whole" foods that did not assume an overtly alternative lifestyle. A few examples are *Natural Food Feasts from the Eastern World* (1976), *The Down-to-Earth Natural Food Cookbook* (1973), *Health Food Cookery* (1972), and *The Whole Grain Bake Book* (1980).[94] These books shared an approach to eating in which some foods were portrayed as villains and others as heroes, giving the genre as a whole a dramatic tone.

In Eleanor Levitt's *The Wonderful World of Natural Food Cookery*, published by Hearthside Press in 1971 (and bought and republished by the more mainstream Dover Publications in 1979), a crowd of food villains appeared together in the author's glossary of food terms. Caffeine "makes your heart beat faster and does you no good at all." Coffee was dismissed because "The caffeine isn't good for you and the 'Danish' that often goes with it is even

worse." Next in the alphabet of evil came cold cuts, which were "full of preservatives, nitrates, nitrites and other chemical poisons." After cold cuts,
Levitt warned against cake and cookie mixes, because they were "all too likely to contain saturated oils, bleached flour or hydrogenated fats, or all three."
Convenience foods such as readymade dinners, "canned or frozen, cost far
more and offer much less protein than similar dishes prepared at home."[95]

Like some other natural foods advocates, Levitt warned against using
baking soda because of fears that it depleted vitamin B. She also issued a
much less common warning against the use of spices, claiming that, "Most
natural food buffs are opposed to salt, pepper, cloves, mustard, nutmeg, vinegar, and other sharp seasonings as irritants to the digestion." This kind of
warning linked Levitt's work to older ideas about human digestion rooted
in theories developed before the birth of the science of nutrition. Her book
thus mixed folk wisdom with contemporary science and also contemporary
mistrust of science, as when she advised, "Frankfurters are used only rarely
in our household, and even then we buy only the organic kind—without
synthetic coloring, artificial flavoring, phosphates, or starchy binders."[96]

Among the heroes Levitt introduced to her readers were carob powder,
"Healthful Hors d'oeuvres and Snacks" such as hummus and falafel, and the
"Federation of Homemakers," a group of women who lobbied for informative food labeling. Levitt's foodways synthesized diverse influences, including *Gourmet*. Introducing a recipe for bean sprout and chicken salad, Levitt
noted that it had been supplied to a *Gourmet* reader who had asked for "the
best way of serving these bean sprouts." It is interesting that Levitt was a
reader of *Gourmet*, and had located one of the few instances in which the
magazine addressed the growing fashion for health and natural foods.

For the most part, writers in *Gourmet* ignored the new dramatic turn in
food writing to publish a consistent stream of articles about eating in France
and other countries, drinking wine, and preparing French food at home in
America. The gourmet movement had its own heroes—green salad and vin-
aigrette—and villains—Jello salad and maraschino cherries.[97]

Mainstream health food cookbooks tended to locate heroic food in a
past time. This mythical era was constructed with rich pastoralist language.

Thus, Jean Hewitt, editor of the *New York Times Natural Foods Cookbook*, published in 1971, introduced her collection with the assertion that "Around the turn of the century, before the advent of large-scale mechanized farming and modern food production methods, people took the special pleasures of fresh, natural and unrefined foods for granted." Eating "naturally" was not something new, she reassured readers, but a return to something true. Like the writers of Americana cookbooks discussed earlier, she believed that America had an edible past.[98]

Ignoring the issues of spoilage and limited variety that had made processed foods so popular, Hewitt offered "the textures, tastes and nutritional benefits of the natural, fresh foods that Grandmother knew" and the "old-fashioned goodness and flavor," attributed to the food of the late nineteenth century. Printed on recycled paper, the eclectic collection of recipes was dedicated to "the thousands of people across the country who believe in, and practice, the natural way of eating for good health." Hewitt drew the line of distinction early, establishing a special audience, in what was an attempt by the nation's best-known newspaper to cash in on the counterculture.[99]

Hewitt's intended audience would agree that, "A casual glance in the average shopping cart at a supermarket reveals quantities of low- or non-nutritive snacks and beverages, and highly processed convenience foods of uncertain nutritive values." Like Lappé and other health food writers, Hewitt admitted, "It isn't always easy to switch from a highly-processed-food diet to meals prepared only from natural foods."[100]

Sounding an early note of alarm about national obesity rates, Hewitt argued that it was truly important to make this transition as much as possible. Obesity was "one of the most serious medical problems in the country," Hewitt declared, and suggested that it was "perhaps not unconnected to these so-called 'empty-calorie' foods that tend to displace the basic nutritious foods in the diet which are needed to maintain proper weight levels and health."[101]

In urging readers to forgo these convenience foods, Hewitt sounded a note from the language of food advertising in the 1920s. Certain foods were "touted as time-savers," but, she warned, "purchasers pay dearly for the built-

in maid service" because the food they get so quickly did not supply nourishment. The built-in maid who had been the selling point for consumers in
the first half of the twentieth century was now seen as an interloper, stand-
ing between a family and its proper feeding. Instead of doing all the work for
the home cook, Hewitt promised, "This book . . . challenges the reader to
know exactly what he is eating by preparing dishes from basic ingredients."
Because food was a matter of life and death, it was a subject for serious work,
contemplation, and action.[102]

The two dominant narratives of the second half of the twentieth century
were of health, both personal and global, and of pleasure, embodied in a stereotyped haute bourgeois French cuisine. These two themes came together
in 1982, in Alice Waters's *Chez Panisse Menu Cook Book*.[103] Having opened
her now-famous restaurant in 1971, Waters produced her first cookbook for
an audience that already enjoyed her cooking and as a way to share her culinary philosophy with a wider audience than those who could visit the restaurant. Writing in the *New York Times*, Craig Claiborne and Pierre Franey
deemed it among the "commendable and inventive cookbooks," that they
claimed had only in the last dozen years begun to appear in book stores.[104]

The Alice Waters Revolution

The *Chez Panisse Menu Cookbook* began with Waters's credo: "Food must
be experienced." Waters worried that her readers could not understand the
food through words and wished "I could just sit people down and give them
something to eat; then I know they would understand." Her dogma and
desire both reflected the gourmet's insistence on pleasure as discursive and
also echoed the countercultural command to "be here now," living fully in
the moment. From both traditions, she carried forward an emphasis on an
idealized authenticity that was found in the moment. Waters's text placed
the aesthetic sense in the foreground of palate development, so that the
sense of beauty was venerated above nourishment in the experience of food.
This introduced a very important shift in food writing parallel to technological developments in printing that gave photography a more central role

in cookbooks in the late twentieth century. Waters's emphasis on aesthetics fit well with these developments and made it easier for her to advocate a new approach to foodstuffs as material culture.[105]

Both her gourmet and her hippie sensibilities decried whatever she perceived as inauthentic or phony in cooking. Waters's narrative of the emergence of her personal palate repeated the themes of gourmet genre cookbooks. Her culinary awakening followed the usual path, occurring in her unsuspecting youth when she visited France. As had happened for Julia Child, a transformative meal involved fish, in this case trout cooked with almonds.[106] Waters's epiphany emphasized the element of time: "The trout had just come from the stream and the raspberries from the garden. It was this immediacy that made those dishes so special." The short distance, both chronological and spatial, between source and plate (or life and death) was important because it allowed no opportunity for "processing," but also because it made it possible for Waters and her friends to eat in the moment, enjoying French food in a Zen way.[107] This sense of urgency was captured in the title of an interview with Waters in *Vogue* in 1982, "*Tres* Fresh."[108]

While gourmets of the 1940s and early 1950s had admired a French "way" with ingredients, this attention to material had been obscured through the 1960s as the popular notion of French food had come to be an elaborate formality and richly sauced repertoire. Waters, too young to have participated in the first wave of the gourmet movement, discovered it for herself through her own dissociation from mainstream American culture. In rejecting the "unnatural" in American foodways, Waters landed not in Asia but in France, enabling her to claim the remnants of French status for her essentially countercultural approach to foodstuffs.

Unlike her gourmet forebears, Waters emphasized the communal in writing about the food served at Chez Panisse. Although credited as the author on the book's cover, the title page informed readers that the text was written "in collaboration with Linda P. Guenzel," that there was a recipe editor, and also an illustrator. A note on the copyright page of the cookbook confessed, "The truth of the matter is that the restaurant and this book exist only because our customers have constantly expanded our horizons along with their own." The epigram was symptomatic of Waters's insistence that the restaurant existed as a discourse between customer and herself. In her opening remarks, as noted above, she perceived herself as a messenger, sharing a vision with others. Later in the book's introductory material, she insisted on using the term "suggest" to describe her menus, cautious about enforcing rules with readers.

Yet although she claimed she was only suggesting, Waters also revealed a stronger will to transform the diner and reader. When visitors came to the restaurant, she wrote, "I want to insist that they eat in a certain way, try new things, and take time with the food." Claiming to value highly the "necessity and importance of feedback from the kitchen to the dining room and back again," Waters nevertheless demanded final authority. The experience was not communal except in the sense that all customers ate the same meal.[109]

Waters's personality-driven narrative was also a harbinger of the celebrity chef cookbook that became steadily more popular through the end of the twentieth century, remaining vital to the genre in the twenty-first century. Although famous chefs and personalities like Duncan Hines had written popular cookbooks in the 1940s and 1950s, Waters introduced a new style in which the chef's personal philosophy was central to the engagement between reader and book. The book was possible because the restaurant had been successful and the restaurant had been successful because of one woman's vision of what food should be.

As Waters remembered, this vision was as political as it was culinary: "All I cared about was a place to sit down with my friends and enjoy good food while discussing the politics of the day." Waters did not separate the palate from the political, remembering, "The timing and the location encouraged my idealism and experimentation. This was during the late sixties, in Berkeley. We all believed in community and personal commitment and quality. Chez Panisse was born out of these ideals. Profit was always secondary." Presenting her countercultural credentials, Waters swore that the restaurant, wildly successful by 1982, had been not a self-aggrandizing capitalist trip, but a collective effort to feed people hungry for more than food.[110]

The ideal of nourishment Waters employed in her text reflected her intense sense of the authentic. Railing against supermarket produce, she argued, "We as a nation are so removed from any real involvement with the food we buy, cook, and consume. We have become alienated by the frozen and hygienically sealed foods." Like Isaiah crying out in the wilderness, she wanted "to stand in the supermarket aisles and implore the shoppers, their carts piled high with mass-produced artificiality, 'Please . . . look at what you are buying!'" For Waters, the average American's encounter with food was sterile because much of it had been processed in factories or shipped long distances. She pitied those who did not share her gift for discrimination, who "cannot see a lovely unblemished apple just picked from the tree as voluptuous, or a beautifully perfect pear as sensuous, or see that a brown-spotted two-foot-high lettuce, its edges curling and wilted, is ugly and offensive." Waters believed that these shoppers did not understand, that "Food should be experienced through the senses," yet she did not suggest how else one could experience food. Distasteful to Waters as they might be, processed foods like McDonald's french fries, have taste, smell, and texture; their fans can enjoy them on all these levels.[111]

Waters took up the language of distinction and blended it with the dominant themes of social health that emerged from the counterculture: "I strongly believe that much of what has gone wrong with American food has been the result of mechanization and the alienation that comes with it." Even in France, it was becoming harder "to find hand-kneaded and -shaped bread and homemade aioli."[112]

Touching food as part of the process of cooking was all-important to Waters, as she echoed Edward Espe Brown's call to use physical intuition to cook. Where Brown had told readers, "your life, your love, will bring these words into full creation," Waters encouraged them to "learn to trust your instincts. A good cook needs only to have positive feelings about food in general, and about the pleasures of eating and cooking." Her own instinct seemed to guide her toward French foodways, a process she portrayed as natural. As in her fury in the supermarket, she again portrayed herself as assaulted by American food culture, claiming, "I personally cannot eat massive quantities of food, so to me, heaped-up plates are truly offensive." Rejecting this custom, which she associated with America, she preferred, "The small courses of a French service."[113]

Although her cuisine and personal food culture seemed deeply centered in an idealized French way, Waters made two important distinctions that set her work apart from earlier gourmet books. She rejected mainstream French food as performed in America, setting the cooking at Chez Panisse in opposition to "the 'classic' *haute cuisine*, which abounds in many French restaurants in this country." Using quotation marks around the term classic suggested that Waters herself knew better than the average diner or chef at a French restaurant in America, unaware that what they were eating was not actually authentic to French tradition. Waters claimed that Chez Panisse's food was "more visually and aesthetically pleasing" than what she considered a popular charade, again emphasizing senses other than taste in the definition of her foodways. She characteristically credited a book of photography, *La Belle France*, as a source of inspiration, mentioning in particular a photograph of a French man in a garden picking a peach, one natural ingredient.[114]

The embrace of regional French foods, instead of standardized haute cuisine, eventually produced a watershed moment in the life of the restaurant and, consequently, in the genre of American food writing. After exhausting all the regions of France for menus, even wandering out into French imperial history to borrow from Morocco and Louisiana, Chez Panisse chef Jeremiah Tower "ultimately" created a menu to reflect the regional ingredients of Northern California. The menu included local delicacies, such as Tomales Bay oysters, Big Sur Creek smoked trout, Monterey Bay prawns, preserved California geese from Sebastapol, dry Monterey jack cheese, and copious amounts of California wine. This was, as Waters remembered, "the first time we made a really concerted effort to serve the ingredients available to us here in the Northern California area, and it truly set a precedent which has been followed since then." Where once Waters and her staff had focused on finding ingredients locally for the sake of freshness, they now moved into a phase of letting the ingredients lead the cuisine, celebrating California produce instead of simply "sourcing" it for French-inspired dishes.[115] And just at the moment when chefs at Chez Panisse began to see food differently, there emerged new ways to convey that new vision to the reading public.

*   *   *

In the late 1980s, new processes for cheaply printing high-quality digital color photographs helped to increase the numbers and sizes of pictures in cookbooks and food magazines. Today, large format, brightly illustrated cookbooks are the norm in the publishing industry. The archetype of this form is *Modernist Cuisine: The Art and Science of Cooking*, a multivolume "kitchen manual" published in 2011 that sells for nearly five hundred dollars and is most famous for its amazing cutaway photographs of food being cooked.[116] In the *New York Times*, reviewer Michael Ruhlman described the book as the manifesto of "a cultural and artistic movement every bit as definitive as Impressionism in 19th century France or Bauhaus in early 20th-century Germany."[117] The shift to the pictorial that made this revolutionary work possible began in the 1980s, with the trendsetting 1985 *Glorious American Food*, by Christopher Idone. Idone's background was in catering large and lavish events like the opening of the Temple of Dendur exhibit at the Metropolitan Museum of Art. His dedication to image showed in the large photographs of food and place settings that dominated the text. Idone recalled the origins of his pictorial approach: "One of my first teachers was a chef who insisted 'You don't cook with books. You don't cook with your tongue. You cook with your eye.'" Idone concluded that, "the eye as well as the palate has to be won." In service of this maxim, "this book is photographic, leading you by the eye though a variety of situations to show how everything—the food, the season and occasion—contributes to the rightness of things."[118]

When a new food magazine, *Eating Well*, published its first issue in 1990, publisher James Lawrence promised "a magazine which is at once impeccably well-informed and graphically striking."[119] For a magazine that claimed to be seriously dedicated to hard reporting about food safety and food sys-

tems, this emphasis on appearances reflects the pervasiveness of the growing association of visual pleasure with culinary satisfaction. Ten years later,
Walter Scheib, chef at the White House, received food magazines with particular pages marked by Laura Bush or her social secretary. When such suggestions arrived in his kitchen, Scheib wrote that he understood, "I wasn't
just to use the recipe, I was also supposed to mimic the presentation." Recreation of the photograph, not the flavor, became Scheib's (unsatisfying)
new job.[120]

The cookbook now often became primarily a thing of beauty, like the
fashion magazine, an object of aspiration. Its existence as a visual object frequently overshadowed its potential as an object of mechanical use. While
cookbooks had always served a role as fantasy fiction, the new food photography made the fantasy a more immediate experience.

Photography gave food a celebrity treatment, one that fit very well with
the rise of the celebrity chef as both public figure and cookbook author.
Where words had once determined the genre of food writing, images and
personalities now dominate. The pictorial turn that cookbooks took in the
early 1990s was not neutral in its affect on cuisine. The medium itself privileged certain foodways over others. The delicacy of nouvelle cuisine preparations and the playful showiness of the movement's iteration in America
made for excellent photographs because the food had already been staged
by the chefs. Photographers and their editors found unique visual interest in
the materials of cooking, fetishizing raw ingredients.

Presenting the viewer/reader with a fresh red pepper or just-sliced loaf
of bread called for action. The photographer created a work of art with the
ingredients and a camera; the viewer created another art piece with the ingredients and her own kitchen. Presenting food both as art and the subject
of art also helped to support the vision of cooking as high culture and chef
as genius that was so central to late twentieth-century cookbooks and food
writing.

CHAPTER 6

THE PALATE OF PERSONALITY

CHEFS AND COOKBOOKS AT THE END
OF THE TWENTIETH CENTURY

THE *GOURMET COOKBOOK*, published in 1950, was one of the first cookbooks to achieve trophy status.[1] Humorist Nora Ephron recalled that owning it "made me feel tremendously sophisticated. For years I gave it to friends as a wedding present." The book was "an emblem of adulthood, a way of being smart and chic and college-educated where food was concerned." It wasn't, however, any use in the kitchen: "I never really used it in the way you're supposed to use a cookbook—by propping it open on the kitchen counter, cooking from it, staining its pages with spattered butter."[2] By the middle of the twentieth century, what had once been text-heavy guidebooks to middle-class American foodways became both objects to be enjoyed aesthetically and souvenirs that connected readers with famous chefs.

The Time-Life series, too, drew the reader's attention to pictures and vignettes instead of primarily to recipes. Nika Hazelton, who wrote the German cookbook in the series, later confided that she thought of the books as "a joke," because there was no collaboration or even consultation in production of the text, recipes, and photographs. The book was not composed by an author but packaged by a media company.[3] Although these two examples paved the way for the celebration of cookbooks as decorative objects, it was not until the 1980s that the entertainment aspects of the cookbook became a focus of the industry.

The New American Chefs

In 1986, chef Jeremiah Tower boldly titled his cookbook *Jeremiah Tower's New American Classics*.[4] Inside, a large copy of Tower's signature sprawled across two pages immediately following the table of contents. The signature asserted that Tower was making his mark on American food. The parallel to John Hancock's signature on the Declaration of Independence also seems intended, as Tower proffered something "new," perhaps even revolutionary, yet at the same time "classic." The year before, introducing her book, *Cooking with the New American Chefs*, Ellen Brown had made the same allusion.[5] Writing about Tower and others in a new generation of restaurant chefs, Brown observed, "They are concocting dishes nightly bearing personal signatures as large as John Hancock's on the Declaration of Independence. And they are shaping the next chapter in the history of American food." It may be that Brown shared this notion with Tower, who then incorporated it into his book, or it may be that the idea suggested itself to them both independently. Whether or not the "new American chefs" really did change what and how Americans ate, it is clear that American cookbooks and food writing changed because of them.

The new generation, some of whom first worked professionally at Chez Panisse, wrote about food in ways that supported the rise of both the celebrity chef—a phenomenon based in singularities—and the eclecticization of American foodways, a trend based in multiplicities. Their approach to food remains dominant in the genre of cookbooks, embracing the emergence of food TV and enabling the rise of food blogs as well as the proliferation of diverse voices in the world of food publishing.

Tower had been responsible for the momentous change in cooking at Chez Panisse when he first looked to his local Californian surroundings for inspiration. Tower and Waters told the same tale as an origin story of the New American cuisine. The work fulfilled Angelo Pellegrini's directive, issued nearly forty years earlier, to make a new cuisine out of America's bounty of foodstuffs. As Waters noted, "the menu was in the plainest of English," which Pellegrini would have approved.[6] While Tower helped reorient the gourmet palate toward American ingredients, he also helped construct a new identity for the professional chef as genius.

Chefs like Tower claimed to be artists, not mere craftsmen, as much philosophers of taste as they were producers of edible materials. The new chef was a cultural agent and member of the thinking class as Ellen Brown implied when she celebrated "the new breed of American-born and college-educated chefs" who "are responding to a climate of educated palates." They "draw from their imaginations to create personal styles," relying on personal inspiration rather than culinary tradition. Unlike previous generations of restaurant chefs trained through a system of kitchen apprenticeship, "Some [of the new generation] bring to cooking philosophies developed in unrelated academic areas such as Chinese philosophy and electrical engineering." These alternate routes to the kitchen, Brown implied, enriched national cuisine as young cooks let go of the age-old hierarchies of culinary training to find their own paths through fields of study considered more intellectual.[7]

In his first cookbook, chef Wolfgang Puck defined the new chef as self-made and self-expressive: "You don't need to be a Cordon Bleu graduate to do it. Think of cooking as an outlet for your ideas, a release for the artist in you." He said that his two very successful, restaurants, Spago and Chinois, were "my two playgrounds where I can excel at what I best like to do."[8] A review of Spago noted that "There were 21 Rolls Royces in the parking lot" the night the restaurant opened in 1982. On the menu were pizzas topped with "goat cheese, fresh tomatoes, Santa Barbara shrimp, duck sausage made there, fresh basil, fresh oregano." That the reviewer described them as "probably as fine as pizza can be, carried to a new dimension" by their toppings, reflects the bold move Puck was making in elevating pizza to the elite dining room.[9]

Brown's reference to the "educated palates" of the American dining public suggested a symbiotic change in the audience as well as in the artists. In economic terms, the new goods and the new market for those goods had helped produce each other. The generation who had become Julia Child's devoted audience had used food as a route to higher cultural status. Cooking French food had made middle-class Americans feel as if they were participating in French high culture. With the rise of the "new chefs" they began to see cooks in restaurants who reflected their own cultural background, people who came to cooking not as a trade but as an outlet for cultural and personal expression.

As Marian Burros noted in the *New York Times* in 1982, this shift also had to do with a change in immigration laws. In 1969, the United States strictly limited the number of chefs who could immigrate to the United States, suddenly choking the previously steady supply of French and Swiss cooks for American restaurants. In place of their preferred foreign chefs, restaurateurs had to hire Americans. Then, in the 1970s, the Department of Labor reclassified chefs, who had been "lumped in with domestics," as "professionals" and "choosing a chef's toque over a doctor's stethoscope or a lawyer's briefcase became respectable."[10]

When Ellen Brown wrote that the new chefs were college-educated, she suggested that food could now be represented as an intellectual enterprise instead of either exclusively a source of sustenance or a source of pleasure. The distinction also affirmed that chefs had formerly been considered members of the service industries, not the elite, despite the economic success and renown some had achieved.

The 1970s were also a period of major transformation in the publishing industry. What had been small publishing companies owned by individuals, or families, like the Knopfs and the Browns, became subsidiaries of major corporations. In an attempt to make publishing more profitable, corporate executives gave business managers and publicity specialists new authority over manuscript acquisitions. Part of this process involved the public portrayal of not only authors but also of editors and publishing executives as glamorous characters. It was in this era that gossip columnist Liz Smith cleverly transformed the National Book Award from "a typical book-business-get together" of "men in tweedy suits and odd footwear and young women in off-the-rack dresses," into a celebrity-studded black tie and ball gown event. Legendary Simon and Schuster editor Michael Korda recalled that journalists "began to treat publishing as a 'hot' business." The new character of publishing supported the emergence of the chef as celebrity because celebrity gave added value to the book-as-product. Korda notes, too, that success changed the foodways of the business when "book publishers, most of whom had hitherto eaten at rather modest restaurants, swiftly took over the new Grill Room of the very expensive Four Seasons restaurant, making it a kind of exclusive club." The *Four Seasons Cookbook*, with a foreword by James Beard, was published in 1971.[11]

Cookbook author and restaurant consultant Barbara Kafka reflected a little later in the era that "The new generation of American chefs were people with educations, eager for invention and fame." Because of their backgrounds and ambition, "Cooking had left the [domestic sphere] and the working class at the same time." Chef Jasper White commented on the transformation of the Culinary Institute of America's student population. In the 1970s, White recalled, it was not "anything like it is today . . . It was attracting a different crowd, more working-class kids who really wanted to become chefs because they thought it would be a great way to make a living. There was no glamour."[12]

Perceptions of the field had changed so much over twenty years that chef Andrew Dornenberg offered gritty reality "to transcend popular 'glamourized' media images of chefs to portray what it's *really* like to work in a kitchen."[13] In her foreword to Dornenberg's *Becoming a Chef*, cooking school teacher and cookbook writer Madeleine Kamman encouraged those who pursued culinary training to recognize their own social importance: "Enjoy your kitchen career and do not ever suffer those prophets of doom who will try to tell you that after all, if you become a chef, you will be practicing 'just another craft.' If you learn well, practice, and persevere, you will live to become a true culinary artist whose plates will be models of good taste, in both senses of the term, for a new generation of cooks."[14]

The newly popular American chefs fed this notion in their writing, disconnecting themselves from any one culinary tradition in order to claim the ascendancy of the individual's educated choice of cuisine. Chef Mark Miller wrote in the preface to his 1989 *Coyote Cafe* cookbook that in the late 1960s, "For the first time, an educated, creative elite was entering the cooking profession, experimenting with innovative techniques and ingredients." Miller implied, perhaps unintentionally, that all previous generations of chefs had been ignorant, uninspired, and plebian. Anne Greer, credited with establishing a national fashion for a new version of Southwestern cuisine (she invented cilantro pesto) also claimed, "A young, urban, sophisticated population with an adventuresome palate" had enabled the emergence of the new chefs and that "Americans today have a new appreciation for food in a cultural sense."[15]

Miller's menu featured dishes associated with Mexico, such as salsas, tamales, and swordfish *escabeche*, but also roamed farther afield to include ceviche, and a curried oyster dish based on something he had tasted in Martinique. He identified lobster enchiladas as "one of the trademark dishes" of the restaurant, noting that it "may seem a little contradictory: lobster is usually thought of as rare and refined, while enchiladas have the opposite reputation. However, this recipe shows just how elegant an enchilada can be!" He suggested "an older, fuller Chardonnay" as the dish's perfect companion, and further elevation to high culture status.[16] When the Coyote Cafe opened in 1987, Ruth Reichl reported that so many famous chefs were in attendance that more than one guest noted, "if a bomb were dropped on this party, it would set back American cooking 20 years." The remark expressed the collective understanding that American food was making progress toward some unspoken ideal through the work of Miller's generation.[17]

What Miller and Greer emphasized was the free way chefs now treated regional and national cuisines and also class cultures. More like undergraduates selecting eclectically from a course catalog than keepers of any one culinary flame, the new chefs celebrated their ability to pick and choose among foodways. Ellen Brown praised Greer's cross-cultural productions, quesadillas filled with brie and mango—a traditional borderlands food with new ingredients—and her grits soufflé, which gave continental treatment to a traditional food of the American South.

Cooking as Personal Expression

Even James Beard, often credited by the new generation as the "father of American cuisine," blurred culinary boundaries in his 1981 cookbook, *The New James Beard*. Just as some of the new generation—Larry Forgione, Anne Greer—credited him as their guru, Beard seemed to take inspiration from their generation himself. Explaining that he had not intended to up-date his 1970 edition of *The New James Beard* so soon, he wrote, "something had been quietly happening, I came to realize: a shift straight across the whole spectrum of my cookery, all the way from menu making right down to how I now wrote recipes. . . . The new me had to write a new book." Beard wanted to introduce "a new, flexible approach to ingredients, to the way we put them together, and the way we plan a meal." He invited readers to "Feel Free," because "Cooking has entered a grand era of liberation, not just in how we cook, but whether we cook, and what." The new Beard implied that the route to satisfying food was a process of self-discovery: "Take nothing for granted—not even your own palate, for it can change. Mine has." Get-ting in touch with one's personal taste, not with trends or traditions, was the best way to find success in the kitchen.[18]

While the new freedom encouraged in cookbooks in the early 1980s seems to have been the product of the loosening of old cultural ties that began in the 1970s, it also manifested trends and themes associated with the "Me Decade," in which self-direction and personal fulfillment were valorized. The new regionalism that emerged in the 1980s, most notably in restaurants and cookbooks by Mark Miller and Paul Prudhomme, also had an analog in American intellectual life, as universities saw the rise of area studies and identity studies that created opportunities for the recognition and celebra-tion of American diversity.[19]

Miller charted a James Beard-ian, individualistic voyage of discovery in the introduction to his *Coyote Cafe* cookbook. First turning his attention away from Santa Fe, where his restaurant was, Miller returned in memory to the first glory days of Chez Panisse and the coterie of inspirational peers he worked with there. His culinary origins were rooted not in family connec-tions to one geographic region, but in ideological kinships. He was neither a New England chef cooking New England food nor a Southwestern chef cooking food of that region. Instead, he was a chef from New England by way of Berkeley, who felt inspired to cook the foods of New Mexico.[20]

In explaining how a person with French Canadian ancestors raised in New England came to open a Southwestern restaurant in Santa Fe, Miller offered the justification of personal taste. His parents, it turned out, had had a friend from Guadalajara, Mexico, who brought Mexican treats when he visited. This early introduction to food of one Mexican region, readers were supposed to understand, somehow led naturally to his recent dedication to New Mexican flavors. Miller felt the need to explain his culinary career, but not to establish anything like "authenticity" in connection to the region. His very explanation subtly argued that lovers of food had an international palate, access to all flavors and techniques. The important thing was to be authentic to the self, not a nationality.

Miller explained, "This book and its recipes are a reflection of my own personal taste in food. Most of the recipes are traditionally Southwestern, while others introduce personal touches, new ideas, or techniques derived from other cuisines. Many of these recipes have been adapted from my travels."[21] The repeated use of the term "personal" and Miller's emphasis on the first person possessive pronoun "my" signal the new paradigm in which the cookbook became a personal expression of an individual chef, enhanced by and enhancing celebrity chef culture.

Ellen Brown noted that Jasper White, another of the new generation, "terms his food 'just my personal style,'" while Wolfgang Puck claimed, "What I am doing is my own personal statement . . . I'm very much an idealist, and think everyone should have their own style."[22] Michael Roberts, known best as the chef of Trumps in Los Angeles, also offered cookbook readers his personal journey.

In *Secret Ingredients*, Roberts related his development from an NYU student in musical composition who cooked for stress release to a full-time chef learning on the job, to his studies in France and his emergence as a star chef of the new generation in 1980s Los Angeles. Roberts's life before his restaurant, Trumps, opened, was a quest for his authentic culinary voice. In his first job as a chef, at an "international hodgepodge" restaurant, he recalled, "Many of the ingredients and flavors intrigued me, and finally I gave up striving for culinary authenticity, put away the cookbooks, and began to improvise. Here at last was a peek at the self-expression I had not achieved through music." Placing the emergence of his talent in the context of other forms of cultural expression, Roberts used many analogies to portray cooking as art. Turning to literature he mused that "Ingredients are to recipes as words are to sentences. . . .We can combine and recombine them in many different ways, giving them very different tastes depending on their context."[23]

The world of fine art supplied another way to understand his work: "A painter creates a painting by organizing colors and shapes in some coherent way. . . . Cooking, likewise, is the act of taking basic ingredients and organizing them in a coherent way, using food as the medium and flavor as the message." Just as Alice Waters had first envisioned the meals at Chez Panisse as a communication between the kitchen and the customers, Roberts conceived of food as statement. His own "artistic impulses led me toward combining elements of different cuisines to form something new," so as to have something relevant to convey.[24]

This mode of writing cookbooks made the restaurant central to American food writing because this was the venue in which the chef could establish his or her personal voice with visible success. To some extent, restaurants had been ascending in the cosmos of food writing since Craig Claiborne first began to review them in 1962 for the *New York Times*. By writing "frank" reviews instead of extended promotions, as had been the tradition, Claiborne made restaurant dining competitive in a new way. Not only were restaurants competing for the critical reviewer's favor, but diners who were not reviewers were also now competing with each other to be correct, or in agreement with Claiborne before his reviews came out.

As Pete Wells, who became *New York Times* restaurant reviewer in 2011, wrote of the phenomenon, "Within a few years, nearly every major newspaper had to have a Craig Claiborne of its own. Reading the critics, eating what they had recommended, and then bragging or complaining about it would become a national pastime."[25] Where previously dining out had been socially competitive in the sense that eating at the most expensive restaurant revealed one's own wealth, it now became a contest of discovering the soon-to-be anointed place and most impressive chef first.

The theater of restaurant dining both required and offered more opportunities for audience participation. As Wells argues, "Claiborne and his successors told Americans that restaurants mattered. That was an eccentric opinion a half-century ago. It's not anymore." Tasting one of Jeremiah Tower's "new American classics" at his restaurant was a public engagement with celebrity, whereas making a recipe oneself from the *Gourmet Cookbook* was not. To eat Tower's vision as prepared by Tower (or his staff) connected the consumer to Tower's celebrity—the diner became part of the performance.[26]

Cookbook author Nika Hazelton wrote about the new phenomenon of performative culinary appreciation in 1980: "The kutlturny, status-symbol-conscious crowd fill more and more cooking schools, like groupies surrounding a pop star." Offering a mocking assessment of this trend, she reminded readers that "These higher cooking interests require a certain amount of education, leisure, and money," while she herself offered guidance in an "American Home Cooking," which she thought had been lost partly to the gourmet trend and partly to the working class's reliance on convenience foods.[27]

By the 1990s, prominent American chefs, while still cultivating personal celebrity through cooking, also claimed allegiance to what James Villas called an American "table of our own."[28] Larry Forgione, who named his restaurant An American Place, dedicated his 1996 cookbook "to my grandmothers . . . for the honesty in their cooking, and to James Beard, the father of American cooking, friend and mentor." Like Wolfgang Puck, Forgione posited a golden age of American cooking to which he offered return passage.[29]

Writing as if he had grown up in the 1850s instead of the 1950s, Forgione declared, "American food is my passion—that is, real American food. What's real about my American food is that it has all the fresh, ripe flavor that I remember from childhood. Back then, we were more closely linked to our food sources. The person who grew the food sold it directly to the person who cooked the food who in turn brought it to the table all warm and delicious." For Forgione, the "real" America was rural and agricultural and existed outside the industrial food chain that had dominated American food culture for nearly one hundred years. Nothing urban and nothing mass-produced could be either desirable or authentic.[30]

Forgione's recipes harked back to historical figures and cookbooks, as when he wrote of General Robert E. Lee's Favorite Soup, "I saw a similar recipe in an old community cookbook published around 1920." The Confederate general apparently favored a tomato-based vegetable soup. Elaborating on his own art as historical reenactor, Forgione noted, "The sherry reveals this as an old Southern recipe. When I first made the soup, I used dry sherry, as I am sure they did in the nineteenth century. However, I eventually switched to cream sherry, because it has a richer, less alcoholic flavor." In recognition of newer food traditions, his book also included Buffalo-Style Chicken Salad with blue cheese dressing.[31]

When chef Stephen Langlois was hired to create a restaurant that honored the aesthetic legacy of architect Frank Lloyd Wright, he, like Forgione, turned rhetorically to America's rural past. He first "rushed off to the library," where he discovered "that there had been a simple, delicious and somewhat homey style of cooking practiced in the Midwest for generations." Framing this as a realization, Langlois assumed that the reader shared his initial assumption that there had been nothing delicious in Midwestern food history. Langlois and his restaurant, Prairie, which opened in 1986, were on a mission to share the revelation: there are good things to eat west of New York and east of Los Angeles! Langlois's research continued at state fairs and in small restaurants in rural towns. He "even traded recipes with a grandmother or two," and "pored over old church and settlement cookbooks looking for useful recipes." Although he updated the recipes because "People today are eating foods that are lighter, healthier, and, most of all, fresher than ever before," his stated starting point was the rural past, not the eclectic urban present or any mixture of the two.[32]

Multiculturalism in American Cookbooks

The multiculturalism of Wolfgang Puck's success—an Austrian cooking Chinese food in Los Angeles—like Mark Miller's success as a New Englander introducing Southwestern foodways to an elite white audience, were part of the third important shift in cookbook writing that happened in the 1990s. Publishers offered American cookbook readers an ever-expanding range of cuisines to attempt and to assimilate into their everyday foodways. Betty

Fussell gives Craig Claiborne much of the credit for expanding American interest in multicultural foodways. Because Claiborne "was the first to write in detail about exotic Szechuan, Vietnamese and Thai cooking and to document them with recipes," his readers in the *New York Times* felt empowered to embark on their own culinary tourism. The new international cookbooks made it possible for Fussell and her cohort to believe that "We, too, could play host to the world's great chefs and learn Chinese cooking from Virginia Lee, Italian from Marcella Hazan, Indian from Madhur Jaffrey, Mexican from Diana Kennedy."[33]

While the new American chefs claimed access to a multicultural cannon of cuisines, publishers increasingly offered readers a diversity of national and regional palates. The gourmet generation had privileged knowledge of French food above all others and although it remained central to the cannon of food knowledge, the generation who came of age with chefs like Waters, Puck, and Tower celebrated their own openness to world cuisines. The concept of world food, like that of "world music," is complicated in that it assumes a norm from which "world" elements vary. Although the stereotype is generally a positive one, it creates a false sense of the norm—American middle-class food in this case—as not of "the world."[34]

In part the new interest in the ethnic was the result of the countercultural rejection of Western society's dominant culture. As philosopher Lisa Heldke explains, using herself as an example of a type of eater, "I collect eating adventures—as one might collect ritual artifacts from another culture without thinking of the appropriateness of removing them from their cultural setting." Determinedly adventurous eaters like Heldke heap praise on ethnic cuisines, but do so within an unspoken hierarchy that has the potential to devalue the very chefs they attempt to celebrate.[35]

To categorize ethnic foods as the opposite of "fancy" cuisines—specifically French and "Nouveau" American—was to limit economic opportunities for these chefs. It also determined that ethnic cuisines would be enjoyed only on American terms—as adventurous departure from a norm, but never normal in their own right. In one example that reflects, even as it gently challenges, the persistence of this pattern, *Gourmet* invited readers in 2001 to find out "just how haute Vietnamese food can get."[36]

In 1994, *Saveur*, a new food magazine, began publication seemingly to speak to and for this new generation of American eclectics. Just five years later, the venerable old *Gourmet* was reinvented to also serve a new audience less interested in tradition than in innovation and informality. In a sense they were both new magazines. Both also retained much of what *Gourmet* and it's more middle-brow rival *Bon Appétit* had established as effective tricks of the trade, such as artistic instead of (strictly) instructive illustrations, travel pieces, and recipes that seemed to be tailored for contemporary home cooks with unlimited time in the kitchen. *Saveur* also joined *Gourmet* in addressing the reader as a singular individual who consciously established her persona through food choices. *Saveur* assisted its readers in creating themselves. In doing this, *Saveur* did not, probably could not, jettison the food connoisseur's map of the world established by *Gourmet* in its early years.

In its pilot issue, *Saveur* editor Dorothy Kalins asked her readers if when traveling they "head for the market first, then the museum? Would you rather bring back olive oil than perfume?" Assuming a traveler, Kalins also assumed a person who cooked, not one who just dined out. The *Saveur* reader headed not for the Michelin-starred restaurant, but to the market for ingredients perhaps to use in a rented kitchen, perhaps for a picnic, perhaps just for "inspiration" and as a way to understand a new culture. And in traveling, this ideal reader was not only self-educator but also self-transformer, bringing the foreign substance home to consume in the domestic context. *Saveur* addressed a reader who was both adventurous and inventive, not just enjoying what foreign restaurants offered, but assimilating herself into another culture.[37]

The analogy of perfume to olive oil also both helped Kalins to suggest an eroticism in cooking reminiscent of the writing of M. F. K. Fisher, and established her assumed reader as female (perfume rather than cologne). This assumed female reader was also fearless: "When you feel like cooking, do you deliberately search out recipes with a long list of ingredients and prep time?" This would be starkly at odds with the most ubiquitous recipe offerings from women's magazines, which promised that speed was compatible with satisfaction. Kalins seemed to invite the reader to wallow in the experience of cooking, asking, "Do you see the world food first?" Yet she also acknowledged that this was an often-unattainable ideal: "If (like me) you answer this description, you know it's only half the story. Because you also know how often you've rushed through a meal and all you remember is the chewing." The reader was not a guiltless eater but was sometimes caught up in the latest health trends: "You buy so much stuff with 'lite' and 'free' marked on it, that you start forgetting the flavor of the real thing." Authenticity is here associated with richness and bounty. She also acknowledged the impermanence of culinary fashions: "You recall the flat aftertaste of fleeting food trends—from Cajun to Pacific Rim." The following of fashion she also associated with loss of real tastes.[38]

In reaction to a cacophony of food voices in contemporary culture, Kalins invited the reader to "Enjoy food. Stop worrying about it. Trust your palate and your heart." Like Beard and Miller, she elevated self-direction above expertise either scientific or cultural. A photograph of the magazine's staff enjoying a dinner party in a private apartment supported the mood of informality Kalins suggested as she urged readers to let go of assumptions and taboos. The space was small, the clothes and table settings informal, faces were flushed with drinking, and wine glasses were full—the scene was appealingly replicable in the ordinary reader's home.[39]

For all its seeming looseness, however, *Saveur* included a small proscriptive feature in which readers had the chance to scoff collectively at recent food-related trends. This, like *Glamour* magazine's "Don't" feature, enabled readers to establish their common identity negatively as well as through positive choices about what to eat. The first appearance of this section was titled "Not in *this* lifetime," and listed foods the magazine's editors did not want to try: "All these dishes—which have appeared recently on menus in various corners of America—are probably really, really good. But, er, we'll have the tuna melt." Rejecting what they implied as overreach or pretension, the editors managed to be both exclusive and democratic at the same time. It is hard to know, however, from the modern vantage point just what was objectionable about "Jamaican yams and coconut milk rice with gunga peas." You had to be there, it seems, to get the joke.[40]

In the first official issue, the list was titled "Never eat at a restaurant where…" and included establishments that served more than five flavors of margaritas and the kind of place where "the menu is Italian rustic, but the owners are named Missy and Biff." The theme appeared to be authenticity, as judged by the savvy editor and readers. The rule about only cooking what you are—like the advice to beginning writers to write only what they know—could be applied to invented characters Missy and Biff, whose names make them comically preppy, but perhaps not to Alice Waters attempting French country cooking or to Mark Miller at the Coyote Cafe or Wolfgang Puck at Chinois.[41]

Although *Saveur* seemed to valorize a particular understanding of authenticity, it also celebrated the personal search for this quality, acknowledging that new truths could be discovered and embodied, though somehow drawing the line at margaritas, Missy, and Biff. The magazine celebrated characters who, like the new American chefs, brought professional or intellectual backgrounds not related to restaurants or cooking schools into their work with food. This archetype—the lawyer who becomes a cheesemaker, for example—had become a stock character in food writing by 2012. Because it is easily associated with a recent turn to the artisanal, borne of disenchantment with corporatized culture, it is revealing to find it emerging earlier in the 1990s.

Culinary Converts

The premier issue of *Saveur* featured a couple, Paul Rizzo and Marcia Durgin, who started their professional lives as environmental chemists, working in a laboratory. They then became interested in baking, left scientific work behind, and opened a bakery in Doylestown, Pennsylvania. There they produced French style breads, pies, tarts, brioches, and also cookies and brownies, joining French and American baking cultures. The couple's journey of personal discovery, in which they learned the truth about their own natures and thereby became more authentic, led to communal enlightenment. As the profile in *Saveur* explained, Rizzo and Durgin "didn't set out to turn the people of Doylestown into addicts of real bread. But that's just what they've done." Just as the chemists found their true callings in baking, Doylestown awoke from what would have been more than two hundred years of misery, to learn the taste of "real bread." The construction of what was in fact an imported food—French-style bread—as authentic or "real" in the rural Pennsylvania context is a good example of how some definitions of authenticity overrode others in the construction of these popular redemption-through-food narratives.[42]

In the next issue of *Saveur*, a former math teacher and pharmaceuticals salesman returned to his rural roots to become owner of a cherry orchard and maker of cherry butters and preserves as a "connoisseur's connoisseur." Writer Allison Engel titled the piece "The Cherry Orchard," although there was no apparent parallel with the Chekhov play. Instead the allusion was a nod to the reader as someone in touch with high culture. The farmer, Tom Cooper, was inspired to make his career/life change "not [by] a stint at culinary school or some flavor epiphany in Europe." He was not, in other words, Julia Child. His epiphany was more in the style of the American-grown transcendentalists. Thinking back to his father's life as a tree farmer, Cooper said, "I remember my father walking down his rows of blue spruce, and kind of patting them with satisfaction." *Saveur* celebrated a certain relationship with nature in Cooper's story, complemented by a particular relationship to the customer.

Thinking about his father's work, Cooper recalled, "His business was about giving customers good value and growing superior trees. I wanted to recapture that ethic." The implication that the world of pharmaceutical sales lacked this "ethic" was important to the establishment of the escape to authenticity as a theme. According to writers in *Saveur*, Rizzo and Durgin brought something "real" to a community that had only known the inauthentic, at least in bread. Cooper reestablished what he defined as older, truer patterns of ethical commerce.[43]

Saveur defined a new kind of authenticity that was intriguingly tied to national identity, rooted in a mythologized America. Thus, Tom Cooper was worth knowing about as much for the fact that his journey to the farm did not take him to France first, as for the cherry butter—a distinctly American product—that his farm produced.

In this vein, the magazine celebrated the 150th anniversary of iceberg lettuce with an attempt to validate what had been reviled. Mocking the voice of the food snob, the piece began: "iceberg, cursed iceberg, the butt of jokes, the bane of all true 'gourmets.' Surely iceberg has no merits for the serious cook or eater." Answering this dogma of the gourmet with a "Ha!" *Saveur* went on to applaud the lettuce for its reliable crispness in sandwiches, placing it within American food culture, and then also noting its essential role in two foreign dishes, *petits pois à la française* and Chinese minced squab. Arguing that iceberg lettuce had culinary value because it was good in sandwiches suggested that the editors also placed the common sandwich on the same level as the two foreign dishes, implying an equality of cuisines that could help establish *Saveur's* as the authentic voice of the omnivore.[44]

The theme of American food authenticity was set in opposition to a stereotype of gourmet sophistication and trendiness again and again in early issues, where it was important to establish tone. The magazine celebrated the food of a Maine fishing camp, by first mocking urban food writing: "The trendy urban name for fare like this today is comfort food. At West Branch Ponds Camps, owner Carol Stirling—whose family has run the camp for three generations—just calls it meat and potatoes." The terms "family" and "three generations" and "just" in contrast to "trendy" and "today" establish Stirling's authenticity, which in turn is transferred to the reader because she or he appreciated the distinction.[45]

Likewise, the magazine editors assumed readers would understand and identify with what writer Robin Gourley meant when she wrote in a separate article of "a recent trend toward over-refinement and flourless [cake] recipes." As antidote, Gourley offered her cake recipe with the explanation that "this beauty is from the 'leave well enough alone' school. It is a cake from the heart of my family."[46] Again, family, the past, and the concept of simplicity valorized both the recipe and the reader who could appreciate it.

This veneration of past foodways was another feature that *Gourmet* had established as central to American food writing. Anne Mendelson, *Gourmet's* in-house (but valiantly even-handed) historian wrote, that an "intangible, but supremely important, element of the magazine's identity" through most of its history until the 1970s "was an intense fixation on the past as the standard of meaning. Every year—it seemed nearly every issue—brought more memoirs of vanished worlds." While Mendelson argued that this obsession had mostly been relinquished by the 1980s in *Gourmet's* pages,

Saveur seems to have adopted it, perhaps as a way for a new young magazine to establish a sense of institutional history.[47]

Driving home the argument that food like Carol Stirling's camp fare was more "real" than what readers might find in fashionable urban restaurants, writer Cynthia Hacinli claimed, "This way of eating has all but gone the way of the caribou in our age of demon cholesterol and prettified camera-ready food." Hacinli implied that Americans were paradoxically both too scared of food and too enthralled by it to truly understand it. Despite the dig at the new emphasis on food photography, *Saveur* supplied artistically composed photos of Stirling's cornmeal-crusted trout with bacon and her blueberry pancakes, probably suspecting that by 1994 readers could not or would not live on words alone.[48]

To support the identification of the magazine with instinct and authenticity, the last page regularly featured a photograph of a moment in what might be called the life of food. One of these images captured a Bronx fishmonger in the moment before his friends dropped a large dead octopus on his head. The photograph could serve to establish the magazine as one dedicated to informality, and "regular" folks, as when it published a feature article on ketchup—the gourmet's kryptonite.[49]

Yet for all the antigourmet rhetoric, the magazine featured reviews of expensive restaurants, articles on foreign travel, and ads for luxury brands such as furniture designer Roche Bobois. That the seeming contradiction between the everyman persona and the voice of the connoisseur did not prevent the magazine from thriving and in fact outliving *Gourmet* suggests American readers wanted to have two cakes—both dacquoise and devil dog—and eat them too.[50]

The New *Gourmet*

In 1999, Ruth Reichl became chief editor of *Gourmet*. Reichl had been the chief restaurant reviewer for the *New York Times*. One reader referred to the magazine after Reichl became editor as "this new version of an old favorite magazine."[51] Reichl's new *Gourmet* seemed to be following the lead set by *Saveur* to loosen up old strictures, in terms of both content and layout.

The most immediately obvious difference between the pre- and post-Reichl *Gourmet* was visual. Fashions in graphic design had largely not affected the look of *Gourmet* over the years, and it had certainly not joined in the 1970s loose, handcrafted style. By 1999, however, graphic design had been revolutionized technologically in ways *Gourmet*'s new editor was willing to take advantage of.

In the 1980s, new computer languages made it possible for layout editors to easily manipulate sections of digital text. No longer bound to columns, they could take a more playful approach to the page. New software also made it possible to make rapid changes in layout.[52] Desktop publishing programs Adobe Photoshop and QuarkXPress enabled editors to see many possibilities for layout in rapid succession.[53] Once it was possible to scan and digitize images, one desktop publishing program, Adobe PageMaker, used the physical mockup board as a model and enabled editors to cut and paste digital items. Because the new technologies made it possible to blur the boundary between text and illustration, readers began to expect more visual variety and excitement from the printed page.[54]

Some of the ideas *Gourmet* picked up, like the use of sidebars and floating collections of data, had helped make *Spy* a popular magazine for urban elites of Reichl's own generation. Making the magazine look like its hippest contemporaries could help bring new readers to an old magazine and thus new markets to loyal advertisers. The mix-and-match ecumenicalism of this generation of cooks was reflected well in the new graphic style of *Gourmet* that atomized stories, deconstructing them into interesting pieces jammed together at surprising angles.

After disrupting the visual landscape of the beloved magazine, Reichl made another forthright territorial shift by including pieces about restaurants all over the country, not just New York and Los Angeles. Noting, "American food has matured, and we want to recognize that by including new cities," she initiated the transformation by contributing a column about restaurants in Minneapolis. The choice of Minnesota can be seen as symbolic, reorienting the magazine so that its center was squarely in America, not just a littoral America, taking in the costal cities, but the continental United States, white bread basket and all.[55]

Underscoring the magazine's new geography, Reichl's first issue featured an article on "five decadent burgers." This piece complemented Reichl's argument that American food had "matured" by assuming a reader who had "matured" in perspective toward American food so that "decadent" could meaningfully describe the dish once considered the antithesis of good food[56].

Under Reichl's direction, *Gourmet* treated American food of the present on equal terms with French food of the past. The magazine had begun to make this shift before her arrival, too, as Jane and Michael Stern's column, first titled "Two for the Road," and then "Road Food" began to appear regularly in 1994. An annual "All American" issue, first appearing in 1986, also acknowledged that there was at least enough going on in American food for one whole issue every year. The Sterns' column, which Reichl continued to run, had a very particular subject area: the "simple" folk cuisine of primarily rural America.

One reader described his understanding of the column, "I have surmised that the editors want to showcase so-called American culinary tradition by frequently reviewing small-town, homey-type restaurants." The reader, noted, "I appreciate this, and often enjoy the recipes that may reveal a secret to fried chicken or what's different about southern-style cornbread." However, the formula could take the magazine too far beyond its core values as when *Gourmet* featured "a restaurant that uses ready-made piecrusts and Cool Whip!" Disappointed, he rebuked the editor: "Talk about dumbing down your magazine." The Sterns' columns emphasized the folksy over contemporary realities in American food, defining authenticity as a kind of innocence of food trends.[57]

The Sterns gave *Gourmet* language to judge mainstream American food on its own terms. In describing Stroud's, a fried chicken restaurant in Kansas City, for example, they wrote, "*Polite* is not exactly the word that comes to mind when thinking of adjectives for Stroud's. Not that it's rude—in fact, everybody is very friendly—but there is a delectable outlaw cachet about the old tavern that adds spice to the dining-out experience." Stroud's existed, and excelled, within in its own system of norms remote from the usual expectations of urban elite diners. Reichl's *Gourmet* took American food seriously on its own terms.[58]

Like the New American Chefs, whom Reichl had come of age with and helped promote through her writing, she changed perceptions of both food and food writing and what was fair game in the genre. Even before she became editor of *Gourmet*, Reichl helped pioneer the food memoir, a genre that also emphasized origins.[59] Now the subject of academic study from diverse disciplines, the story of self as maker and consumer of food had its beginnings for American readers in the writings of M. F. K. Fisher. Fisher largely had this field to herself until the 1980s, however, when publishers brought out several successful new works in this genre. By 1997, one reader could claim, "The distance between books of recipes surrounded by personal stories and novels laced with recipes seems to be getting shorter every day."[60]

Food Memoirs

Nora Ephron's *Heartburn*, published in 1983, was an early and influential culinary memoir. Although the novel is mostly focused on the lightly fictionalized breakup of the author's marriage, recipes regularly appear as expressive of the narrator's identity and experience. In reflecting on the early stages of her courtship with the man who would later betray her, Ephron wrote, "The first time I made dinner for Mark I made potatoes. The first time I made dinner for just about anyone I ever cared for I made potatoes."[61] One of the story's villains, Thelma Rice, steals the narrator's husband, but is forever damned by the assessment that her puddings are "gluey."[62]

Novelist Laurie Colwin's essay collections, *Home Cooking* (1988) and *More Home Cooking* (1993), also implicitly argue that telling someone what and how you cook is another way of telling them who you are. Many of the essays collected in these two volumes had first been published in *Gourmet*, where personal culinary adventures like Samuel Chamberlain's Clementine stories, had long found a home. Colwin's essays, however, were the opposite of travelogues. Colwin tied her cooking and food-based entertaining history to her development as an independent adult in a modern urban context. As her title implied, the book stayed very close to her own domestic sphere—her tiny Manhattan apartment.

Using the term "home cooking" as the title for the collection of Colwin's essays, her publishers also reflected the ways in which food memoirs could demystify culinary rhetoric. Because the food memoirist wrote about herself as a person in daily interaction with food, readers were less likely to encounter the extremes of professional preparation. Far from bragging about her glamorous show kitchen, Colwin recalled the many years she spent without a kitchen sink, running to the bathtub to drain her pasta. She also frequently admitted that she could bore her culinary audience. Beginning an essay "The Same Old Thing," with the statement that "Many of my closest friends are sick of my baked chicken," she joined in to mock herself: "when I point out that I know a million variations on this theme, they rightly point out that they have had them all, and more than once." No domestic diva, Colwin did not attempt to sell herself to readers as a culinary expert to be emulated, but instead to use experiences of cooking and eating to create a sense of empathetic community between author and reader.[63]

Colwin's sketches of herself as a cook revealed a unique self, a person who was impulsive and open-hearted, valuing personal bonds above social capital. The "home cooking" she wrote about was the quirky meals she ate alone as often as it was the meals she created for others. The theme of nourishment, of both self and community, implicit in her title acted as a sort of counternarrative to the emergence of the nouvelle cuisine and the New American chefs who were of her generation.

Colwin's readers, like her friend, novelist Anna Quindlen, who wrote a profile of her in *Gourmet* in 2001, were fans of her voice more than of her palate, reading her essays as a way to spend time with her, but not necessarily to get any one of her one million recipes for roast chicken. The popularity of Colwin's memoir-with-recipes indicated that readers were eager for the personal voice in food writing. These voices could be very judgmental—Colwin's was—but the judgment was of the individual not the caste, making it more a matter for amusement than of anxiety over proprieties left unperformed.

Reichl's sensualist memoir, *Tender at the Bone*, shared Colwin's focus on personal authenticity.[64] Reichl's memoir was published in 1998, the year she took charge at *Gourmet*. Having promoted the distinctly individualist chefs of the New American generation, Reichl joined their ranks as chronicler of her own food story. Slightly scandalous in its details about an affair Reichl had with Colson Andrews, who became editor in chief of *Saveur*, the memoir gave readers access to the bedrooms as well as kitchens of the characters who had by 1999 come to wield a new kind of cultural authority in America.

Perhaps the most popular food memoir of the time was Anthony Bourdain's *Kitchen Confidential*, which provided new opportunities for readers already thoroughly engaged with the restaurant as source of cuisine and the chef as its presiding genius, to learn the secrets of the trade. Declaring "food, for me, has always been an adventure," Bourdain promised his readers, "it's all here: the good, the bad, and the ugly." Making the "bad and the ugly" part of their culinary knowledge, readers who were attracted to Bourdain's tale reinforced the distance between the professional and domestic kitchen while seeming to get closer to the real action. Readers were presumably not intentionally learning to re-create the bad and ugly elements of Bourdain's experiences.[65] Even before the advent of reality television, the real had become a powerful concept in food writing. Only writers who eschewed the glamorous could really be trusted.

Publishers of *Taste of Home* magazine seemed to address the hunger for the personal and the real when they introduced their new food magazine in 1993. More than one thousand men and women who were described as "country cooks" and "no-nonsense cooks" edited the magazine. *Taste of Home*'s first issue was introduced to potential subscribers in terms that were flatly antigourmet: "It's down-home and practical—its recipes call for ingredients most cooks readily have on hand. You won't have to run to a specialty food store for goat cheese or sun-dried tomatoes . . . and that's a promise!" Suggesting a cultural divide between "specialty: and "normal" foods, the magazine's publishers seemed to encourage readers to construct their identity in opposition to contemporary food trends. The suggestion here is that food writers had been abusing their audience by making them feel materially inadequate and showing disregard for their real lives.[66]

In a profile of the staff as a group, *Taste of Home*'s publishers revealed subtle hostility toward urban and career-oriented Americans. The magazine described the one thousand staff members collectively as "common-sense cooks" who "aren't 'professionals' who test food in some high-rise office building." Placing the term professional in quotation marks implied that this was an assumed identity, even a fraud, and that cooking and professionalism must be antithetical. The test kitchen, or indeed any kitchen in a high-rise building, was represented as an inauthentic space from which real food could not emerge. Unlike the urban professional, the *Taste of Home* cooks "practice their trade at home, day in and day out. They're probably a lot like you—friendly, down-home, practical and real." Arguing that the reader and writer shared authenticity and the quality of being friendly implied that those who made food their profession were by nature fraudulent, pretentious, and, to make matters worse, cold-hearted.[67]

The publishers of *Taste of Home* clearly believed that a market existed for an antigourmet food magazine in the early 1990s. As evidence, they could offer readers the story of the magazine's naming. Asked to choose from a list of titles, one of the magazine's multiple volunteer editors, Janet Siciak of Bernardston, Massachusetts, wrote, "I'm sure you want the title of your magazine to conjure up the kind of expectant anticipation you get when you're offered a peek into a dear friend's heirloom recipe collection."[68] Siciak and the magazine's publishers here gave high value to old recipes local to their user's geographical and taste communities, and not part of the sphere of public food writing. Novelty had a very low value in this food culture.[69]

This editorial assumption was supported by the contemporary restaurant trend for "comfort food," which celebrated the so-called classics of American cooking, really the kinds of foods found on luncheonette menus since the 1920s—meatloaf, macaroni and cheese, chicken pot pies, puddings, and layer cakes. When Phillip Stephen Schulz published his *As American as Apple Pie*, a collection of multiple versions of twelve dishes he considered archetypically American, he included the concept of comfort food to define the American aesthetic: "As a nation what we choose to prepare for ourselves most often are the homely and familiar dishes on which we were raised long, long before microwaves or macrobiotics came into our lives." The "homely," was that which existed outside trends. It was "well-remembered comforting foods . . . the dishes that gave us emotional security as kids." While the magic of comfort food might not always work "When we lose our jobs, spouses, or big bucks in the stock market," there was nonetheless, "a real measure of contentment in eating what we know best." Schulz's assumed "we" were those who knew baked beans, apple pie, chili, fried chicken, pot roasts, and waffles best.[70]

While the notion of the food of childhood might be inclusive, the particular foodways represented were not. Although claiming that "our cooking is basically imprecise, and much improvised by the immigrant hands that stirred each pot, Schulz identified his collection of slightly archaic recipes of primarily Northern European-American heritage as "America's best home fare," subtly, though most likely unintentionally delegitimizing the more recent immigrant's sense of home in America.[71]

One of the first books to use the term "comfort food" was *Better Homes and Gardens Comfort Food*, published in 1992. The introduction to this short collection incorporated many of the tropes that make the idea of comfort food interesting. Immediately differentiating its contents from the newly popular restaurant-based cookbooks, *Comfort Food*, like *Taste of Home* magazine, referred only to the home kitchen: "Sharing favorite foods with family, friends, and neighbors is one of our country's most comforting and memory-making traditions." Americans were represented here as generous, but only within the boundaries of their local communities. Comfort food was given an insular character that was further reinforced as the editors assigned it a palate: "In Comfort Food we celebrate America's love of simple, familiar foods." Readers apparently did not need to be told what "familiar" was, as editors assumed homogeneity in their tastes, further reinforcing this with the term "simple," also not defined. Both terms carried a meaning implicitly hostile to the notion of a pluralistic America in which identities might be complex and cultural elements not all familiar to all participants.

Martha Stewart's 1999 *Favorite Comfort Food* cookbook acknowledged that Americans "inhabit a culinary melting pot of markets, restaurants, chefs, and neighbors who bring us every taste from every corner of the earth," yet even this phrasing placed the "we" of readership apart from the "them" of the multicultural. The flavors of the melting pot were produced outside the home, coming as close as the neighbor arriving with a potluck dish, but not emanating from the reader's own kitchen. As if to underscore the theme of cultural homogeneity, the cover was noticeably white, featuring Stewart herself lying on her stomach on a white covered bed in an entirely white room, sock-feet kicked up behind her, just about to eat a grilled cheese sandwich.

Taste of Home's collective identity was white, a notable fact in an era in which popular culture was increasingly multicultural and restaurant chefs were becoming famous for their adaptations across cuisines. The magazine included no photographs of people who did not appear to be white in the first year's issues and a search of the thousand editors' names revealed none that would indicate Latino, East Asian, or South Asian heritage. The first editor profiled was Mennonite. Editors assumed readers were Christian, able to make use of the regular feature "our grace," which reprinted readers' private family mealtime prayers. Like the "Sugar and Spice" section of *Gourmet*, "our grace" gave readers opportunities to showcase their own personae, in this case in terms of faith and family instead of privilege and sophistication. Photographs of readers of *Taste of Home* showed people who were middle-aged and older, with a special feature serving recipe needs of "empty nesters."

Taste of Home's presentation of white middle-class Christianity as the national norm can also be read as a statement in the culture wars of the 1990s. As academics and activists argued for the reality and richness of the nation's cultural diversity along with the importance of identity politics, cultural conservatives resisted with statements asserting the supremacy of Western culture and Judeo-Christian values.

Actual recipes in the magazine, letters from readers, and some of the regular columns, however, challenged the construct of a common larder and culinary identity in *Taste of Home*. A column titled "Checking with the Experts," for example, both loosened the seeming Luddism of the magazine and blurred the no-advertising policy by offering advice on new food technologies and products.

In the very first issue, editors in this section encouraged readers to try a cherimoya—a tropical fruit not then or now a common sight in mainstream American supermarkets.[72] Also in the first issue, "empty nester" Dorothy Pritchett of Wills Point, Texas, shared her recipe for "festive chicken," featuring bacon-wrapped chicken breasts marinated in soy sauce, hot sauce, paprika, ground ginger, minced garlic, and sugar—a personal foray into fusion.

In the magazine's second issue, publishers noted that while heaping praise on *Taste of Home*, readers also had many requests, including more vegetarian recipes and more "ethnic" dishes. Having sent in her own recipe for cashew chicken, Ena Quiggle of Goodhue, Minnesota, rhapsodized: "We love eating ethnic foods, especially Oriental dishes."[73] Despite what the founders of the magazine had imagined, American cooks really did want to try new things. While *Taste of Home* readers sought novelty from their own cohort of cooks, the publishing industry banked on the appeal of professional chefs as taste makers.

In Reichl's first issue of *Gourmet*, Anne Mendelson asked, "Should Chefs Write Cookbooks?" Mendelson cut right to the chase: "Not to waste time being polite, I believe that in the aggregate [cookbooks by chefs are] about as useful as cognac in the gas tank." Chef-authored cookbooks were largely useless, she argued, for two important reasons: chefs do not use cookbooks and chefs are not trained in the difficult art of recipe writing. The ability to cook like a chef, she suggested, was opposite to the skills needed to write recipes for home cooks.

Seemingly resigned to the fact that her own assessment would have no bearing on publishers' behavior, Mendelson explained the real significance of the celebrity chef cookbook: "Whether I like it or not, there's another side to this question ... [chef cookbooks] point to profound changes taking place in the interests and underlying value systems of American cooks and diners." While there were more and more cookbooks, she argued, fewer and fewer people were using them to cook. This was evidence of "a major shift in food hobbyists's perspectives over a fairly short span of time." Where one generation had bought books to cook with, the next were buying them to look at.[74]

Reflecting back to the time when Julia Child was alive and in her prime, Mendelson remembered, "Thirty years ago, excited would-be learners used to spend hours or days busting their own personal chops to make venerable French or other European or maybe even American dishes that advanced their practical kitchen skills and knowledge." Cookbooks helped readers to transform themselves from amateurs to experts, a work of tangible, edible self-improvement. Thanks to the rise of the celebrity chef, however, "their counterparts today look more to restaurant meals for the elements of a culinary education." And "throngs of cookbook buyers reveling in a big, ornate volume with some restaurant connection honestly think they've got their money's worth because, in a way, they have . . . the book stands for the restaurant in many admirers' estimation." The expansion of the restaurant industry, tied closely to the expansion of middle-class wealth during the 1990s, had made restaurant dining more accessible so that it had replaced home entertaining as the high-status way to experience food. Restaurants, Mendelson argued, instead of home cooking, thus became the source of popular understanding about food.[75]

When the Food Network began airing in 1993, it expanded on this trend, further inflating the celebrity of well-known and emerging chefs and bolstering their status as authorities on culinary matters. In the same year, *New York Times* food writer Florence Fabricant wrote a profile of Shep Gordon, the first Hollywood agent to sign chefs. Determined to win for chefs the same kind of pay and perks that rock stars had come to expect, Gordon signed most of the big names of the era, including Wolfgang Puck and Larry Forgione. Forgione noted that because Gordon had signed so many of the most well-known chefs, he had real power to establish rates for chefs cooking at special events. Making Gordon's agency sound like a guild or labor union, Forgione argued, "if we're organized, someone who's putting together an event can't shop around and try to get someone cheaper or for free." By 1993, celebrity chefs, ostensibly competitors, had developed a shared sense of their value in American culture.[76]

This status rose even though the kind of cooking from which they derived their fame was only peripherally related to home cooking. Television allowed the two dominant trends of the era—the photo-centric cookbook and the celebrity chef—to merge by providing a strictly visual performance platform in which the viewer need never be confronted with textual evidence of food. Mendelson longed for a return to the days when the home cook strove to be prouder of her own creations than of which restaurants she had dined at: "Rightly or wrongly, I look at chef's cookbooks and wish that other kinds of cooking still mattered more to food mavens than the last word in multistar restaurant cooking." Acknowledging herself in the minority she asked, "Prejudice?" and answered with charming honesty, "Sure."[77]

*   *   *

Mendelson's call for more attention to the home kitchen was about to be answered by the myriad individuals outside of the publishing industry or professional food world who sat down at desktops and laptops to write up food blogs and contribute to the many recipe sites that blossomed in the early twenty-first century. By writing about what they did and how it turned out, food bloggers and recipe site contributors added a new element of reality to the cookbook, now made virtual. They brought the format to life by adding new recipes regularly, revisiting old ones, trying someone else's way and commenting on their own alterations. Food writing on the Internet democratized the genre, making it clear to those who did not yet know, that recipes can not be copyrighted.[78]

The rise of food blogs also revealed that no two cooks are alike. Indeed, the premise of many cookbooks, even those that encouraged creativity, was that the reader could become the author through following a recipe. Because recipe sites publish comments, however, we can now see how very differently each cook uses a single recipe. As Celia Barbour discovered in her 2007 survey of the comments sections of popular recipe sites, each cook makes a recipe his or her own. As she notes, "Cooks have always adjusted recipes, for all kinds of reasons," but recipe sites allow us to see the process almost in action and to hear the rationale of the cook. One commenter, for example, substituted orange Kool-Aid for orange zest, while another replaced green beans and asparagus with calamari and shrimp. These comments, generally devoid of any sense that the writer is doing anything more than tweaking the recipe, suggest that cooks often use recipes as launching pads for personal flights of fancy. The comments can also reveal common themes in cooking across a broad section of the population. As Barbour noted, the most common adjustment on American sites was to add cheese, reflecting, it would seem, a national preference, at least among cooking site commentators.[79] The dominance of celebrity chefs with recipes unfriendly to the home kitchen hardly mattered, as visitors to food blogs and recipe sites could see that no one cooked by the book anyway.

In this liberated world of home cooks talking to home cooks, perhaps it was inevitable that food writing, having turned intensely personal, should also become deeply political in a new genre that turned each cook into an activist and each meal a meditation on the origins of things.

CHAPTER 7

ORIGIN STORIES

A NEW DISCOURSE IN
TWENTY-FIRST-CENTURY COOKBOOKS

BLOGS, RECIPE SITES, Twitter, and Instagram have all helped to democratize food writing. We no longer have to wait for a new restaurant to be
reviewed in the local newspaper; now we can read Yelp or Urbanspoon reviews from opening night. And nobody needs to crack the spine of a cookbook to find 408,000 recipes for zucchini fritters, as I just did in ten seconds
online. That many of these recipes will be duplicates copied from one blog
to another only highlights the communal nature of cooking-by-Internet.

If a great many more people than in the last thirty years are now writing
about food, there are also more people worrying about food. This particular
kind of worry focuses on the food chain—who gets what kinds of food and
how. The terms "obesity epidemic" and "food deserts" are central themes in
contemporary discourse about food in America. Critics and policy makers
argue that there is too much of the wrong kind of food and too little of the
right kind.[1]

Interest in and anxiety about the food chain are clearly an outgrowth of
the natural food movement of the 1970s and its consequent cooptation by
the food industry. But it is also a product of the New American chef's focus

on the local and the singular in American food. That interest itself can be traced back to the gourmet's insistence that many American foods weren't foods at all and to his veneration of French ingredients.

When she hired a forager for her restaurant, Alice Waters drew attention to the food supply chain, and by serving the forager's findings in her famous restaurant, she made them precious. This provoked middle-class Americans who wanted to be in-the-know to think differently about where food should come from. Where once the elite were marked by their distance from the dirt of agriculture, Waters and the new American chefs reversed the stereotype, defining processed food as lower class and making "just picked," the most highly valued descriptor.

Gourmet's 2001 "Produce" issue tapped into the emerging locavore movement and the great success of farmers markets. Both of these trends built off the fetishization of the fresh and singular ingredient that emerged from Waters's kitchen.

Chef Jeff Crump, who had worked as an intern at Chez Panisse, recalled a moment of personal culinary epiphany when Chez Panisse chef Russell Moore asked him how the raw corn he was shucking tasted. Crump, he recounts, "gave the wrong answer: 'It's not cooked . . . Why would I taste it?" Moore took an ear, tasted it, and advised Crump to set it aside (for the staff meal) and look for the "'real good stuff,'" in a shipment arriving the next day. The next day's corn came from the famous Chino's fruit and vegetable market in San Diego. Crump recalls, "I still get chills when I think about it. It was one of those rare moments when you discover sheer perfection." The emphasis on single ingredients echoed the rise of the celebrity chef who was not just the interpreter of generations of knowledge, nor the voice of a people, but originator of his or her own wisdom. For Crump, the discovery of corn's potential gave his own personal vocation larger meaning.[2]

Long before the term locavore was coined, however, nouvelle cuisine had taught chefs and diners to treat the dinner plate in new ways. Emerging parallel to the rise of the New American chefs, nouvelle cuisine in America supported the idea that chefs were artists and foodstuffs were precious. For all its reputation as absurdly rarified, nouvelle cuisine in America had consistently celebrated the essence of materials, showcasing ingredients through minimal cooking time and maximum attention to display. The new style of cooking and presentation had such a profound impact on professional chefs and cookbooks that it seems to have been completely absorbed into the culture, shaping expectations for what we will find on a plate when we sit down to dine in a restaurant.[3]

Nouvelle Cuisine in America

Nouvelle cuisine was a trend in restaurant cooking that emerged in France in the late 1960s. Nouvelle chefs emphasized freshness and favored crisp vegetables over longer-cooked ones. They were also known for their stocks, which were reduced for an unusually long time to create condensed flavors. In 1973, two French restaurant critics celebrated the movement with a list of their "ten commandments of nouvelle cuisine." These were,

> 1. Thou shall not overcook. 2. Thou shall use fresh, quality products
> 3. Thou shall lighten thy menu. 4. Thou shall not be systemically
> modernistic. 5. Thou shall seek out what the new techniques can
> bring you. 6. Thou shall eliminate brown and white sauces. 7. Thou
> shall not ignore dietetics. 8. Thou shall not cheat on thy presentation.
> 9. Thou shall be inventive. 10. Thou shall not be prejudiced.[4]

The critics, Henri Gault and Christian Millau, played on nouvelle cuisine's paradoxical reputation for both simplicity and fussiness.

Julia Child criticized the new movement, writing in *New York* magazine in 1977 that it was overhyped and ought not to replace older styles of French cooking. She reduced it to a few dishes, which had become standard in the industry, noting "Almost any restaurant of any pretensions [now] has its little salad of green beans more or less lavishly garnished," a seafood mousse, poached fish, and julienned carrots.[5] The advocates of nouvelle, particularly Gault and Millau, were bullies, Child claimed, forcing reluctant chefs to change their cooking style or risk bad reviews. Although concluding enthusiastically, "It's not that I don't appreciate the *nouvelle cuisine*. I love it! We need it!" she simultaneously defended her own turf as American guru of

French *cuisine bourgeoise*, "Please let's not throw out the comfortable old glories, at least not while I'm still around."[6]

When nouvelle cuisine came to America, its impact was first primarily felt in restaurants. Very few cookbooks used the term nouvelle cuisine. The first was written by famous restaurateurs, the Troisgros brothers themselves, and published by William Morrow in 1978. Writing in *New York*, William Bayer and Paula Wolfert designated *The Nouvelle Cuisine of Jean & Pierre Troisgros*, "the recipe book of the season."[7] Bayer and Wolfert acknowledged the fame of the nouvelle cuisine movement by noting that "their famous salmon scallops with sorrel sauce are [in the book] and their equally famous vegetable terrine." When Bayer and Wolfert tried a few of the recipes, they blamed themselves when the results were disappointing. The fish that came out too dry "in the hands of the Troisgros must be sublime," and "our home-made stock lacked the background taste of a restaurant stock."[8] The cult of the celebrity chef here unbalanced the power relation between critic and author. Here it was the author, not the customer, who was always right. Bayer and Wolfert celebrated the book's French-ness, noting, "This isn't a book for your Aunt Ida in Tulsa, who may not be intrigued" by flavor combinations such as duck livers with celery root. That it lacked a common touch seemed to make the book all the more desirable.[9]

Soon after the Troisgros' own book, two French-trained Americans, David Liederman and Michele Urvater, published *The Nouvelle Cuisine in America*. This 1982 book brought French techniques to American ingredients. The authors noted, "We are Americans, conscious of our audience, familiar with American kitchens and our native produce, and aware of how our culture differs from the French." More in the spirit of Angelo Pellegrini than Julia Child, they "attempted to . . . create an American nouvelle cuisine."[10]

Unlike gourmet authors of the 1940s and 1950s, Liederman and Urvater did not urge readers to seek out French ingredients, but instead encouraged them to eat locally. The authors argued, "Since the essence of the nouvelle cuisine lies in its use of the freshest ingredients, chosen for their taste, texture, and color, we created our own recipes and adapted some French ones with the American seasonal market in mind." They were even specific as to having chosen New York City as their region and had "used the best of what was available to us." They chose New York because the city had access to good fresh seafood. Reader/cooks farther inland might need to substitute ingredients, and this was fine, Urvater and Liederman assured them, but only if everything was fresh. If you had to ask "'What if we only have frozen bass available to us?'" the authors advised, "don't do that recipe—do another one."[11] Freshness was one of the ten commandments, after all.

Freshness was not to be confused with spontaneity. Liederman and Urvater warned readers that the nouvelle cuisine was not easy. In words that would have enraged Peg Bracken, they admonished, "we should say right off that you must be prepared to be both host/hostess and chef—inevitably you will find yourself spending a good deal of time in the kitchen." Aware that "most people are caught between wanting to impress guests with an elaborate meal and wanting to spend time with them," they asked readers to concede that "achieving both is simply not consonant with making a great meal." Here was a return to the gourmet's mantra that really good food takes time. Part of what was so time consuming about nouvelle cuisine was that where formerly restaurants as well as home cooks had served meals on platters from which individual diners were served, nouvelle chefs made each plate a work of art. Fanning carrot slices and drizzling reductions to make a "delectable display" for each diner joined together ideas of chef as artist and individual foods as worthy of such treatment.[12]

Sourcing the New American Cuisine

The rise of the new American chefs also supported an interest in origins, as the tale of Jeremiah Tower's California meal in 1976 should remind us. In his introduction to *The Four Seasons Cookbook*, James Beard recounted the "prospecting for sources of prime foods" that took place just before the famous New York restaurant opened. Beard identified sources with distinct individuals: "A man was discovered in Oregon who raised tiny French carrots, because he had learned to like them in Europe," and "various vendors were signed up to supply an almost constant flow of wild mushrooms." Meanwhile, "the finest fruits were hunted down, and routine delivery of potted herbs was arranged." The restaurant became a nexus between obscure producers and eager consumers of "prime foods." An unusual ritual nurtured this relationship when "patrons are invited to select their favorite [raw vegetables] from baskets of the market's choicest offerings, and the kitchen is banked with pressure cookers, so that the vegetables can be rushed from basket to table in a matter of minutes. By giving carrots and beans the same high status treatment usually reserved for live lobsters, the Four Seasons made an implicit argument for the glory of the vegetal.[13]

Stephen Langlois, chef at Prairie in Chicago, and one of the new American chefs, wrote in 1990 of having established "a network of local suppliers" who could bring him foodstuffs that were often works of culinary re-enactment. One source, for example, "makes ice cream the same way his father did in 1935," and another provided "cheeses made by descendants of the original Swiss settlers, using traditional methods that have been handed down from generation to generation." Langlois trusted his audience to take it on faith that the 1935 style of ice cream making was better than anything contemporary and that the traditional Swiss methods produced exceptionally tasty cheese. Here, methods of long use were conflated with the concept of high quality. Cookbooks portrayed the new foraging, which included locating small-batch producers as well as rummaging through the undergrowth in a way that gave high value to the local and traditional and low value to what could be described as large-scale, distant, and innovative.[14]

Chefs, however, weren't always consistent in how they valued sources. Larry Forgione, for example, claimed to have coined the phrase "free range" in regard to chickens and celebrated the "explosion of interest in fresher, better indigenous ingredients," but he also praised high-speed long-distance delivery of foodstuffs. Forgione also drew inspiration from the very opposite of locavorism: "The one thing that really changed *my life* as a professional cook was overnight delivery. It opened up possibilities that had never existed before." As "local went national," Forgione rejoiced that "I could get a bushel of just-picked baby white asparagus from Michigan, sparkling fresh shrimp flown straight from Key West." The foodstuffs still reflected his passionate commitment to "American specialties," but modern storage technologies allowed him to cook *all* of America all the time, an opportunity he would not deny himself in favor of locavorism.[15]

When Hillary Clinton hired Walter Scheib as White House chef, she specifically gave him a mandate to celebrate American products and dishes. Staying on to serve the Bush family after Bill Clinton's two terms, he found it much more difficult after the September 11, 2001, attacks and the anthrax mailings that followed to connect to the small-scale producers who had supplied him during the pre-9/11 years. Scheib recalled that "While I was previously willing to sample unsolicited foods that were sent to me via FedEx or in the mail—from syrups to juices to smoked salmon—those items were now automatically discarded before I ever saw or heard of them." Scheib, with the encouragement of Clinton, had been largely responsible for opening the kitchen door to these purveyors. By hiring Scheib to cook innovative American food as well as to start a garden on the roof, Clinton had also created a prominent venue for a kind of national localism. The White House locavorism had to depend on the kinds of long-distance sourcing that Forgione delighted in because its kitchen had to create an illusion of one great continent-sized backyard.[16] By writing about American food nationally instead of locally, a new cohort of food writers in the early twenty-first century made the discussion of origins a discourse of crisis.

The Omnivore's Dilemma

In 2006, journalist Michael Pollan published *The Omnivore's Dilemma*, a very successful book that asked Americans to think carefully about food origins. This book made Pollan a dominant voice in American food writing.[17] The book followed in the wake of two other very popular investigative works about food, Eric Schlosser's *Fast Food Nation* (2002) and Morgan Spurlock's film, *Supersize Me* (2004).[18] Both Schlosser and Spurlock uncovered unappetizing truths hidden in plain sight about the fast food industry that has had such remarkable success in American culture. It is quite clear, after reading these books, what you *don't* want to eat, which perhaps gave new attention to the question of what you *do* want to eat.

In attempting to answer the question and also drawing on the interest in farmers markets that has been growing since the 1970s, Pollan traced the origins of food "all the way from the earth to the plate."[19] Pollan's exceptional skills in researching and telling a story won a large audience for the book, particularly for his section on the central role corn plays in American food production.[20] At Chez Panisse, one chef recalled that Pollan's work changed the way the restaurant purchased beef. Phillip Dedlow explained how knowledge could be disruptive: "After we learned from Michael Pollan about all the horrors of feed lots and sick cows and all that, Alice decided she didn't want to use any more corn-fed beef, and we've been searching for over a year now for grass-fed beef that tastes good."[21]

Taste, though sometimes privileged by both Pollan and Waters, was not the only consideration. Dedlow explained, "And it has to be humanely raised and killed. No chemicals on the land. Totally organic. It hasn't been easy to find." Yet, inspired by Pollan's expose, the Chez Panisse crew continued to search, making daily work out of a new genre in food writing, the discourse of origins, which draws attention to the sources of foodstuffs, valuing foods differently based on two categories of provenance: industrial and local.[22]

By 2006, many urban devotees of food writing had already absorbed this discourse. They were accustomed to weekly interactions with food growers and producers at farmers markets and community-supported agriculture programs that allowed them to meet the farmer who grew their food. Some had even become their own farmers on a small scale with plots in community gardens or through the "eat your lawn" movement.[23]

This discourse, in which knowledge of the origins of foodstuffs was valued, perhaps helped to spark Pollan's own curiosity and provided an eager audience for *Omnivore's Dilemma*. Knowledge of origins, however, was not sufficient. Knowing, for example, that the potatoes in your salad were grown in Idaho and peeled and parboiled in a mechanized facility, then canned and distributed by Del Monte did not give the salad any special value in this discourse. In fact, it turned knowledge into anguish. Pollan explained that if, while biting into a typical fast food burger, "the eater could accurately picture the feedlot and the slaughterhouse and the workers behind it or knew anything about the 'artificial grill flavor,'" then this bite would be "impossible to enjoy." To knowledge must be added a sense of responsibility.

Knowing the origins of the canned potatoes must invoke sorrow for the ecological impact of pesticide use on the potato field, sorrow for the loss of nutrients as the peel was removed, sorrow for the impact on the ozone of the machinery that processed the potatoes, and the trucks that distributed them, even perhaps sorrow for the cook and diner who were too ignorant to use local organic potatoes. As Canadian chef Crump wrote in 2009, "Even worse," than the "terrible" taste of out-of-season fruits and vegetables, was the realization that "some people don't know the difference between the exquisite, local, seasonal food around them and the tasteless, rigid fare on offer in the supermarket." The discourse of origins is also, as Langlois's identification of his traditionalist sources suggests, a dramatic discourse of descriptive detail and suggested action: find out everything, respond emotionally, and seek out particular qualities while avoiding others.[24]

In the discourse of origins, the right kind of knowledge restored pleasure to consumption. Paul Springstubb, a "young professional" interviewed by Evan Jones in 1985, visited the Cleveland farmers' market because "I discovered that this was the place to get food direct from the farm—you knew where it came from."[25] If, instead of feedlots, Michael Pollan argued, the burger eater "can picture the green pastures in which the animal grazed," even with full knowledge of death and dismemberment, "a pleasure of another order . . . based on knowledge rather than ignorance and gratitude rather than indifference," would ensue.[26]

In *Omnivore's Dilemma*, Pollan provided action rhetoric, an element missing from his earlier study of agricultural evolution, *The Botany of Desire*.[27] *The Botany of Desire* provided new ways to think about plants as agents in their interactions with humanity, but did not suggest that readers adopt any behavior based in this perspective. *Omnivore's Dilemma*, on the other hand, tapped into the very desire for culinary guidance that it seemed at first to lambaste.

Pollan advocates in *Omnivore's Dilemma* the knowledge-seeker approach to eating.[28] He argues that those who take the investigative approach to eating will find "in practice few things in life can afford quite as much pleasure." Knowledge, in other words, is appetizing, while "the pleasures of eating industrially, which is to say eating in ignorance, are fleeting." Here we read a revival of the old trope of American food writing: most Americans (excluding the author) eat what they eat because they don't know any better.

As is also traditional in critiques of American food since the 1930s, this willful ignorance is set in contrast to the foodways of France. Italy has also now joined the small pantheon of sensible eaters, a status it did not hold securely when the French-American dichotomy first appeared in the 1920s. Pollan argues that if Americans had a culture "in possession of deeply rooted traditions surrounding food," they would "not be shocked to discover that there are other countries, such as Italy and France, that decide their dinner questions on the basis of such quaint and unscientific criteria as pleasure and tradition, and eat all manner of 'unhealthy' foods." Eating "such demonstrably toxic substances as foie gras and triple crème cheese," French and Italian diners, Pollan claims, "wind up actually healthier and happier in their eating than we are." Because America is "a relatively new nation drawn from many immigrant populations," and thus lacks common traditions, Pollan argues, Americans allow professionals who are driven by profit motives to prescribe their food choices.

While critics like Pellegrini saw the diversity of American immigrant foodways as a positive aspect of the nation's foodscape, for Pollan it means that Americans have no shared guidelines for "sensible" eating. Where other critics saw the potential of diverse culinary traditions to "improve" American cuisine, Pollan argued a problematic lack of cohesion, implying that shared ethnicity would result in improved health and environmentally friendly food production practices.

Having established the American eater as hapless ignoramus, Pollan assigned the role of villain to an awkward amalgamation of professions, "the food scientist and the marketer." Although the two professions have completely different educational paths, practices, and goals, Pollan joined them together as equally driven by the motive to make money off of "our anxieties about what to eat."

This trope is familiar from the dawn of the gourmet, who came into being partly in resistance to the emergence of nutrition as a science and to the emphasis on innovation in food marketing of the 1920s. What seemed to Pollan a newly discovered plot to rob Americans of their common sense is very similar to the multiheaded monster (Prohibition, convenience, and nutritional science) that hid under the gourmet's bed in the 1940s.

As it did in the 1940s and 1950s, this distrust of experts also contains a formal problem. The basic assumption is that knowledge of food facts is antithetical to pleasure, yet the critic presents his own set of facts, which must be assumed to be unlike other facts in that they *serve* pleasure. The falseness of all other prophets is proven by the truths of the one preaching to you now. Food writing, in addressing issues of desire, and behavior often (unsurprisingly) follows the contours of religious writing. In her food memoir *Julie and Julia*, Julie Powell describes her immersion in Julia Child's *Mastering the Art of French Cooking* as "what prayer must feel like. Sustenance bound up with anticipation and want."[29]

Pollan addressed the problem of the one true prophet in his *In Defense of Food*, when he asked readers "Who am I to tell you how to eat?" After "advising you to reject the advice of science and industry," how can he "blithely go on to offer my own advice[?]" Pollan's answer, which seems to have satisfied many readers, is that "I speak mainly on the authority of tradition and common sense." These are two properties that cultural historians understand to be entirely unstable. Both traditions and common sense are culturally constructed and change over time. Both (as Pollan's popularity proves) are powerful ideals for moving people to action, even if that action is only buying a book and talking about it at cocktail parties.

The unstable ground of "tradition" was critiqued brilliantly in a 2001 article in *Gastronomica* by food historian Rachel Laudan, who argued that "if we romanticize the past, we may miss the fact that it is the modern, global, industrial economy (not the local resources of the wintry country around New York, Boston, or Chicago) that allows us to savor traditional, peasant, fresh and natural foods" like packaged pasta and canned tomatoes. According to Laudan's calculations, it takes no more than fifty years to establish a culinary tradition as everlasting in the popular imagination. She offers two very compelling examples by noting that the French only adopted the baguette nationwide after the Second World War and that tequila was "promoted as the national drink of Mexico during the 1930s by the Mexican film industry."[30] The idea that some cultures have fixed cuisines while America does not is also a familiar theme in writing about American food as something always in the process of becoming.

By establishing himself as bearer of the true food gospel, Pollan seems to empathize with readers' existential crises. He describes the typical American's relationship to food: "And so we find ourselves where we do, confronting in the supermarket or at the dinner table the dilemmas of omnivorousness . . . the organic apple or the conventional? And if the organic, the local one or the imported? The wild fish or the farmed? The transfats or the butter or the 'not-butter'?" According to Pollan's "common sense," having "a surfeit of choice brings with it a lot of stress," that makes us "no longer so sure of our senses." This material abundance, as Pollan's critics have pointed out, is really only a problem for the affluent. For Pollan's imaginary shopper, cost is notably not considered in making the choice between similar goods. *The Omnivore's Dilemma* is about how to make choices amid plenty, not how to improve global access to nutrition. Familiarity with Pollan and his ideas has become a status marker independent even of what actually ends up on the reader's table.[31]

Pollan's work fits neatly into the particularly middle-class genre of self-improvement literature that has a long history in America. Consumption of this literature is a marker of middle-class status because it assumes a fairly high level of literacy and financial resources to make sometimes costly changes in consumer behavior. Self-help literature requires a reader who is neither completely hopeless nor already complacent. Pollan's vision of the individual overwhelmed in the marketplace is familiarly antimodern, employing nostalgia for a mythical time as a tool to create dissatisfaction with the present. His proposed crisis also echoes Waters's account of her own desire, while walking through supermarkets, to wake shoppers from their intellectual slumber, to sound the alarm about the food they are buying. Pollan's shoppers are aware, but this very awareness creates a "dilemma" from which they also need rescue.

Pollan compared the bewildered modern American shopper unfavorably to the "hunter-gatherer picking a novel mushroom off the forest floor," and determining whether it is poisonous by "consulting his sense memory" of communal wisdom. This lucky character (whose life expectancy was lower and likeliness to die in battle over resources much higher than Pollan's) did not have more than two choices: eat it or don't eat it. According to Pollan, this limited knowledge-bordering-on-ignorance was bliss.[32]

In the service of reclaiming prehistoric man's freedom from choice-based anxiety, Pollan paradoxically proposes a new set of questions for the marketplace. Instead of asking "eat it or don't eat it?" the reader enlightened by Pollan asks: Where did it come from? Which parts of its origin story matter to me? What impact does its production have on the environment? Would I be willing, if the chance arose, to kill or grow it for myself? Among these questions, however, the reader/forager must be careful not to ask "what does nutritional science tell me about this?" because for Pollan this represents inauthentic knowledge.

Cookbooks and food guides that embrace the discourse of origins portray the reader as a person on a quest. The author offers herself or himself as guide for this journey of spiritual enlightenment. Thus, Marilou Suszko, author of *The Locavore's Kitchen*, dedicated her book to "family and friends who respect my quest for the best in the food we share" and cautioned readers that "the journey to create a locavore kitchen does not happen overnight." As with other kinds of lifestyle literature, including religious texts, the reader is first constructed as unfinished and in the act of becoming, an act transpiring in the encounter with the author's words.[33]

Despite Julie Guthman's avowal that *Omivore's Dilemma* "made me crave corn-based Cheetos" it had a galvanizing effect on other writers, some of whom wrote consciousness raising pieces like Pollan's own while others put his ideas to work in cookbooks. *Gourmet* published a short piece by Pollan about a farmer who was featured in *Omnivore's Dilemma* in 2002 and the magazine continued until its print version's demise to publish articles about food politics, a somewhat new undertaking for the magazine of "the good life." *Bon Appétit*, for its part, has published columns about cooking with farmers market produce, but not about food systems or food politics.

In a culinary call to action, food writer Ann Vileisis borrowed Pollan's villains, claiming that "a relentless legion of admen and home economists" worked for fifty years "to convince America's skeptical homemakers to adopt the new products and new ways to think and 'know' about foods." This evil team, Vileisis argues, talked American cooks right out of their taste buds. They erased Americans' "traditional knowledge" of "specific intimate details of the food" we cook.[34]

In order to "build a healthier food system," readers should join the "emerging trend of consumers striving to bring knowledge and stories of foods back into their kitchens and lives." Vileisis shares Pollan's perspective on foods as pseudo-texts, portraying food as material in which stories inhere. Amy Cotler in her lifestyle manual *The Locavore Way* also finds narrative in food, promising readers, "While the best part of eating locally is the food itself, its context and the stories behind it enrich the experience of eating it." Chef Jim Denevan likewise laments, "In a typical American restaurant, most ingredients are without provenance or story." These writers echo Waters's encouragement to cooks to listen to their food. In emphasizing origins, these contemporary food writers invest the edible with narrative life, if not quite human-level agency.[35]

In an example of putting the discourse of origins into practice in cooking, Suszco's *The Locavore's Kitchen* "presents an opportunity for you to think and act like a locavore in your own kitchen with information about what you choose to eat," and asks "Do you have what it takes to become a locavore?" Echoing Pollan's claim that the examined dinner is the one most worth eating, Suszco promises that "Locavores embrace shopping for their food. For them, it's not a chore, it's a pleasure, an adventure, and often a welcome challenge with delicious rewards."[36] Like the gourmets of the 1930s and 1940s, and like Julia Child in the 1960s, Suszco wants to reorient American cooks so that they think of daily meal preparation as fun, not work.

In a dialogue published in 2011, two *New York Times* writers, Amanda Hesser and Virginia Heffernan, debated whether this reorientation is possible.[37] Hesser, the cookbook author and compiler of the *Essential New York Times Cookbook*, attempted to convince Heffernan, a cultural affairs reporter, that "home cooked" meals in which nothing is pre-prepared can bring joy to the cook as well as the eaters. Heffernan, whose recent celebration of Poppy Cannon as a proto-techie and life hacker had caused a small stir among cooking advocates, argued that almost no one has time to cook the way Hesser does.

In response, Hesser situated food knowledge on the same plane as other cultural literacies, urging Heffernan, "if you're a thoughtful person—and I know you are—then why not eat thoughtfully? And why not address feeding your children the same way you address their education?" Particularly focusing on Heffernan's role as a parent, Hesser argued, "Food is a gateway to the world. I would argue that parents who don't feed their children well and don't expose them to other foods are limiting their future." Heffernan's rejoinder was that people who love to cook and people who hate it simply have different talents to offer the world. She drew a distinction between foodies who "like cooking, and. . . try to find ways to do it with more love and consciousness and art," and techies like herself who "dislike cooking, and . . . try to find hacky ways around it." In drawing this distinction she attempted to glorify her own foodways as contemporary and authentic and suggest that Hesser's approach is dishonest. Heffernan will "never believe that foodie eating is more convenient than hacky eating," making it impossible for Hesser's points to be addressed.

Because of her cultural milieu—exactly that in which Hesser lives (it becomes clear that the women even live in the same New York City neighborhood)—Heffernan was defensive about her lack of interest in food and cooking. She bristled when Hesser quoted Brillat-Savarin's maxim, "tell me what you eat and I will tell you who you are," and challenged its viability. This suggests that she does not like the person her food choices tell us she is, the person who feeds a family on takeout pizza, organic boxed macaroni and cheese, and four-minute meals from FreshDirect (the grocery delivery chain).

Hesser accused Heffernan of a kind of inauthenticity, too, suggesting that her approach to food is the result of marketing strategies, not her true feelings: "I really think you're making the assumption—which food marketers have promoted for the past 100 years—that eating well takes too much effort." The question of what "eating well" means to both women was not finally explored in the exchange. It seems that Heffernan actually agreed with Hesser that "eating well" involves time and local ingredients and intellectual considerations but that it is unreasonable to expect this behavior of everyone. Rather than expressing joy in her own cooking style and pleasure in her four-minute meals, she ended up reinforcing Hesser's argument that there are right and wrong ways to relate to food and meals. The kind of thinking that drives locavore cooks, that food is worth thinking about deeply and that there is pleasure in this intellectual work, seems to have been normalized, at least in the upper-middle-class intellectual circles in which Hesser and Heffernan both live and publish. Heffernan's frustration is that she can't live up to the food ideals of her community, so she is attempting to force change in the ideals so that her own approach to food has validity.

Locavore Food Writing

The same ideals Heffernan rages against were the framing device for Barbara Kingsolver's very popular food memoir, *Animal, Vegetable, Miracle*, which, like Hesser and Heffernan's exchange, blends the personal and the polemical.[38] Well-known novelist Kingsolver's *Animal, Vegetable, Miracle* is a locavore food memoir/manifesto, which blends an account of the pleasures and problems of trying to eat locally for a year in the Appalachian Mountains with a detailed critique of American food systems.[39] Kingsolver's humor and admissions of "weakness" for things like coffee and chocolate, which could not be found locally in her region, appeal to readers unsure of their own virtue. These admissions also support the trope of the food—in this case the local food—as a character with a moral imperative. Kingsolver's family is portrayed as responsible not only to local farmers—other humans like themselves—but also to the land, its produce, and the animals who are raised as food. In the very first sentence of her memoir, Kingsolver identifies her narrative as a "story about good food." She thus sets the scene, as have other American food writers before her, with a hero, an implied villain, and a concept—good food—in need of definition and defense.

Kingsolver introduces both heroes and villains as essential to the journey that set the narrative in motion: "We did have a cooler in the back seat packed with respectable lunch fare," but, stopping at a convenience store they acknowledged that with "more than two thousand miles to go" between Tucson and Virginia, "we'd need to . . . indulge in some things that go crunch." Kingsolver can expect that her readers will know what she means by "respectable lunch fare," and why gas station market snacks are something to "indulge" in while offering justifications for doing so. The reader must already share with the author her definitions of good and bad food or the description makes no sense. She seeks their approval, too, in reassuring the readers that salty snacks are not *all* she will provide her family. She does know better.[40]

Like other American food writers before her, Kingsolver argues that the French *really* know better. Lamenting, "Oh, America the Beautiful, where are our standards?" she asks how "Europeans," who are "ancestral cultures to most of us" have "somehow managed to hoard the market share of Beautiful?" Kingsolver applies the capitalized adjective more to behavior than to sceneries or architectures. What is "beautiful" about Europeans in Kingsolver's estimation is that "They'll run over a McDonald's with a bulldozer because it threatens the way of life of their fine cheeses." Her reference to an event in France in 1999 when a sheep farmer attacked the construction site of a new McDonald's, ties French eaters to the concept of traditions and invests them with deep wisdom and proper priorities. Americans, in contrast, are dangerously confused.[41]

Kingsolver finds the origins of this confusion in a half-baked idea of freedom. Our ancestors, she explains, "Came here for the freedom to make a *Leaves of Grass* kind of culture . . . pierce our navels as needed, and eat whatever we want without some drudge scolding: 'You don't know where that's been!'" For Michael Pollan, Americans' weakness was in paying too much attention to experts whose credentials he doubted; for Kingsolver, the problem is an addiction to self-determination, or *not* listening to those who know better. For both writers, a simple solution would be to find a French way to be American.[42]

Kingsolver's personal approach to the problem was to re-create the back-to-the-land movement on a small scale by moving to a rural region she knew could support locavorism. For those who lacked access to their own piece of arable America, new approaches to the existing marketplace created fellowship based on food shopping.

Attention to food sources has created communities both virtual and local as those Hesser might term "thoughtful" eaters explore their options in neighborhood markets and make connections with like-minded people across various web platforms. Food blogger Brett Laidlaw described his food gathering activities as "shop-forage-source." The process "goes something like this: Au Bon Canard *duck* breast from Clancey's, and I've got that *black-*

berry jam *from Bide-A-Wee fruit*, and that braid of *shallots from the Dallas market* is still holding out . . . need to check if I have enough *Hope Creamery butter*, and pick up *raw milk* from Renee" (italics in original).[43] Although his food aesthetic is eclectic, it is interesting that this shopping list includes items (except perhaps for the blackberries) American writers have strongly associated with French cuisine. It also attests to the success small food pur-veyors have had in branding their products. Hope Creamery butter may not be a household name nationally, but it clearly has meaning within Laidlaw's community and would suggest to readers more generally a small batch local producer—they can insert their own version into their own shopping lists.

Laidlaw explained that "a taste for the authentic is what informs ev-ery aspect of this book" and, by implication, his peripatetic shopping. The multivendor approach, he promises readers is "really not as exhausting as it sounds. It is, in fact, a genuine pleasure." Part of that pleasure comes, he explains, through the human interactions that accompany each visit. The theme of connection that Laidlaw draws on here is also a common theme in contemporary food writing. Editors at *Gourmet*, for example, employed this theme in their article about Cambodian immigrant farmers in Western Massachusetts who "are growing food to build the community they're in— and to rebuild the one they were forced to leave behind."[44] As food became more interesting to academic scholars, too, the study of just how food cre-ates and maintains communal identities became a rich topic for study.[45]

Narratives of origin argue that finding the source of one's dinner almost inevitably creates human community, that quality famously missing in cri-tiques of modernity.[46] Russ Parsons dedicated his *How to Pick a Peach*, a kind of brief practical encyclopedia of his favorite fruits and vegetables, "to all the talented farmers who work hard so we cooks don't have to." For Par-sons, farmers and cooks conspire to bring the best (or worst) out in food. Susan Wiggins, reviewing two books about locavore living, asserts that "Sustainable eating promotes intimacy with your family, partner, fishmonger, farmers, and foodshed," with the unquestioned assumption that both read-ers and producers would desire and find value in these intimacies.[47]

In *Organic Marin*, an example of the location-specific food guides that fol-lowed *The Omnivore's Dilemma*, author Tim Porter introduced his collection with the words "Food creates community." Porter attributed the statement to a "young organic farmer from Bolinas" and elaborated that these "three little words. . . . Encompass a huge idea: the connection between food and community, between farmer and family, between land and table." Consideration of this "link," Porter argued, is "missing in much of today's commodity-based agribusiness." Not only do individual farmers become characters in this new food literature, but the cookbook itself creates a relationship between the farmer and the reader. To buy from the Marin Farmers Market is to create human community, which has as much (in fact more) value than the recipes readers are invited to try. This approach insists on cooking as not only an "agricultural act," as poet Wendell Berry famously named it, but also a social act.[48]

Kingsolver wrote cynically that, "It's fair to say, the majority of us don't want to be farmers, see farmers, pay farmers, or hear their complaints." She claimed that most Americans don't really believe farmers exist anymore, "Except as straw-chewing figures in children's books." Kingsolver then gave first place in her acknowledgments to "the hands that feed us," a list of farmers from her local farmers market with the recognition that "I couldn't have survived without you." Giving farmers a place in the public eye, this new kind of food writing displaces the longstanding tradition of making the cook/reader or the food itself hero of the food narrative.[49]

Pollan also supports this theme in his "food rules," when he urges readers not to eat alone. Although citing research that suggests eating with others makes us eat more, Pollan nonetheless theorizes that "when we eat mindlessly and alone, we eat more," and that "the shared meal elevates eating from a mechanical process . . . to a ritual of family and community." There are broader benefits than just slimness, he implies, if readers will transform eating "from mere animal biology to an act of culture." The French are offered here as models of conviviality. Pollan quotes psychologist Paul Rozin, who found that "Although they eat less than Americans, the French spend more time eating, and hence get more food experience while eating less." This behavior seems an "eminently sensible approach to eating," from Pollan's perspective. Like gourmet food writers of the 1940s and 1950s, Pollan is cheerfully sure Americans will become good eaters if they will only mimic the French. Rozin's study comparing attitudes to food transnationally ends

with the suggestion that "on the psychological level, Americans may have
something to learn from the French."[50]

The entity identified as "good" or "real" food thus has added value in
that it is not solely beneficial to the body, as Pollan implies his ideal diet is,
but also beneficial to the *social* body because it both supports human community and sustains the human environment. Food is "no mere *thing* but a
web of relationships among a great many living beings." Indeed, his suggestion, as he celebrates "the French paradox,"—eat foie gras, don't get fat—is
that physical health is a matter of having the correct social attitudes toward
food. Either live like the (mythologized) French, guided by age-old culinary
traditions, or, if you are not French, adopt an attitude of persistent curiosity
about food. Be French or be nosy. Ask questions, but don't worry.[51]

Pollan's *In Defense of Food* and *Food Rules* capitalized on his newfound
status as food guru to give advice unadorned by investigative narrative. In
In Defense of Food Pollan attacked nutrition as "bad science," which American eaters should feel free to ignore. He also reinforced the notion of foodstuffs as bearers of a narrative. Because so many Americans do not apparently listen to food the way that Alice Waters can, Pollan proposed to speak
on food's behalf, like Dr. Seuss' Lorax, who speaks for the trees. The book
cultivates a Lorax-like sense of urgency, too, suggesting that if we do not
begin to listen to our food, to its stories of origin, we will soon find ourselves
left only with "edible foodlike substances" that are not "real" food.

To eat food that has an ideal degree of reality, Pollan argues, the reader
must grow her own vegetables. This work endows the gardener with "an
omniscience about your food that no amount of supermarket study or label reading could hope to match." Here again, food almost acquires agency:
"This is food, so fresh it's still alive, communicating with us by scent and col-
or and taste." For "the good cook" such food is "a basket of possibilities"; she
or he helps the food to achieve its true destiny through the use of culinary
arts. Barbara Kingsolver, in a similar mood, concludes *Animal, Vegetable,
Miracle* with her ecstatic reaction when a turkey hen on her property hatch-
es chicks. Referring back to an earlier part of the narrative when this same
hen was purchased and raised by Kingsolver herself, she declared: "this time
[the chicks] would be raised right, by a turkey mother, ending once and for

all in our barnyard the indignity of unnatural intervention." Kingsolver and her daughter dance in the barn to celebrate what they perceive as their own success in setting nature back on its course.[52]

The 2009 *Locavore Way*, which used quotes from Pollan as epigrams, advised "Local food doesn't require much of you. All you have to do is let your ingredients star by allowing their flavors to shine." Echoing Edward Espe Brown's Tassajara bread book, the authors assure us that the vegetables know what they want to do, the cook's role is to let them do it. The cookbook *Earth to Table* begged readers to give both farmer and fresh produce "credit," as if food's being had intention in relation to the eater.[53]

The essential action rhetoric of *In Defense of Food* was distilled into Pollan's very brief guide, *Food Rules*. The two most often repeated of Pollan's "food rules" are "Eat food. Not too much. Mostly plants," and "Don't eat anything your great-grandmother wouldn't recognize as food."[54] The two rules are interdependent in that the "food" readers are exhorted to eat is not whatever we find edible, but in fact what our great-grandmothers "recognized" as food.

Sociologist E. Melanie DuPuis succinctly summed up the problems with Pollan's sense of food history in her discussion of the history of diet advice: "Unfortunately, as history has shown, unless we also want to return to our great-great grandmother's enema bag, [Pollan's] may not be the best advice."[55] Readers must just hope that their particular great great grandmother was not one of the millions of sufferers of "dyspepsia" addressed by endless advertisements in popular magazines of the nineteenth century.

What is important about Pollan's rule is that it supplied contemporary readers with a golden age in food history, an edible past. This is a familiar rhetorical move in food writing, from the Southern regionalist cookbooks of the early twentieth century to the back-to-the-land collections of commune cooks.

The discourse of origins by its nature requires a usable past. Ann Vileisis, for example, cleverly revisits Martha Ballard, the late eighteenth-century Maine midwife made famous in Laurel Ulrich's Pulitzer Prize-winning history, *A Midwife's Tale*. Ballard knew "the garden stories of her knobby potatoes, the contours of the cornfields that supplied her bread flour, and the muscle it took to transform raw ingredients into satisfying meals." The idealized knowledge presented here is sensory, personalized, and practical. Underlying the description of Ballard's way of knowing her food is the notion that this multilevel awareness made her in some way, whether physically or ethically (or both) happier than contemporary shoppers who "know very little about what we eat; and, sensing a 'dark side' to our food's production, many of us don't even *want* to know."[56]

Pollan's imagined golden age is an era stretching back to the beginning of human civilizations and ending with the emergence of nutritional science. During this long, happy time, he estimates that humans ate "without a lot of controversy or fuss."[57] Food historians disagree, finding that controversy has never been absent from human food choices.[58] Those scholars who chronicle periods of famine also find a good deal of "fuss" about food and recognize that absence of choice, far from bringing joy, often stemmed from lack of food altogether.[59] But for Pollan, the relevant moment is the just-dawning future, in which his readers must enter food markets and kitchens empowered by a sense of knowledge but only of a certain kind. Whereas Ann Vileisis offered a communal past in which Americans "knew" food in the correct way, Pollan reassures readers that the knowledge they need to eat "well" is already somehow encrypted in their family narrative. Although he may seem to offer just another diet in his *Food Rules*, he claims to be actually reminding readers of wisdom they once had.

Crump also invokes a communal wisdom in food choice in his cookbook *Earth to Table*, arguing that the knowledge of "good food" is inside us but is often dormant and needs to be coaxed out. The first step is to trust our bodies, which Crump claims will not crave blueberries in February or beef stew in July. This can be difficult, however, "partly because industrial-scale farming, shopping, and eating have permitted our culture to forget a great deal that we once knew about food." Instead of accepting the idea that tastes change over time, Crump encourages the reader to revive ancestral longings: "there are some things we have to remember *how* to want if we want to do it right."[60] Like the countercultural cooks of the 1970s, Crump celebrates the adaptability of the palate, which can be guided by the intellect.

Whether readers possess this food knowledge intuitively or not, their grandmothers and mothers may well have encountered advice like Pollan's before in the gourmet cookbook trend. *The Omnivore's Dilemma* and *In*

Defense of Food fit neatly into preexisting genres of food writing, blending many of the gourmet's values with a little of the counterculture's alarmism. One of Pollan's food rules even recapitulated the gourmet's devotion to wine, "Have a Glass of Wine with Dinner." Although not embracing wine's role in the diet, as Pellegrini had, by recommending it for small children and at breakfast, Pollan professed faith in its health-giving powers. Somewhat contradictorily for someone who rejected nutritional science in food choices, he pointed to "abundant scientific evidence for the health benefits of alcohol" and then steered the reader toward using wine (rather than beer, bourbon, or rum) to achieve these benefits because "a diet particularly rich in plant foods," like the one he recommends, otherwise known as "the French and Mediterranean diets . . . supplies precisely the B vitamins that drinking alcohol depletes." Congratulating himself on his good luck in liking what is good for him, Pollan remarks, "How fortunate!"[61]

This self-satisfaction (Pollan saying he already follows all his own food rules) earned the book some criticism, particularly from those involved in food science and related professional and academic fields. Among the criticisms advanced in an article in *Gastronomica* is that Pollan's suggestions are "elitist and impractical for a majority of people to follow, especially those who live in challenged economic conditions, in areas where the growing season is short, or who have busy working lives." Another argument against Pollan's antimodernism made in this same article is that science has done much to fight dietary diseases in the past and will most likely be involved in essential global health projects in the future.[62]

Gregory Ziegler, a professor of food science, professionally alarmed at Pollan's arguments, also pointed out that Pollan's distinction between "refined" and "natural" has itself false origins as it rejects the millennia-long history of crop cultivation and food processing as refinement. Ziegler notes that "despite cacao's ancient origins predating the Mayan culture," the beloved substance is not consumed in its "natural" state, but "'refined' using steel roller mills" and thus a "food like substance," that he suspects many would not want to give up. Kingsolver's special dispensation for chocolate, noted in *Animal, Vegetable, Miracle,* supports his suspicion. Faulting Pollan for his "selective use of science to support his opinions," Ziegler's most interesting criticism comes from research in his own field: "In a recent paper in the *Journal of Food Science*, colleagues confirmed consumer preferences for refined over whole-wheat bread. We make white bread because that's what people want." Far from experiencing stress from having the choice, Americans ate what they liked, following their own cultural traditions.[63]

Crump complicates this simple representation of the food market in his introduction to his farm-to-table restaurant cookbook. Noting that "Marketers know what we want," and that advertising portrays food of almost supernatural freshness, Crump deduces that we really do seek food we can describe as "wholesome." As he notes, "there is hardly an industrial-grade fast-food burger that is not advertised with images of dewy, plump tomatoes, wholesome bread straight from the oven." Although "the reality of flaccid vegetable matter, a soggy bun and tasteless meat" is what we get, "we are so mesmerized by the promise of fresh, wholesome food that we can be tricked into eating something else." For Crump, advertisers' ability to exploit our pastoralism proves that these yearnings exist. Fighting back against critics who fault Pollan's ideology for elitism, Crump argues, "the desire for food grown and prepared with care is not elitist or limited to a band of hippies. It's what we *all* want," and the many authenticity-signifying grandmothers and farm scenes that grace our food packaging prove it.[64]

The pursuit of origins is also easy to parody, as one episode of the satirical TV show *Portlandia* suggests. In the episode, "Farm," main characters Carrie and Fred enter a farm-to-table restaurant and, although supplied many details about a chicken they might order for dinner, including its name, their appetite for meal omniscience is unsated until they drive off to the farm itself and end up joining the polygamous cult of the charismatic farmer. Much is being spoofed here: the restaurant's pretensions to education, the couple's naïve faith that knowing about the chicken makes it fair to have him killed for their personal consumption, and the reverence in which farmers are held in some food subcultures like the farm-to-table dining scene.[65]

Famous food blogger Julie Powell also mocked farmers' market cuisine in a paean to what she argued was Julia Child's more democratic approach to food. While Victorians displayed their wealth by eating strawberries in December, Powell wrote, the new cult of freshness demands that "we demonstrate our su-

periority by serving our dewy organic berries only during the two-week period when they can be picked ripe off the vine at the boutique farm down the
road from our Hamptons bungalow." She described this aesthetic as "the privileged activity of someone who doesn't have to work for a living."[66]

Despite the mockability of his program, Pollan's tone of "common sense,"
has also drawn followers who, as cookbook writers and publishers have long
noted, like to be told what to eat. They do not necessarily follow advice, but
they like to get it. DuPuis is intrigued with Pollan's certainty that this question recurs unanswered in American minds. Musing that "Maybe we should
stop asking 'What to eat?' long enough to consider why we continue to ask
the question." For Pollan, just as for nutritionists, food marketers, and food
writers, the question is their "bread and butter," preferably French bread and
grass-fed cow's milk butter. For DuPuis, the question is a diversion. Asking,
as Pollan appears to, what we should eat in order to remain healthy (or slim
as the two are constantly conflated) is for DuPuis a symptom of social dis-
engagement—the opposite of the community that locavore and discourse-
of-origins writers believe they are promoting. Dupuis asks, "Why do we
continue to think the creation of better bodies will solve our political problems? Perhaps the truth is the other way around: We need to stop trying to
solve our social problems through our stomachs and think about the ways
in which this type of politics simply justifies current inequalities."[67] By keeping the focus tightly on the individual as consumer of real or unreal foods,
Dupuis suggests, we lose sight of the context in which food is grown, sold,
cooked, and consumed.

* * *

Tracie McMillan's *The American Way of Eating* takes up DuPuis's challenge,
and in doing so adds another cast of characters to the contemporary discourse of origins.[68] Largely absent from Pollan's analysis of the food chain,
food workers—pickers, packers, stockers, and cooks—are the focus of Mc-
Millan's work of investigative journalism. To the question of, "What should
we eat," McMillan would probably answer, "that which does not exploit other
people," placing her emphasis on the human as producer within the indus-

trial food system, instead of on the idealized farmer who is the hero of many locavore works of the early twenty-first century. Crump, for example, swears he "would watch a reality TV show that followed the trials of an articulate farmer pursuing the perfect heirloom tomato." For his part, Denevan goes on the road regularly in a large bus to prepare meals for "farmers and food artisans" across the country, setting up their dining table in the fields from which the produce comes.[69] Crump's insistence that the profiled farmer be "articulate" both hints at snobbery and echoes Ellen Brown's celebration of the "new American chefs" as educated and erudite, not "mere" cooks.

Although articles in *Gourmet* in the 2000s celebrated particular farms and farmers and included serious critiques of industrial farming, the migrant worker, meatpacker, and dishwasher remained in the shadows. McMillan's book may be the first in a series, or it may stand alone. Knowledge-seeking eaters are already paying attention to soil quality, carbon footprints, and their own pleasure. Can they also think about the people in the fields and kitchens?

In a 2007 article in *Gastronomica*, Aaron Bobrow-Strain argued, "Michael Pollan suggests that a dualistic vision of good and bad food is hardwired into our omnivorous nature—an essential element of human biology. That seems a bit simplistic, but the question certainly does seem hardwired into food writers' brains."[70] Doing the research for this book has convinced me that Bobrow-Strain is right, and that words about food continuously construct heroes and villains, right ways and wrong that seem deeply true to readers and writers in the context of their own times and foodways. To the question of why we continue to ask, "What should we eat?" I answer that Americans keep asking the question only partly because they want to know and mostly because it's a narrative question, something like the "What happened next?" that we ask of novelists. And, like novelists, our food writers, polemic or practical, attempt to satisfy our question with variations on the few themes that persistently engage us as readers—home and away, good and evil, love and hate.

WHAT SHOULD WE READ
FOR DINNER?

THE HUNDREDS OF COOKBOOKS I read over the course of this project revealed to me that, like all writing genres, cookbooks exist at the pleasure of readers, serving their needs for inspiration and reflection. Cookbooks can be useful for practical matters, but for the most part they serve other purposes—reinforcing class identities, establishing communal historical narratives, providing, like other kinds of fiction, a diversion from the reader's personal experience of the usual. The cookbooks discussed here all performed at least one of these functions and sometimes all of them and more simultaneously.

For cooking blog author Julie Powell, a cookbook famously became a self-help manual and guide to self-discovery, as well as path to stardom. Powell became well-known first for writing a blog about cooking every recipe in Volume 1 of *Mastering the Art of French Cooking*. Because blogging now offers a platform for public self-expression and rhetoric, it was possible for Powell to get attention for writing a cooking blog using someone else's recipes rather than publishing her own cookbook.

The blog led to a book and the book to a movie, itself a box office success. Powell's original story was of a young woman who chose to use *Mastering the Art of French Cooking* as a way to give her life a structure and, potentially, a meaning. The tale explores her relationship with her husband, friends, and city as she pursues her eccentric goal. The movie—*Julie and Julia*—brought together Powell's tale with the memoir, *My Life in France*, that Julia Child wrote with her nephew Alex Prud'homme. Julie's pursuit of Julia was juxtaposed with the story of Child's own voyage of self-fulfillment through the study of French cuisine.[1] The blog, book, and movie, collectively reinforced the idea that cooking is a way to get in touch with one's true self—a gourmet notion as well as one endorsed in different ways by the 1970s counterculture and the Alice Waters school of cooking and eating.[2]

That Powell could make a compelling tale out of her relationship to a particular cookbook, rather than to food in general as M. F. K. Fisher, Nora Ephron, and Laurie Colwin had before her, reflected the cultural status of the genre at the beginning of the twentieth century. Cookbooks had come to be revered and treasured, rather than simply relied upon. Ubiquity had paradoxically bred rarefication. Because there were so many kinds of cookbooks on the market by the end of the twentieth century, some could stand out from the crowd. The two primary ways in which cookbooks had come to be valued was as works of art and as repositories of tradition.

Since the 1990s, technological developments had made it possible to create cookbooks that were objects of enduring beauty. In the nineteenth century, a strong binding had been the only material requisite for a cookbook. The push toward the beautiful cookbook began in the 1920s, with the introduction of corporate cookbooks, those recipe-collections-as-advertisements that courted middle-class readership with glossy images and unusual layouts. While ink illustrations lent wit and color photography brought style to the cookbooks of the 1940s and 1950s, it was not until the 1990s that publishers and authors could make photography the top priority in a cookbook.

Cookbooks became special as aesthetic objects in this era, but a few titles over the years since the Civil War had acquired the special reputation of being totemic. Kitchens were not considered equipped without these books. The volumes served as quiet guides to the correct performance of one's culture. These books either spoke for a generation or transcended generations. Among those that spoke for a generation were the *Gourmet Cookbook*, *Mas-*

tering the Art of French Cooking, Tassajara Bread Book, Moosewood Cook-book, and *Silver Palate Cookbook.* Transcending generations, the *Fannie Farmer Cookbook* and *The Joy of Cooking* stand alone and indeed still stand on many kitchen bookshelves. One cook may very well own and cook from all of these listed books at one time or another. To possess multiple cook-books makes one part of a distinct reading cohort in which there is a kind of cannon of essential works, emergent over time.[3]

In the twenty-first century, cooking blogs are much more likely than ac-tual books are to speak for a generation of cooks, bringing together in their recipes and images trends in taste, writing style, kitchen design, and some-times parenthood, as many food bloggers talk about their families in the course of talking about the food they make. Powell used what was then the new genre of cooking blog to explore the totemic nature of *Mastering the Art of French Cooking.*

The confessional tone that is common to blogs fit well with Powell's proj-ect of charting her search for self-fulfillment. The preexisting audience for blogs about cooking provided another layer of readership. Powell seems to have settled on *Mastering the Art of French Cooking* as guide for her vision quest without knowing about the book's first life before it became a "classic," when it was a liberationist text for many women of Powell's mother's gen-eration. The book's first cohort of readers, Betty Fussell and Mary Cantwell among them, turned to it for help in mastering *something* in a culture that did not expect women to achieve much beyond domestic duties. Powell, too, sought the book as process rather than product. She had no particular need or desire to cook French food, but did have a compulsion to become some-body.

While the first generation of readers had seen Child as a peer and thus someone to be comfortable with, for Powell Child was a more like an aus-tere grandmother figure, implicitly judging when Powell's work in the kitch-en did not achieve the ideal as portrayed in the cookbook. Eventually the real Julia Child even critiqued the project itself. Powell did not hide from her readership that Child had declared the project foolish, but she did not let this interfere with her own plans.

Powell's ability to share the moments of failure and shame, such as Childs' rejection, as well as kitchen disasters and marital tensions with her readers reflects a major shift in food writing. Failure has become an important theme in the digital world of food writing. Powell has helped to develop this trend, which signals the further transformation of food writing from proscriptive to imaginative literature.

Although many who write about Julia Child have emphasized her own willingness to show mistakes in her television performances, arguing that this was what made her popular, the trope of the noncatastrophic accident remained tied to the televised world of cookery until the advent of the cooking blog. Child flubbed food on television, but her recipes were still pre-tested and presented to the reader as perfect. Occasionally, cookbooks tell readers what will happen if they do things wrong. The 1953 edition of *Better Homes and Gardens New Cook Book*, for example, included a section titled "Reasons for angel- and sponge-cake failures." Recipes themselves, however, propose that the reader who follows along faithfully will produce something perfect.[4]

Recipe websites now make public the fact that very few people follow recipes as written, but there is something even more disruptive to the paradigm of recipe perfection achievable through blogs. Because a blog is a chronicle, we can follow one cook through her or his cooking adventures, from failure to success to failure again. Food bloggers can make amendments to recipes years later and link back to the original. A popular food blog, *Smitten Kitchen*, even includes an index section for "disasters."

An example of how failure can become a compelling theme occurred in November 2008 when the blog's author, Deb Perelman, revised her opinion on the important topic of pie crust. Having previously advocated for a part-lard, part-butter crust, she announced that in fact the all butter crust was best. Furthermore, she noted that over the year since her original post, "I've probably made about 12 additional doughs and I swear, every single time I think of something that wasn't in that post and am certain you've been robbed."[5]

Perelman's new post linked back to an older one, revealing the Deb of the past to have been wrong. Because the original post was not altered, readers can once again observe the blogger seemingly sure of herself, in the usual style of cookbook authors. Knowing that the Perelman of the past and the Perelman of the present do not agree destabilizes the reader's relationship to printed cookbooks. If Perelman can change her mind after publishing a recipe, haven't lots of other cookbook writers done the same? Aren't they robbing the reader of the tastier truth? But when something appears in print, there is very little chance of alteration. Most cookbooks do not appear in revised editions. By revealing her own mistake, Perelman makes herself more trustworthy, while simultaneously encouraging readers to distrust all printed cookbooks and perhaps all who profess culinary certainty.

The public acceptance of failure as part of the cooking life that we find in cooking blogs and recipe sites is part of a larger culture of living in public. From shows about real people losing weight to the hours we spend on Facebook, Americans are increasingly comfortable showing their imperfections for the sake of sympathy, support, or a laugh. Given the nature of celebrity media, most popular culture consumers know it is not possible, whoever you are, to maintain a façade of perfection. Someone will take a picture of you without your makeup on, or with your soufflé flat.

Cooking blogs, recipe sites, and photo-sharing apps allow us to partake in this culture of revelation through our kitchen skills. By posting pictures of the meals we eat in restaurants as well as those we cook for ourselves, we democratize the world of food images and at the same time signal our knowledge of which foods are appropriate to our class culture. The person who posts photos of jars of homemade pickles, for example, probably assumes an audience that will appreciate her artisan skills, rather than worry that she cannot afford the commercial variety.

In the late nineteenth century, American women assembled recipe collections that signaled their belonging in a particular class, collections that included the frugal with the fancy to indicate balance and moderation as hallmarks of middle-class life. Like the cooking bloggers of today, they presented themselves to the public through their recipes. Today's bloggers have the ability to comment much more fully on recipes and their own kitchen experience than their ancestors in this genre did. They also comment as individuals, an important distinction. The community cookbook as representation of a particular, regionally defined group has not yet found a place in cyberspace and there is no indication that it will.

This may be because cookbooks in general do not tend to have a digital presence. While publishers develop cooking apps based on original books, apps are not produced at the community level. It is also likely that because community cookbooks so seldom include truly original material, but are instead collections of recipes from other books, it would be difficult to convince readers to buy a digital cookbook when so many of the same recipes would be available for free online.

This is not to say that paper cookbooks are in decline. Their market seems robust and in some cases, as for *The Smitten Kitchen Cookbook*, a blog produces the audience for a book.[6] According to *Publishers Weekly*, Perelman's book was the sixth best-selling cookbook in 2012. While Ina Garten, a chef who gained her fame long before the days of food blogs, had the top seller of the year, two others among the top ten—Ree Drummond and Lisa Lillien—became famous through their blogs. The others, unsurprisingly, all have television shows.[7]

Food writing helps create cultural knowledge that people can use to orient themselves, whether it is the one true way to make a daiquiri, or the one true way to choose our food.[8] To observe the formation of these certainties and their changing truths over time allows us to understand one of the many ways in which people create communities out of words and how uneasy most of us really are with the relativist French suggestion, "chacun à son goût."

NOTES

INTRODUCTION. WORDS ABOUT FOOD

1. See Janet Theophano, *Eat My Words: Reading Women's Lives Through the Cookbooks They Wrote* (New York: Palgrave Macmillan, 2002).

2. I am hardly the first historian to notice what cookbooks can and cannot offer us as primary sources. Ken Albala, in his history of dietary advice in the European Renaissance, explains, "In examining food preferences found in purely prescriptive literature, we are, of course, one step removed from actual consumption. There is really no way to be sure if anyone consistently followed the advice offered in dietary regimens." Ken Albala, *Eating Right in the Renaissance* (Berkeley: University of California Press, 2002), 164.

3. Scholars identify Amelia Simmons, *American Cookery*, published in 1796, as the first American cookbook, in that it was the first published in America that was not a reprint from Britain and contained recipes for indigenous American foods. Amelia Simmons, *American Cookery* (Hartford, Conn.: Printed for Simeon Butler, 1796).

4. Sarah Kemble Knight, *The Private Journal of a Journey from Boston to New York in the Year 1704* (Albany, N.Y.: F.H. Little, 1865), 4.

5. Andrew Burnaby, *Travels Through the Middle Settlements in North America, in the Years 1759 and 1760*, reprinted from the third printing, 1798), 63. Burnaby was probably referring to the sora, a small water fowl native to the Southern Atlantic coast.

6. Mary Randolph, *The Virginia Housewife: or Methodical Cook* (Washington, D.C.: Davis and Force, 1824), x. Randolph's book went through many editions.

7. "Organic Labels Bias Consumers Perceptions Through the 'Health Halo Effect,'" http://foodpsychology.cornell.edu/outreach/organic.html, accessed July 17, 2013.

8. The most influential discussion of food as language is found in Mary Douglas, "Deciphering a Meal," in which she argues that cuisine functions like grammar to help convey messages. Mary Douglas, "Deciphering a Meal," *Daedelus* 101, 1 (Winter 1972): 61–81.

9. My book follows in the footsteps of Arjun Appadurai, Lara Anderson, and Carol Gold, who located the construction of Indian, Spanish, and Danish cuisine, respectively, in cookbooks. Arjun Appadurai, "How to Make a National Cuisine: Cookbooks in Contemporary India," *Comparative Studies in Society and History* 30, 1 (January 1988): 3–24; Lara Anderson, *Cooking Up the Nation: Spanish Culinary Texts and Culinary Nationalization in the Late*

Nineteenth and Early Twentieth Century (Woodbridge: Tamesis, 2013); Carol Gold, *Danish Cookbooks: Domesticity and National Identity, 1616–1901* (Seattle: University of Washington Press, 2007).

10. Eleanor Lowenstein, *Bibliography of American Cookery Books* (Worcester, Mass.: American Antiquarian Society, 1971). For two examples of cookbook histories that focus on gender and religion, respectively, see Jessamyn Neuhaus, *Manly Meals and Mom's Home Cooking* (Baltimore: Johns Hopkins University Press, 2003) and Lara Rabinovitch, "A Peek into Their Kitchens: Postwar Jewish Community Cookbooks in the United States," *Food, Culture & Society* 14 (March 1, 2011).

11. Fales Library, *101 Classic Cookbooks, 501 Classic Recipes* (New York: Rizzoli, 2012); Luke Barr, *Provence, 1970: M. F. K. Fisher, Julia Child, James Beard, and the Reinvention of American Taste* (New York: Clarkson Potter, 2013)

12. The Lost Cause is a term used by historians and other scholars to describe the perspective of many Southerners after the Civil War. Perpetuators of the Lost Cause legend remember the South's involvement in the war as a noble cause, though doomed. They often downplayed the role of slavery in causing the war.

13. Warren James Belasco, *Appetite for Change: How the Counterculture Took on the Food Industry* (Ithaca, N.Y.: Cornell University Press, 2006).

14. Lucy Horton, *Country Commune Cooking* (New York: Coward, McCann & Geoghegan, 1972); Edward Espe Brown, *The Tassajara Cook Book* (Boston: Shambala, 1986).

CHAPTER 1. THE BEST-FED PEOPLE IN THE WORLD: AMERICAN COOKBOOKS IN THE NINETEENTH CENTURY

1. Amelia Simmons, *American Cookery* (Hartford, Conn.: Simeon Butler, 1798), i. Also see Cindy R. Lobel, *Urban Appetites*, for a discussion of how meal possibilities were made more complex through the introduction of the cookstove and precursors to the modern refrigerator: Chapter 5, "No Place More Attractive Than Home, Domesticity and Consumerism," *Urban Appetites: Food and Culture in Nineteenth-Century New York* (Chicago: University of Chicago Press, 2014), 139–68.

2. For a discussion of Simmons's book in the political context of her times, see Glynis Ridley, "The First American Cookbook." *Eighteenth Century Life* 23, 2 (May 1999): 114–23.

3. Eleanor Lowenstein, *Bibliography of American Cookery Books* (Worcester, Mass.: American Antiquarian Society, 1971). Although Lowenstein's biography gives 835 entries for the era between 1742 and 1860, her list includes all editions and printings of each title. By counting the titles listed in the bibliography's index, I arrived at the number 265.

4. Joel Barlow, an American politician, poet, and revolutionary, *The Hasty Pudding, in Three Cantos* (New York: W.H. Graham 1796).

5. Mary Randolph, *The Virginia Housewife: or Methodical Cook* (Washington, D.C.: Davis and Force, 1824)

6. Louis Szathmary, *American Gastronomy* (Chicago: Regnery, 1974), 7; Nicholas A. Basbanes, *A Gentle Madness: Bibliophiles, Bibliomanes, and the Eternal Passion for Books* (New York: Henry Holt, 1995), 357–59. By the time of his death, the collection included several hundred thousand works dating back to the medieval era in Europe.

7. Mary Douglas introduced the idea that meals have a grammar in her seminal article, "Deciphering a Meal," *Daedalus* 101, 1, *Myth, Symbol, and Culture* (Winter 1972): 61–81.

8. Lowenstein, *Bibliography of American Cookery Books*, 110.

9. Lydia Maria Child, *The Frugal Housewife* (Boston: Carter and Hendee, 1830), 9. Child's book was reprinted four times between 1829 and 1831 and was in its eighth edition by 1832, http://digital.lib.msu.edu/projects/cookbooks/html/books/book_06.cfm.

10. Ibid., 101.

11. Lobel, *Urban Appetites*, 142.

12. Randolph, *The Virginia Housewife.*

13. For a comprehensive survey of vegetarian thinking and writing in the nineteenth century, see Adam Shprintzen, *The Vegetarian Crusade* (Chapel Hill: University of North Carolina Press, 2013). Examples of temperance cookbooks are *Fisher's Temperance Housekeeper's Almanac, 1843: Containing Directions for Carving; With Recipes for Boiling, Baking, Roasting, Stewing, Frying, Potting, Pastry, Preserving, Candying* (Boston: James Fisher, 1843) and *Total Abstinence Cookery: Being a Collection of Receipts for Cooking, From Which All Intoxicating Liquids Are Excluded. Compiled by a Lady* (Philadelphia: E. Cummiskey, 1841).

14. Hellmut Lehman-Haupt, *The Book in America* (New York: Bowker, 1951), 321.

15. Grolier Club, *One Hundred Influential American Books Printed Before 1900: Catalogue and Addresses,* (New York: Grolier Club, 1947), 117.

16. I take the term "the reading class" from sociologist Wendy Griswold, whose work in the sociology of literature will be useful to anyone interested in how reading as a behavior fits into social life.

17. Lobel, *Urban Appetites*, 152.

18. For a history of the women who did the work in middle-class kitchens, see Rebecca Sharpless, *Cooking in Other Women's Kitchens* (Chapel Hill: University of North Carolina Press, 2011).

19. As Andrew Haley notes in his history of the American restaurant, "What the aristocrat took for granted," in terms of cultural cues about dining behaviors, "the middle class had to learn. What the rich ignored, the middle class fretted over. The middle class *ariviste* lacked the knowledge and experience to be nonchalant." Andrew P. Haley, *Turning the Tables: Restaurants and the Rise of the American Middle Class, 1880–1920* (Chapel Hill: University of North Carolina Press, 2011), 59.

20. Katherine Leonard Turner writes, "Working-class people did not frequently read or write magazine articles about how to keep house and cook. They rarely used cookbooks, nor did their recipes find their way into the published books." Turner, *How the Other Half Ate* (Berkeley: University of California Press, 2014), 2. Turner uses the records of settlement house workers and extension agents to reconstruct American working-class foodways.

21. For a history of the historical profession in America, see Peter Novick, *That Noble Dream* (Cambridge: Cambridge University Press, 1988).

22. In the twenty years after the Civil War, the largest new subcategory of American cookbooks was community cookbooks (42 of 247 listed works in the Library of Congress catalog). The South was the region best represented in single-author cookbooks during this period (11 of 247 books). While the raw numbers may seem unimpressive, what matters is that there were not a corresponding number of books dedicated to any other region. Eleven books (in-

cluding one Southern cookbook) used the term "economical" in their titles and four included "science," both signaling an interest in progressive cooking. Eighteen books were associated with cooking schools, institutions strongly associated with progressivism; eight of these were by a single author, Juliet Corson.

23. There is a small but growing body of scholarship on community cookbooks. The best place to begin is Anne L. Bower, ed., *Recipes for Reading: Community Cookbooks, Stories, Histories* (Amherst: University of Massachusetts Press, 1997). Also see Bower's essay, "Recipes for History: The National Council of Negro Women's Five Historical Cookbooks," in Bower, *African American Foodways: Explorations of History and Culture* (Urbana: University of Illinois Press, 2007) and Kennan Ferguson, "Intensifying Taste, Intensifying Identity: Collectivity Through Community Cookbooks," *Signs: Journal of Women in Culture and Society* 37, 3 (2012): 695–717. See also Lara Rabinovitch, "A Peek into Their Kitchens: Postwar Jewish Community Cookbooks in the United States," *Food, Culture and Society* 14, 1 (March 2011): 91. In my own attempt to discern whether community cookbooks broadcast any message collectively, and after reading hundreds of books in this genre, I created a simple database into which I entered all the recipes from twenty community cookbooks, sorting by categories so I could have a clear picture of what the most popular recipes were both across place and time.

24. Los Angeles. Simpson Methodist Episcopal Church. Ladies' Social Circle. *How we cook in Los Angeles: a practical cook-book containing six hundred or more recipes, including a French, German and Spanish department with menus, suggestions for artistic table decorations, and souvenirs, by the Ladies' Social Circle, Simpson. M. E. Church, Los Angeles, California* (Los Angeles: Commercial Printing House, 1894), http://www.archive.org/details/howwecookinlo-san00losa.

25. Ladies Aid Society of the Fulton Presbyterian Church, *The Reappear: A Book of Choice Recipes* (Santa Rosa, Calif.: C.A. Wright, 1908), https://archive.org/details/reappearbookofch-00fult.

26. Helen Lyon Adamson, *Grandmother in the Kitchen* (New York: Crown, 1965), 1.

27. All the cookbooks mentioned in this section are available on the Library of Congress site, "American Church, Club and Community Cookbooks," https://www.loc.gov/rr/scitech/SciRefGuides/communitycookbooks.html-top.

28. George H. Lewis, "The Maine Lobster as Regional Icon: Competing Images over Time and Social Class," in Barbara G. Shortridge and James R. Shortridge, eds., *The Taste of American Place* (Lanham, Md.: Rowman and Littlefield, 1998), 67.

29. A further twist in the legend is that the original customer's name was Wenberg, but when he and the owner of Delmonico's had a falling out, the first letters of the first syllable were reversed, in a way to reclaim it for the restaurant.

30. For more about the urbanization of America and the emergence of commerce as entertainment, see William Leach, *Land of Desire: Merchants, Power, and the Rise of a New American Culture* (New York: Pantheon, 1993) and Alan Trachtenberg, *The Incorporation of America* (New York: Hill & Wang, 1982).

31. Cora A. Wood, *Recipes for the Chafing Dish* (Buffalo, N.Y.: McLaughlin Press, 1904), 9.

32. See Marcie Cohen Ferris, *The Edible South: The Power of Food and the Making of an American Region* (Chapel Hill: University of North Carolina Press, 2014), chap. 6, "The

Reconstructed Table" for an excellent analysis of how Southern cookbook writers reimagined Southern cuisine after the war.

33. For a fuller discussion of the Lost Cause, see Barbara L. Bellows and Thomas Lawrence Connelly, *God and General Longstreet: The Lost Cause and the Southern Mind* (Baton Rouge: Louisiana State University Press, 1995) and David Blight, *Race and Reunion: The Civil War in American Memory* (Cambridge, Mass.: Harvard University Press, 2002).

34. Martha McCulloch Williams, *Dishes and Beverages of the Old South* (New York: McBride Nast, 1913), 21–22.

35. Marion Cabell Tyree, *Housekeeping in Old Virginia* (Richmond: Randolph & English, 1878), vii.

36. See Cynthia Wachtell, "Sir Walter Scott's Legacy and the Romance of the Civil War," in her *War No More: The Antiwar Impulse in American Literature 1861–1914* (Baton Rouge: Louisiana State University Press, 2010), chap. 3. See also Kenneth Greenberg, *Honor and Slavery* (Princeton, N.J.: Princeton University Press, 1997) for an explanation of how Southern men invented and practiced a culture of honor in the antebellum period. His subtitle, *Lies, Duels, Noses, Masks, Dressing as a Woman, Gifts, Strangers, Humanitarianism, Death, Slave Rebellions, the Pro-Slavery Argument, Baseball, Hunting, Gambling in the Old South*, is just a hint of the fascinating behavior he uncovers.

37. Tyree, *Housekeeping in Old Virginia*, viii.

38. Celestine Eustis, *Cooking in Old Creole Days* (New York, R.H. Russell, 1904), xiii.

39. Ibid.

40. The Christian Woman's Exchange of New Orleans, *The Creole Cookery Book* (New Orleans: T.H. Thomason, Printer, 1885), iii.

41. Eustis, *Cooking in Old Creole Days*, xiii, xvi.

42. Minnie Fox, *Blue Grass Cookbook* (New York: Fox, Duffield, 1904).

43. Ibid., vi–x.

44. Ibid., xiii. Food historian and cookbook writer Jessica B. Harris argues that hospitality was a cultural attribute Africans introduced into the English colonies. Harris quotes Judith Martin (Miss Manners), who claims "southerners [learned] to practice African manners," because white elites were raised by African American nurses: "It is not from the British that what came to be known as southern graciousness was developed." Jessica B. Harris, *High on the Hog: A Culinary Journey from Africa to America* (New York: Bloomsbury, 2011), 109.

45. Fox, *Blue Grass Cookbook*, xiii.

46. For a discussion of how the idea of devotion was commercialized in the form of Aunt Jemima pancake mix, see Doris Witt, *Black Hunger: Soul Food and American Culture* (1999; Minneapolis: University of Minnesota Press, 2004), esp. chap. 1.

47. Williams, *Dishes and Beverages of the Old South*, 16.

48. Ibid., 10.

49. Abby Fisher, *What Mrs. Fisher Knows About Old Southern Cooking* (San Francisco: Women's Co-op Printing Office, 1881).

50. Lucy C. Andrews, "Southern Prize Recipes," *American Kitchen Magazine* 6, October 1896–March 1897, 224.

51. For a comprehensive history of the politics of beaten biscuits, see Witt, *Black Hunger*, esp. chap. 2.

250 NOTES TO PAGES 31–37

52. Williams, *Dishes and Beverages of the Old South*, 29.

53. Howard Weeden, *Bandana Ballads* (New York: Doubleday & McClure, 1899), 70.

54. Junior League of Charleston, *Charleston Receipts* (Charleston, S.C.: Walker, Evans & Cogswell, 1950), 174.

55. Freda De Knight, *Date with a Dish: A Cookbook of American Negro Recipes* (New York: Hermitage, 1948), 308.

56. Williams, *Dishes and Beverages of the Old South*, 30.

57. An American cookbook published in India in 1933, on the other hand, argued that it made sense to use Southern U.S. food as a model for cooking in India because of climate similarities. Louise Rankin, *An American Cookbook for India* (Calcutta: Thacker and Spink, 1933), vii.

58. Other writers have referred to these books as both domestic science cookbooks and home economics cookbooks, but these terms are misleading because they imply a connection to a national movement in education that they were not part of. They might usefully, although not elegantly, be called cooking school cookbooks because the best known of them were associated with cooking schools, but this gives a false impression that they were teaching manuals, which they were not. The term progressive reflects a shared interest in organizing cooking practices around rational principles. This was an interest common to a wide range of contemporary movements, all inspired by the notion that superior methods could and should be found to approach all aspects of human existence.

59. No date [c. January 1897], no author, "Good Living," *Providence Journal*, Clipping in Box 2 Papers of Ellsworth Milton and Alice Statler, Kroch Library of Manuscripts and Rare Books, Cornell University. Oscar Tschirky, *The Cook Book by "Oscar" of the Waldorf* (Chicago: Werner, 1896).

60. Juliet Corson, *Miss Corson's Practical American Cookery and Household Management* (New York: Dodd, Mead, 1885), v.

61. I have been interested to see that twenty-first-century food writers (Mark Bittman, for example) have been shifting away from the rational school as too restrictive, favoring a more improvisational approach to food. They intend this new approach to do the same kind of democratizing work Farmer and Parloa had hoped to accomplish. The rules they believed would give more women access to the delights of cooking are now seen as keeping interested amateurs away. Once seen as liberators, level measurements have become the palace guards.

62. Maria Parloa, *First Principles of Household Management and Cookery* (Boston: Houghton, Mifflin and company, 1882)

63. M. F. K. Fisher, *The Art of Eating* (Cleveland: World, 1954), 17. Laura Shapiro provides a more contemporary but similar critique that "Cooking School Cookery emphasized every aspect of food except the notion of taste." Shapiro, *Perfection Salad: Women and Cooking at the Turn of the Century* (Berkeley: University of California Press, 2009 [reissue]), 68.

64. Shapiro, *Perfection Salad*, 109.

65. Sarah Tyson Rorer, *Mrs. Rorer's New Cook Book* (Philadelphia: Arnold, 1902), 278. Rorer did recommend soy sauce for several recipes, but her "Japanese Fish Sauce" included Worcestershire sauce and walnut ketchup in equal proportions to soy.

66. Shapiro, *Perfection Salad*, 106.

67. Fannie Merritt Farmer, *The Boston Cooking-School Cook Book* (Boston, Little, Brown, 1896) 1.

68. Shapiro, for example, claims of the cooking school authors, "By ennobling the recipes over the results, and disdaining the proof of the palate, they made it possible for American cooking to accept a flood of damaging innovations for years to come." *Perfection Salad*, 68.

69. For an excellent discussion of how the American conversations about food became a moral discourse at the end of the nineteenth century, see Helen Zoe Veit, *Modern Food, Moral Food* (Chapel Hill: University of North Carolina Press, 2013).

70. Steve Fraser, *Every Man a Speculator* (New York: HarperCollins, 2005), 257–58.

71. Corson, *Miss Corson's Practical American Cookery*, v.

72. Ibid., vi.

73. Ibid., v. Contemporary nutritional science based in recognition of vitamins and calories only emerged in the early twentieth century. Prior to this era, however, ideas about what was healthful food changed over time to accommodate new materials as well as new ideas. The best book on the topic of changing ideas about health and food is still Ken Albala's *Eating Right in the Renaissance* (Berkeley: University of California Press, 2002). Although Albala's book is about Europe in the Renaissance, the patterns he reveals have had a lasting impact on how the Western world thinks about health and food.

74. Corson, *Miss Corson's Practical American Cookery*, vii.

75. Farmer, *The Boston Cooking-School Cook Book*, 10.

76. Parloa, *First Principles of Household Management and Cookery*, 60.

77. Common contemporary kitchen guides usually warn cooks that spices lose their flavors over time and advocate frequent replacement, a practice easier in our era of cheap spices than in Parloa's, when curry powder would still have been something of a luxury. Halford sauce was a vinegar-based savory sauce eclipsed by the rise of Lea & Perrin's Worcestershire sauce. Mushroom ketchup, along with ketchups made from walnuts and grapes, was gradually pushed off the American table by Heinz's tomato product.

78. For example, the Cookbook Publishers company promises, "We've made it easy for your community to share recipes and raise thousands of dollars for charitable giving, special projects or to mark a memorable event," http://www.cookbookpublishers.com/community-cookbook/, accessed May 27, 2014.

79. Louis Van Dyke and Billie Van Dyke, *The Blue Willow Inn Bible of Southern Cooking* (Nashville, Tenn.: Rutledge Hill, 2005), 20.

CHAPTER 2. AN APPETITE FOR INNOVATION: COOKBOOKS
BEFORE THE SECOND WORLD WAR

1. Frigidaire Corp, *The Frigidaire Key to Meal Planning* (Dayton, Ohio: Frigidaire Corp. 1933).

2. See Robert S. Haller, *The History of New Thought: From Mind Cure to Positive Thinking and the Prosperity Gospel* (West Chester, Pa.: Swedenborg Foundation Press, c. 2012) for a history of positive thinking in the United States. Haller writes that by the beginning of the twentieth century, larger social issues such as class conflict and labor unrest "took a back seat" in public discourse to "a plethora of literature touting the self-made nature of poverty, the importance of individual hard work and achievement and the promise of material comfort that was only a wish away. New Thought's readers learned that the only barriers to personal

health, happiness and prosperity were self-made, meaning that failure was due to personal fault" (216).

3. Mary Green, *Better Meals for Less Money* (New York: Holt, 1917), iii.

4. *Publishers Weekly* 92, 1, July 7, 1917, 10 The digital archive Hathi Trust provides access to *Publishers Weekly* archives from 1873.

5. Ibid., 4.

6. Wartime cookbooks also built on the preexisting genre of community cookbooks because they were often compiled by the same groups who had published charity cookbooks before the war. Where prewar cookbooks raised money for local projects, recipe collections like the *"Win the War" Cook Book* from St. Louis raised money for international causes as well as helping readers conserve resources for military use. Reah Janette Lynch, *"Win the War" Cook Book*, St. Louis County Unit, Women's Committee, Council of National Defense, 1918.

7. Nina Teicholz, writing an opinion piece in the *New York Times*, reflected on the lasting legacy of this shift: "For two generations, Americans ate fewer eggs and other animal products because policy makers told them that fat and cholesterol were bad for their health." "The Government's Bad Diet Advice," *New York Times*, February 20, 2015.

8. C. Houston Goudiss and Alberta M. Goudiss, *Foods That Will Win the War and How to Cook Them* (New York: World, 1918).

9. Charles Johanningsmier, "The Industrialization and Nationalization of American Periodical Publishing," in Scott Evan Casper, Joanne D. Chaison, and Jeffrey David Groves, eds., *Perspectives on American Book History: Artifacts and Commentary* (Amherst: University of Massachusetts Press, 2002), 331.

10. *Borden as Guardian of the Public Health* (Book One) (New York: Lesan Advertising Agency, 1932?), 4.

11. David M. Katzman, *Seven Days a Week: Women and Domestic Service in Industrializing America* (New York: Oxford University Press, 1978), 223–65.

12. Ruth Schwartz Cowan explores the complicated impact of these new technologies and products in *More Work for Mother: The Ironies of Household Technology* (New York: Basic, 1983).

13. See Katherine J. Parkin, *Food Is Love: Advertising and Gender Roles in Modern America* (Philadelphia: University of Pennsylvania Press, 2006), for a fascinating history of advertising and market research about women and food in the twentieth century.

14. Jane Busch, "Cooking Competition: Technology on the Domestic Market in the 1930s," *Technology and Culture* 24, 2 (April 1983): 222–45, 228.

15. Lizzie Black Kander's *The Settlement Cook Book* was originally published as *The Way to a Man's Heart* (Milwaukee: The Settlement, 1901). Under the title *The Settlement Cook Book*, and after 1954, the *New Settlement Cook Book*, it remained in print and sold approximately two million copies by 1991.

16. Carolyn Goldstein, *Creating Consumers: Home Economists in Twentieth-Century America* (Chapel Hill: University of North Carolina Press, 2012), 159.

17. Gesine Lemke, *How to Make Good Things to Eat* (Chicago: Libby, McNeil, and Libby, 1900), 8.

18. *Foods from Sunny Lands* (New York: Hills Brothers, 1925).

19. Commercial date agriculture was only successful after growers imported varieties from the Middle East in the first years of the twentieth century. Donald R. Hodel and Den-

nis V. Johnson, *Imported and American Varieties of Dates (Phoenix Dactylifera) in the United States*, Agriculture and Natural Resources Publication 3498, University of California, 2007.

20. California Fruit Growers Exchange, *For Vigorous Health: Sunkist Recipes for Every Day* (Los Angeles: California Fruit Growers Exchange, 1935), 13.

21. See Douglas Sackman, *Orange Empire* (Berkeley: University of California Press, 2005) for the most comprehensive study to date of the rise of Sunkist.

22. California Fruit Growers Exchange, *For Vigorous Health*.

23. Ibid., 100.

24. Ibid., 104.

25. Ibid., 2. Historian Douglas Sackman writes of acidosis that it is "a real and dangerous malady, but diet has little or nothing to do with it." Sackman argues that rather than being a real threat, "Like neurasthenia, acidosis fed on preexisting cultural anxieties about loss of vigor in the modern, corporate, machine-driven world." Sackman, *Orange Empire*, 111.

26. Busch, "Cooking Competition"; Mark H. Rose, *Cities of Light and Heat: Domesticating Gas and Electricity in Urban America* (University Park: Pennsylvania State University Press, 1995), 108.

27. California Fruit Growers Exchange, *For Vigorous Health*, 42.

28. *Frigidaire Frozen Delights* (Dayton, Ohio: Frigidaire Corporation, 1927)

29. *Frigidaire Recipes* (Dayton, Ohio: Frigidaire Corporation, 1929).

30. Ibid., 90.

31. Melissa Clark, "Mayonnaise: Oil, Egg, and a Drop of Magic," *New York Times*, May 22, 2012.

32. John Roberson and Marie Roberson, *The Famous American Recipes Cookbook* (Englewood Cliffs, N.J.; Prentice-Hall, 1957), 192.

33. General Foods Corporation, *Correct Salads for All Occasions* ([s.l.]: General Foods Corporation, 1931).

34. *Frigidaire Recipes*, 68.

35. Ibid., 85.

36. *Frigidaire Key to Meal Planning*, 6.

37. *Frigidaire Recipes*, 54.

38. Busch, "Cooking Competition," 239.

39. Research Kitchen of American Stove Company, *Lorain Cooking* (1924; St. Louis: American Stove Company, 1926), 17.

40. Jean Prescott Adams, *The Business of Being a Housewife* (Chicago: Armour, 1921), 3.

41. *Frozen Delights*, 25

42. See Susan Strasser, *Never Done: A History of American Housework* (1982; New York: Macmillan, 2013), esp. chap. 4, "At the Flick of a Switch," for a discussion of changing roles for women and the advent of electrical appliances.

43. Changing gender roles and changing beauty norms reinforced each other as middle-class women became more active in public life and the active figure—characterized as slim—became the cultural ideal. This transition is most thoroughly treated in Peter N. Stearns, *Fat History: Bodies and Beauty in the Modern West* (New York: New York University Press, 1997, 2002). Stearns cites two forces as driving the change: the growing interest in athleticism that emerged in the late nineteenth century and changing clothing fashions related to the reshaping and even rejection of the corset.

44. Seattle Public Library, *A List of Books for Women in the Home and in Business* (Seattle: Seattle Public Library, 1909).

45. Lulu Hunt Peters, *Diet and Health with Key to the Calories* (Chicago: Reilly and Lee, 1918), 18.

46. Edna Sibley Tipton, *Reducing Menus for the Hostess of To-day* (New York: D. Appleton, 1925), 1.

47. Hillel Schwartz, *Never Satisfied: A Cultural History of Diets, Fantasies, and Fat* (New York: Doubleday, 1990), 174.

48. Vance Thompson, *Eat and Grow Thin: The Mahdah Menus* (New York: E.P. Dutton, 1914), 34.

49. Ibid., 17.

50. Ibid., 15.

51. Ibid., 12.

52. Fannie Hurst, *No Food with My Meals* (New York: Harper & Brothers, 1935), 26.

53. Ibid., 27.

54. Ibid., 52.

55. Ibid., 16–17.

56. Ibid., 22.

57. Peters, *Diet and Health*, 24.

58. Tipton, *Reducing Menus*, 57.

59. Marion White, *Diet Without Despair* (New York: M.S. Mill, 1943), 30.

60. Ibid., 73

61. Ibid., 125.

62. Betty Crocker, *Picture Cook Book* (Minneapolis: General Mills, 1950).

63. New York Times food and diet bestsellers list, September 2016. *The New York Times* publishes a monthly list of bestsellers on its digital edition. http://www.nytimes.com/books/best-sellers/food-and-fitness/, accessed September 4, 2016; readers can click through to previous lists.

64. "About the Authors," http://www.skinnybitch.net/authors.html, accessed May 27, 2014.

65. Dean Ornish, *The Spectrum: A Scientifically Proven Program to Feel Better, Live Longer, Lose Weight, and Gain Health* (New York: Ballantine, 2007)

CHAPTER 3. GOURMET IS A BOY: MIDCENTURY
COOKBOOKS AND FOOD MAGAZINES

1. *Frigidaire Frozen Delights* (Dayton, Ohio: Frigidaire, Corporation 1927)

2. L. B. Beardsley, Letter, *Gourmet* 2, 4 (April 1943): 3. For a brief history of Gourmet's first ten years, see Andrew F. Smith, "Earle McAusland's Gourmet," in Smith, *Eating History: Thirty Turning Points in the Making of American Cuisine* (New York: Columbia University Press); also see Ann Mendelson, "60 Years of Gourmet," *Gourmet* 61 (September 2001): 71.

3. Cookbooks for men are discussed at length in Jessamyn Neuhaus, *Manly Meals and Mom's Home Cooking* (Baltimore: Johns Hopkins University Press, 2003). While Neuhaus argues that men were brought into the kitchen because women were entering the workforce, I

see the attempt to put men into oven mitts as part of a change in thinking about and marketing American food and wine.

4. M. F. K. Fisher, *Serve It Forth* (New York: Harper & Brothers, 1937), 117–18.

5. Allan Ross MacDougal, *The Gourmet's Almanac* (New York: Covici-Friede, 1930), 71.

6. A 1911 guide to the restaurants of Europe, *The Gourmet's Guide to Europe*, published in New York, indicates that the term was used in the United States before 1930, but it does not seem to have been associated with home cooking until MacDougal published *The Gourmet's Almanac*.

7. No author, "Brief Reviews," *New York Times*, January 26, 1930.

8. Helen Buckler, "Why Live Without Cooks?" *Saturday Review of Literature*, January 25, 1930, 674.

9. Charles Browne, *The Gun Club Cook Book* (New York: Charles Scribner's Sons, 1946), iii.

10. "Latest Books Received," *New York Times*, September 20, 1931; "Dr. C. Browne, 71, Ex-Congressman," *New York Times*, August 18, 1947.

11. Theodore Hall, "Yea, There's Need for a Book, When the Man Is the Cook!: A Batch of the Best Are Selected for the Bachelors. Here's How to Escape the Ills of Eating Delicatessen," *Washington Post*, November 18, 1934, B7.

12. M. W. "About the Various Pleasures of Eating: Serve It Forth," *New York Times*, June 20, 1947.

13. David Strauss, *Setting the Table for Julia Child* (Baltimore: Johns Hopkins University Press, 2011), 75.

14. Ibid., 70–75.

15. Fisher, *Serve It Forth*, 114.

16. Mrs. D, McQuilkin, Garden City, L.I., "The members of our family have had a discussion as to the correct pronunciation of the name of your magazine. Will you be so kind as to settle the point in question? I think your magazine is excellent. I know good food and am interested in the preparation of it—but I'll never be a gourmet since I don't care enough for different foods." "Sugar and Spice," *Gourmet* 2, 2 (February 1942): 3.

17. Ann Hark, "Common—But Good!" *Gourmet* 3, 12 (December 1943): 10; John J. Rowlands, "Apple Butter," *Gourmet* 6, 10 (October 1946): 26; Louis P. De Gouy, "Yankee Shore Dinner The Old New England Clambake," *Gourmet* 1, 8 (August 1941): 14.

18. In 1934, writer Andre Simon, who had cofounded the Wine and Food Society of London, traveled to America and helped establish sister associations in Boston, Chicago, Los Angeles New Orleans, New York, and San Francisco. Thomas Pinney, *A History of Wine in America: from Prohibition to the Present*, vol. 2 (Berkeley: University of California Press, 2005), 108–9.

19. Mary Grosvenor Ellsworth, *Much Depends on Dinner* (New York: Knopf, 1939), 31.

20. Charles Browne, *The Gun Club Cook Book* (New York: Charles Scribner's Sons, 1930) (viii).

21. Richardson Wright, Introduction in Jeanne Owen, *A Wine Lover's Cookbook* (New York: Barrows, 1940), xii.

22. Hall, "Yea, There's Need for a Book, When the Man Is the Cook!" B7.

23. Wright, Introduction, xii.

24. Book Review, *New York Herald Tribune*, January 19, 1941, 13.

25. Ric Riccardo in Morrison Wood, *With a Jug of Wine* (New York: Farrar, Straus, 1949). Riccardo was, interestingly, the founder of Pizzeria Uno, now considered a profoundly un-gourmet establishment.

26. No author, "A Line o' Type or Two: Fountain Pen Week," *Chicago Daily Tribune*, November 15, 1949, 20.

27. Rexford Tugwell, "Wine, Women, and the New Deal," February 5, 1934; reprinted in *The Battle for Democracy* (New York: Columbia University Press, 1935), quoted in Pinney, *A History of Wine in America*.

28. For example, a talk I attended in September 2010 on "Wine and Philosophy" began with the presentation of American wine consumption statistics in which the speaker, Fritz Allhof, regretted Americans' failure to drink as much wine per capita as most European nations. Mount Holyoke College, South Hadley, Mass., September 2010.

29. Marian Burros, "Thomas Jefferson, Founding Foodie," August 22, 2012, *New York Times*. Felisa Rogers, writing for Salon, identified him as "America's original foodie," in 2011, http://www.salon.com/2011/07/02/jefferson_culinary_history/; the University of Mississippi Press published John Hailman, *Thomas Jefferson on Wine*, in 2006.

30. Pinney, *A History of Wine in America*, 114–15.

31. Peter Greig, "The Choice of Wine," *Gourmet* 1, 1 (January 1941): 34.

32. No author, *Bon Appétit* 1, 1 (November–December 1956): 8.

33. Pinney, *A History of Wine in America*, 88.

34. Greig, "The Choice of Wine," 25.

35. Thanksgiving itself had, of course, become established as an archetypal American holiday through a vigorous campaign in print. Pinney argues that labeling and bottling were primarily a way for winemakers to present a product that was easy for regulators to assess in the post-Repeal market, which was much more complexly monitored than the pre-Prohibition industry.

36. William Bird, *A Practical Guide to French Wines*, quoted in MacDougal, *The Gourmet's Almanac*, 226.

37. Advertisement, Wine Advisory Board, 1942.

38. I have not yet determined the date of this advertisement, but it appears to have been made in 1953 or shortly thereafter, as Sills began appearing on the show *Opera Cameo*, sponsored by Gallo that year. Beverly Sills, *Bubbles: A Self Portrait* (Indianapolis: Bobbs Merrill, 1976), 55.

39. Cora Brown, Rose Brown, and Bob Brown, *The Wine Cook Book* (Boston: Little, Brown, 1934), 319.

40. "Vitamic Discovery to Aid Humanity," *New York Times*, March 21, 1921, 14. The article was about the announcement by Dr. H. B. Cox that he had "succeeded in extracting the vita-mic properties from fruits and vegetables," making it potentially possible to provide vitamin supplements independent of food material.

41. Ellsworth, *Much Depends on Dinner*, iii.

42. Advertisement, "Sportsman's Special Offer," *Gourmet* 1, 10 (October 1941): 35.

43. See Kimberly Wilmot Voss, *The Food Section* (Lanham, Md.: Rowman and Littlefield, 2014), for the history of newspaper food columns.

44. MacDougal, *The Gourmet's Almanac*, 53.

45. Browne, *The Gun Club Cook Book*, vii.

46. For a comprehensive history of Pyrex, see Regina Blaszczyk, *Imagining Consumers* (Baltimore: Johns Hopkins University Press, 2002).

47. Ellsworth, *Much Depends on Dinner*, 175.

48. Oscar E. Anderson, *Refrigeration in America: A History of a New Technology* (Princeton, N.J.: Published for the University of Cincinnati by Princeton University Press, 1953), 274.

49. *Gourmet* 1, 1 (January 1941), Earle McAusland, "To you—a lover of good food we introduce Gourmet the Magazine of good living," 5.

50. Samuel Chamberlain, "Burgundy at a Snail's Pace"; Louis P. De Gouy "Game for Gourmets—and Others." *Gourmet* 1, 1 (January 1941).

51. Ann Mendelson, "Gourmet's First Decade," originally published September 2001. Gourmet.com, accessed August 1, 2012.

52. A. H. Deute, "The Stones Grind Slowly," *Gourmet* 3, 3 (March 1942): 14.

53. Mrs. Marvin Hirschberg, Letter, *Gourmet* 12, 6 (June 1952), 2.

54. Josephine Jenkins, Letter, *Gourmet* 12, 8 (August 1952), 2.

55. Editorial response to Jenkins, Letter, 2.

56. The Clementine of Chamberlain's title was a composite of two cooks the family had hired during their time in France. One of the cooks also moved with the family when they returned to the United States on the eve of the Second World War.

57. Nathalie Jordi, "Samuel Chamberlain's *Clementine in the Kitchen*," *Gastronomica: The Journal of Food and Culture* 7, 4 (Fall 2007): 42–52; Samuel Chamberlain, "Clementine in the Kitchen," *Gourmet* 1, 2 (February 1941): 15.

58. Phineas Beck (Samuel Chamberlain), *Clementine in the Kitchen* (New York: Hastings House, 1949), serialized in *Gourmet* 1, 2 (February 1941): 15.

59. Ellsworth, *Much Depends on Dinner*, 163.

60. Ernst Lorsy, "Escoffier," *Gourmet* 4, 1 (January 1944): 10

61. Mary Grosvenor Ellsworth, "La Bonne Cuisine: Clementine in the Kitchen," *New York Times*, November 21, 1943; BR8.

62. Esquire's *Handbook for Hosts* (New York: Grosset & Dunlap, 1949), 71.

63. Ibid.

64. Fannie Merritt Farmer, *The Boston Cooking-School Cook Book* (Boston: Little, Brown, 1896), 287.

65. Walter Buehr, "Café Society 19th Century Style," *Gourmet* 2, 1 (January/February 1942): 17.

66. Eric Howard, "If I Had My Way—When a Man Cooks," *Gourmet* 1, 11 (November 1941): 10.

67. Esquire's *Handbook for Hosts*, 14.

68. Winnie Meeks, Letter, *Gourmet* 5, 11 (November 1945): 2.

69. Wallace, *Garrulous Gourmet*, 168, 169, 16.

70. See Alexandra Kelly and Cynthia Harris, *Hometown Appetites: The Story of Clementine Paddleford, the Forgotten Food Writer Who Chronicled How America Ate* (New York: Gotham, 2008), 262. According to Paddleford's adopted daughter, the food writer "almost never cooked at home except to prepare a steak on the maid's night off."

71. Iles Brody "An Adventure in Taste," *Gourmet* 1, 8 (August 1941): 22. Media historian Kenon Breazeale has argued that *Esquire* actually based its initial success on an aggressively antiwoman tone, which she sums up as the "'Women Are Lousy at [fill in name of activity]'" genre. Brezeale, "In Spite of Women: *Esquire* Magazine and the Construction of the Male Consumer," in Jennifer Scanlon, ed., *The Gender and Consumer Culture Reader* (New York: New York University Press, 2000), 227–44.

72. Brody, "An Adventure in Taste," 8.

73. M. F. K. Fisher, "Gourmets Are Made—Not Born," in Fisher, *A Stew or a Story: An Assortment of Short Works* (Emeryville, Calif.: Shoemaker & Hoard, c2006).

74. Ibid., 111.

75. Ibid., 114.

76. Ibid., 113–15.

77. Nicholas Roosevelt, *Creative Cooking* (New York: Harper & Brothers, 1956), xiii.

78. British Butcher's Apron Advertisement, *Gourmet* 16, 6 (July 1956): 52.

79. M. F. K. Fisher, *The Art of Eating* (Cleveland: World, 1954), 7–8.

80. Ibid., 119.

81. Lizabeth Cohen, *Consumer's Republic* (New York: Knopf, 2003), 148.

82. See Tom Pendergast, "'Horatio Alger Doesn't Work Here Any More': The Emergence of Modern Masculinity," in Pendergast, *Creating the Modern Man: American Magazines and Consumer Culture, 1900–1950* (Columbia: University of Missouri Press, 2000), 111–66.

83. As Pendergast argues in his study of men's magazines, "The growth of modern masculinity created roles for men that suited them to a corporate consumer culture." Ibid., 3.

84. Ibid., 212.

85. See Adam David Shprintzen, *The Vegetarian Crusade: The Rise of an American Reform Movement, 1817–1921* (Chapel Hill: University of North Carolina Press, 2013) for a discussion of how vegetarians worked to construct their own identity in American culture.

86. Angelo Pellegrini, *The Unprejudiced Palate* (1948; New York: Modern Library, 2005), 118.

87. Mark Bittman, "Rethinking the Word Foodie," *New York Times*, June 25, 2014.

CHAPTER 4. MASTERING THE ART OF AMERICAN COOKING:
JULIA CHILD AND AMERICAN COOKBOOKS

1. See, for example, Christopher Kimball, "An American in Paris: Julia Child Celebrated French Cuisine but Embodied Yankee Virtues—Candor, Enthusiasm and Hard Work," *Wall Street Journal*, December 4, 2010. "Julia's commitment to excellence, fueled by a stubborn dedication to the 'correct way' of doing everything, made *Mastering* a watershed cookbook."

2. Susan Marks, *Finding Betty Crocker* (Minneapolis: University of Minnesota Press, 2005); Joan Reardon, *Poet of the Appetites: The Lives and Loves of M. F. K. Fisher* (New York: North Point, 2005); Julia Child, Simone Beck, and Louisette Bertholle, *Mastering the Art of French Cooking* (New York: Knopf, 1961).

3. Peg Bracken, *The I Hate to Cook Book* (New York: Harcourt, Brace, 1961).

4. This was a recurring theme on *Bewitched*, for example, and had become such a com-

mon trope by the 1970s that the *Mary Tyler Moore* show could play on expectations with an episode titled "The Boss Isn't Coming to Dinner."

5. Women of General Foods Kitchens, *The General Foods Kitchens Cookbook* (New York: Random House, 1959).

6. Ibid., 142.

7. It was the first cookbook on the list since 1926, when both *Diet for Health* and Fannie Farmer's cookbook were best sellers.

8. *Betty Crocker's Picture Cook Book* (New York: McGraw Hill, 1950), 5.

9. Ibid., 85.

10. Ibid., 43 (Appetizers); 56 (Chocolate).

11. *Better Homes and Gardens New Cookbook* (Des Moines, Iowa: Better Homes and Gardens, 1953), 4.

12. Ibid., 19.

13. Ibid., 62.

14. James Beard, *The Fireside Cook Book* (New York: Simon and Schuster, 1949), 11; Evan Jones, *Epicurean Delight: Life and Times of James Beard* (New York: Knopf, distributed by Random House, 1990), 149.

15. Angelo Pellegrini, *The Unprejudiced Palate* (New York: Macmillan, 1948), 164.

16. Ibid., 12.

17. Beard, *The Fireside Cook Book*, 11.

18. Ibid., 11, 13.

19. Jones, *Epicurean Delight*, 165. James Beard, *Cook It Outdoors* (New York; Barrows and Company, 1941).

20. Beard's biographer Robert Clark writes of the *Fireside Cookbook*, "While the book understood that its readers' tastes in entertaining and in food might be unformed, it also understood that the display of those tastes to friends and colleagues was serious business, announcing to the world who—in leisure, in aspiration, and in status—their possessors were. Food and the knowledge of it were a full-fledged lifestyle accessory." Robert Clark, *James Beard* (New York: HarperCollins, 1993), 130.

21. Poppy Cannon, *The Can-Opener Cookbook* (New York: Thomas Crowell, 1951), 1.

22. Ibid., 1.

23. Ibid.

24. Ibid., 2.

25. Ibid., 6.

26. No author, "Life Guide: Cookbooks," *Life*, September 29, 1961, 29.

27. Poppy Cannon, *The Electric Epicure's Cookbook* (New York: Crowell, 1961). Laura Shapiro discusses Cannon's ability to exist easily in both the convenience food crowd and the gourmet camp in *Something from the Oven: Reinventing Dinner in 1950s America* (New York: Penguin, 2004), 108–10.

28. Margalit Fox, "Peg Bracken, 'I Hate to Cook' Author Dies," *New York Times*, October 23, 2007.

29. Bracken, *The I Hate to Cook Book*, ix.

30. Ibid.

31. Ibid., 20. Bracken's reference to the "pizza man" reflects the mainstreaming of what

had recently been considered exotic "ethnic" food. The "chicken pie" lady is possibly a reference to the Marie Callender chain of restaurants, famous for its chicken pot pies. This chain was limited to California until the 1960s, but Bracken did live in California.

32. Ibid., 20.

33. Ibid., 25.

34. Ibid, 26.

35. Despite Bracken's distrust, eggplant recipes had appeared regularly in American cookbooks as far back as Eliza Leslie's 1840 *Directions for Cookery in Its Various Branches.* Leslie had recommended a breaded eggplant fritter flavored with marjoram as a breakfast dish that could sometimes be served at dinner. Eliza Leslie, *Directions for Cookery in Its Various Branches* (Philadelphia: Carey and Hart, 1840), 193.

36. Jo Coudert, *The I Never Cooked Before Cook Book* (New York: Stein and Day, 1963), 9.

37. Bracken, *The I Hate to Cook Book*, 103.

38. Pellegrini, *The Unpredjudiced Palate*, 10.

39. Lynn Dallin, *The Stay Out of the Kitchen Cookbook* (Garden City, N.Y.: Doubleday, 1968), xiii.

40. Ibid., 273.

41. Ibid., xii.

42. Ibid., xi.

43. The answer was that there was not room in one book for all the treasures of French cooking and that some—like *pâté feuilleté*—were better learned in a class than from a book.

44. Mary Cantwell, *Manhattan When I Was Young* (New York: Penguin, 1995), 102. The Dione referred to was Dione Lucas, who ran a well-regarded cooking school in Manhattan and published cookbooks.

45. Betty Fussell, *My Kitchen Wars* (New York: North Point, 1999), 159.

46. Ibid., 154. Fussell's adaptation of famous fashion model Jerry Hall's quip that a woman must strive to be "a maid in the living room, a cook in the kitchen and a whore in the bedroom," playfully suggests how important innovative cooking had become to the modern marriage.

47. Ibid., 159.

48. Charlotte Turgeon, *Time to Entertain* (Boston: Little, Brown, 1954).

49. John Marshall, *Classic Cooking: A New Approach to French Cuisine* (New York: Duell, Sloan and Pearce, 1959)

50. Myra Waldo, *The Complete Book of Gourmet Cooking for the American Kitchen* (New York: Putnam, 1960)

51. Evan Jones, *American Food: The Gastronomic Story* (New York: Dutton, 1975), 138.

52. Child's gift for and to the new medium of television has been chronicled in several biographies and particularly Kathleen Collins, *Watching What We Eat: The Evolution of Television Cooking Shows* (New York: Continuum, 2009).

53. See Collins, *Watching What We Eat.*

54. Marcia Seligson, "What We Need Now Is Another French Cookbook," *New York Times,* November 10, 1969.

55. Ibid, B8.

56. Food historian Paul Freedman has described the series as "picturesque and stylized

ethnography," for the scenes of folk life, such as horses pulling wagons, that accompany the recipes. Paul Freedman, panel presentation, "Cookbooks as Dreams of the Ideal," Roger Smith Cookbook Conference, February 29, 2012, video, http://www.ustream.tv/recorded/20780036. See Catherine A. Lutz and Jane L. Collins, *Reading National Geographic* (Chicago: University of Chicago Press, 1993), for a history of *National Geographic* as cultural agent. For an exploration of *Life*'s role in the democratization of taste, see Sheila Webb, "The Consumer-Citizen: 'Life' Magazine's Construction of a Middle-Class Lifestyle Through Consumption Scenarios," *Studies in Popular Culture* 34, 2 (Spring 2012): 23–47.

57. James Beard, "Take Equal Parts of Bounty, Diversity and Ingenuity," Introduction to Dale Brown, *American Cooking* (New York: Time-Life, 1968), 6.

58. Brown, *American Cooking*, 21.

59. Ibid., 22.

60. James P. Shenton et al., *American Cooking: The Melting Pot* (New York: Time-Life, 1971), 18.

61. Ibid.

62. Peter Wood, "A Moveable Feast from the Caribbean," in ibid., 181.

63. Eugene Walter, *American Cooking: Southern Style*, (New York: Time-Life, 1971), 109.

64. Ibid., 111.

65. For a full treatment of Cold War cultural politics, see Steven Whitfield, *The Culture of the Cold War* (Baltimore: Johns Hopkins University Press, 1991, 1996).

66. Linda Wolfe, *The Literary Gourmet* (New York: Random House, 1962), 329.

67. For recent authentication of accounts of postmortem cannibalism in Jamestown, see http://www.smithsonianmag.com/history/starving-settlers-in-jamestown-colony-resorted-to-cannibalism-46000815/?no-ist.

68. Jean Hewitt, *The New York Times Heritage Cook Book* (New York: Putnam, 1972), xvi–xvii, xv.

69. For a history of the complex and important role food played in relations between English settlers and Native Americans in the colonial era, see Michael Lacombe, *Political Gastronomy: Food and Authority in the English Atlantic World* (Philadelphia: University of Pennsylvania Press, 2012).

70. John Roberson and Marie Roberson, *The Famous American Recipes Cookbook* (Englewood Cliffs, N.J.: Prentice-Hall, 1957), 185.

71. Charlotte Turgeon, *The Saturday Evening Post All-American Cookbook* (Nashville, Tenn.: Thomas Nelson & Curtis, 1976), 195.

72. Brown, *American Cooking*, 175.

73. Editors of American Heritage, *The American Heritage Cookbook and Illustrated History* (New York: American Heritage, distr. Simon and Schuster, 1964).

74. Bullock worked as a specialist in historical architecture; she was also information officer at the National Trust for Historic Preservation from the 1950s to the 1970s and "regarded as the nation's leading authority on open-hearth cookery." Robert McG. Thomas, Obituary, *New York Times*, November 11, 1995, 13.

75. Marshall Fishwick, "Thomas Jefferson," in Editors of American Heritage, *The American Heritage Cookbook*, 135. In the *New York Times*, Nan Ickeringill described the *American Heritage Cookbook* as "a fascinating hodgepodge of information about people, places, and

indigenous products that have contributed to America's nourishment." She reprinted recipes for gumbo, cranberry pie, anadama bread, cornbread stuffing, and pecan pie, dishes with a decidedly historical rather than contemporary flavor and featuring native plants. Ickeringill, "Out of Our Past: Our Past," *New York Times*, September 27, 1964, SM111.

76. Narcisse Chamberlain and Narcissa G. Chamberlain, *The Chamberlain Sampler of American Cooking* (New York: Hastings House, 1961), v.

77. Ibid., vii.

78. Ibid., vi. The choice of steak and kidney pie, a British tradition that had not been popular in the United States since the nineteenth century, is surprising.

79. Ibid., vi.

80. Hewitt, *The New York Times Heritage Cook Book*, xv.

81. Ibid., xv.

82. Raymond Sokolov, *Fading Feast: A Compendium of Disappearing American Regional Foods* (1979; New York: Farrar, Strauss, Giroux, 1981), 8.

83. In 1956, the chairman of the board of the National Trust for Historic Preservation reported that sales of cakes made from historic recipes Helen Bullock had adapted were "manna from heaven" because they increased both revenue and interest at historic sites. No author, "Old Recipes Save U.S. Landmarks," *New York Times*, October 20, 1956, 21.

84. Notably lacking from the usual American origin story are the Spanish settlers who inhabited Florida and the Southwest before the English established either Jamestown or Plimouth.

85. Jane Whitehill, *Food, Drink, and Recipes of Early New England* (Sturbridge, Mass.: Old Sturbridge Village, 1963), 23.

86. Letha Booth, *The Williamsburg Cookbook* (Williamsburg, Va.: Colonial Williamsburg Foundation, 1971; distributed by Holt, Rinehart and Winston), 2. An earlier cookbook produced by the site in 1938 was perhaps a bit too authentic seeming to gain a wide audience. It was printed at the site's own printing press and used the "medial s," which is easily confused with a lowercase "f," even though many of the recipes were borrowed from nineteenth-century books that used modern typography. Helen Bullock, *The Williamsburg Art of Cookery: Or, Accomplished Gentlewoman's Companion* (Williamsburg, Va.: Printed for Colonial Williamsburg, incorporated, on the press of A. Dietz and his son, 1938).

87. George Percy, "A True Relation of the Proceedings and Occurances of Moment which have happened in Virginia from the Time Thomas Gates shipwrecked upon the Bermudes," London, 1624. Percy was governor of Virginia during the Starving Time of 1609–1610.

88. In 2006, Edna Lewis, *The Taste of Country Cooking* (New York: Knopf, 1976), was reissued in a thirtieth anniversary edition.

89. Edna Lewis, *The Edna Lewis Cook Book* (Indianapolis: Bobbs-Merrill, 1972)

90. For a discussion of the commemorative aspects of *The Taste of Country Cooking*, see Rafia Zafar, "Elegy and Remembrance in the Cookbooks of Alice B. Toklas and Edna Lewis," *MELUS: Multi-Ethnic Literature of the U.S.* 38, 4 (Winter 2013).

91. Miriam Ungerer, Book Review, "American Food: The Gastronomic Story," *New York* 14, 50 (December 21, 1981): 77–78.

92. Lewis, *The Edna Lewis Cookbook*, 3.

93. Judith Jones, *The Tenth Muse* (New York: Anchor, 2008), 116–17.

94. Lewis, *The Taste of Country Cooking*, 242.

95. Ibid., 30.

96. Ibid., 182.

CHAPTER 5. OPPOSITIONAL APPETITES: COOKBOOKS AND THE COUNTERCULTURE IN THE 1960S AND 1970S

1. Lucinda Franks, "Red Dye No. 2: The 20-Year Battle," *New York Times*, February 28, 1976, 45.

2. Adelle Davis, *Let's Cook It Right* (New York: Harcourt, Brace & World, 1962), 8.

3. Ibid.

4. Lois Palmer, "Let's Cook It Right: Good Health Comes from Good Cooking" (Book Review), *New York Times* (Early City Edition), May 25, 1947, 28.

5. Jane Howard, "Earth Mother to the Foodists," *Life*, October 22, 1971, 67.

6. Mary Ann Cronin, "Keep the Crap Out of the Kitchen," *Off Our Backs* 1, 5 (May 16, 1970): 16.

7. True Light Beavers, *Eat, Fast, Feast* (Garden City, N.Y.: Doubleday, 1972)

8. Ibid., 154.

9. Robert Houriet, *Getting Back Together* (New York: Coward, McCann, 1971), xiii n.

10. Hugh Gardner, *The Children of Prosperity* (New York: St. Martin's, 1978).

11. Elinor Lander Horwitz, *Communes in America: The Place Just Right* (Philadelphia: Lippincott, 1972), 151.

12. Ron E. Roberts, *The New Communes: Coming Together in America* (Englewood Cliffs, N.J.: Prentice Hall, 1971), 50.

13. Agnes Toms, *Eat, Drink and Be Healthy* (New York: Devin-Adair, 1963), v.

14. Ibid., ix.

15. For more about consumer cooperatives, see Tracey Deutsch, *Building a Housewife's Paradise* (Chapel Hill: University of North Carolina Press, 2010), esp. chap. 4, "Moments of Rebellion: The Consumer Movement and Consumer Cooperatives, 1930–1950."

16. For a discussion of the pasteurization movement, see Daniel Block, "Purity, Economy, and Social Welfare in the Progressive Era Pure Milk Movement," *Journal for the Study of Food and Society* 3, 1 (Spring 1999): 20–27; Toms, *Eat, Drink and Be Healthy*, ix.

17. Jane Howard, "Earth Mother to the Foodists," *Life* 71, 17 (October 22, 1971): 67–70, 67.

18. Literary scholar Daniel Cordle argues that "it is suspense—anticipation of disaster, rather than disaster itself—that defines the period," so it is not surprising to find a note of panic in cookbooks of the 1960s and 1970s. He also remarks that "The recurrent image in civil defense literature and discourse was that of the single house, usually suburban, usually middle class." Daniel Cordle, *States of Suspense: The Nuclear Age, Postmodernism and United States Fiction and Prose* (Manchester: Manchester University Press, 2008), 2, 90.

19. Davis, *Let's Cook It Right*, 7.

20. U.S. Department of Defense, *Fallout Protection* (Washington, D.C.: Government Printing Office, 1961), 32, 41.

21. Cronin, "Keep the Crap Out of the Kitchen," 16. It is worth noting here that despite her feminism, Cronin did not critique the cultural expectation that women were responsible not only for feeding their families but also for giving them food they liked.

22. Irma Rombauer and Marion Rombauer Becker, *The Joy of Cooking* (Indianapolis: Bobbs-Merrill, 1951).

23. Anne Mendelson, *Stand Facing the Stove: The Story of the Women Who Gave America The Joy of Cooking* (New York: Scribner, 1996), 263.

24. Natural Food Associates of Albuquerque, *Tempting and Nutritious Recipes for the Avant-Garde Hostess and Homemaker* (Milwaukee: Lee Foundation for Nutritional Research, 1961). According to Richard McCord, the book was still in print in 2009; McCord, *Santa Fe Living Treasures: Our Elders, Our Hearts*, vol. 2 (Santa Fe: Sunstone, 2009), 36.

25. Natural Food Associates, *Tempting and Nutritious Recipes*, i.

26. Bernard Jensen, *Vital Foods for Total Health* (Los Angeles: Bernard Jensen, 1952), 7th page (pages unnumbered).

27. John T. Edge, "Hummus Catches On," *New York Times*, June 15, 2010.

28. Natural Food Associates, *Tempting and Nutritious Recipes*, vi.

29. Euell Gibbons, *Stalking the Wild Asparagus* (New York: David McKay, 1962),

30. John McPhee, "A Forager," *New Yorker*, April 6, 1968 "[During the Great Depression Gibbons's] father left in a desperate search for work. The food supply diminished until all that was left were a few pinto beans and a single egg, which no one would eat. Euell, then teen-aged and one of four children, took a knapsack one morning and left for the Horizon mountains. He came back with puffball mushrooms, piñon nuts, and fruits of yellow prickly pear. For nearly a month, the family lived wholly on what he provided."

31. Craig Claiborne, "Food Forager Makes Use of Bounty of Nature," *New York Times*, June 8, 1962, 36.

32. David L. Goodrich, "Stalking the Weed Eater," *Saturday Evening Post*, July 25, 1964, 22–23.

33. Gibbons, *Stalking the Wild Asparagus*, 5.

34. Ibid., 7. See also Euell Gibbons, *Stalking the Blue-Eyed Scallop* (New York: David McKay, 1964) and .Euell Gibbons, *Stalking the Wild Asparagus Field Guide Edition* (New York: David McKay, 1970)

35. Ibid., 9.

36. Grace Elizabeth Hale, *A Nation of Outsiders: How the White Middle Class Fell in Love with Rebellion in Postwar America* (Oxford: Oxford University Press, 2011).

37. Gibbons, *Stalking the Wild Asparagus*. Wild wine: "I consider myself fairly knowledgeable when it comes to tastes in food, but I am afraid I am no judge of wine. I find most wines nauseating, even those which are highly praised by the experts . . . However, on two occasions I tasted sweet wines made of wild grapes which I thought the finest drinks that had ever passed my lips" (99). Suburbs as foraging sites: "Come with me for an hour's walk in almost any rural or suburban area in the eastern half of our country, and I will point out . . . many edible wild plants to you. . . . I have collected fifteen species that could be used for food on a vacant lot right in Chicago. Eighteen different kinds were pointed out in the circuit of a two-acre pond near Philadelphia" (4).

38. These numbers were obtained using the Worldcat database of books stored in libraries worldwide, searching for books in English under the subject heading "Cooking (Natural Foods)." Some of the titles generated through this search are from English-speaking nations other than the United States, such as England, Canada, and Australia, and I have attempted to leave those out of my count. Some are also reprints of books published earlier in the same time span, but I chose to count those because reprinting indicates the popularity of the theme.

39. Susan Dart, "Natural Foods," *Chicago Tribune*, January 2, 1981, N8.

40. Warren Belasco, *Appetite for Change: How the Counterculture Took on the Food Industry*, 2nd updated ed. (Ithaca, N.Y.: Cornell University Press, 2007).

41. Carl Larsen and James Singer, eds., *The Beat Generation Cook Book* (New York: 7 Poets Press, 1961), no page numbers.

42. Ibid.

43. Ibid.

44. Panama Rose (Ira Cohen), *The Hashish Cookbook* (San Francisco: Gnaoua Press, 1966).

45. Sarah W. Tracy and Caroline Jean Acker, "Introduction," in Tracy and Acker, eds., *Altering American Consciousness: The History of Alcohol and Drug Use in the United States, 1800–2000* (Amherst: University of Massachusetts Press, 2004), 9. As one historian of American drug culture notes, the Beats "enlarged the repertoire of hip drugs and the 'meaning' of using them," because "they believed that drugs had a major and significant role to play in opening closed minds to higher experience." Jill Jonnes, *Hep-Cats, Narcs, and Pipe Dreams: A History of America's Romance with Illegal Drugs* (New York: Scribner, 1996), 215.

46. Marcia Seligson, "What We Need Now Is Another French Cookbook," *New York Times*, November 10, 1969.

47. Alice May Brock, *Alice's Restaurant Cookbook* (New York: Random House, 1969), 3.

48. Ibid., 4. Historian Sam Binkley has persuasively identified the quality of "looseness" as the essential commodity of the counterculture. Of the nonfiction literature of the 1970s specifically, Binkley argues, "Through advisory narratives on diet, relationships, exercise, home furnishing, travel, sex, home economics, cycling, recycling, gardening, massages, home birth, and Volkswagen repair, readers were exhorted to relax into their immediate experiences and live themselves in the daily flow of events." Sam Binkley, *Getting Loose: Lifestyle Consumption in the 1970s* (Durham, N.C.: Duke University Press, 2007), 102.

49. Ita Jones, *The Grubbag: An Underground Cookbook* (New York: Vintage, 1971), 159; Verta Mae (Smart-Grosvenor), *Vibration Cooking; or, The Travel Notes of a Geechee Girl* (Garden City, N.Y.: Doubleday, 1970), xii.

50. Verta Mae, *Vibration Cooking* , xiv.

51. Brock, *Alice's Restaurant Cookbook*, 8; Verta Mae, *Vibration Cooking*, xiv.

52. Brock, *Alice's Restaurant Cookbook*, 30.

53. Alicia Bay Laurel, *Living on the Earth* (New York: Vintage, 1971).

54. Binkley argues that countercultural text design challenged "the typographic control of space" by using hand writing instead of print, spilling text across margins in a style that "sought to represent . . . a certain social informality, intimacy, and group membership against the anonymity and authority" of the typical fact-based layout. Binkley, *Getting Loose*, 107.

55. Raymond Mungo, "Her Hymn to Nature Is a Guidebook for the Simplest of Lives," *New York Times*, March 26, 1971, 34.

56. Robert Dahlin, "Nature & Environment: Nurturing the Whole Earth's Catalogue," *Publishers Weekly*, October 4, 1999.

57. Laurel, *Living on the Earth*, iv.

58. Ibid., 164.

59. Edward Espe Brown, *The Tassajara Bread Book* (Boulder, Colo.: Shambhala, 1970); Edward Espe Brown, *Tassajara Cooking* (Boulder, Colo.: Shambhala, 1973).

60. Ann Hodgman, "Flour Power," *New York Times*, March 30, 2003, C36.

61. Richard Seager, *Buddhism in America* (New York: Columbia University Press, 2000), 99.

62. Brown, *Tassajara Cooking*, 255.

63. Having visited forty-three communes in America and Canada, cookbook writer Lucy Horton noted, "All communes have a shelf of cookbooks, ranging from *Cosmic Cookery* and the *Tassajara Bread Book* to *The Fannie Farmer Cookbook*, with *The Joy of Cooking* the overwhelming favorite." Lucy Horton, *Country Commune Cooking* (New York: Coward, McCann, 1972), 54.

64. Hodgman, "Flour Power."

65. Stephanie Hargman, a historian of counterculture cookbooks, explained, Brown's "guidelines are freeform, to encourage the cook to take cues from the food rather than slavishly follow instructions. Whatever you make, then, ultimately becomes your recipe, and that recipe might just be a one-time performance." Hargman, "The Political Palate: Reading Commune Cookbooks," *Gastronomica* 3, 2 (Spring 2003): 29–40, 37.

66. Brown, *The Tassajara Bread Book*, 2.

67. Ibid., 2.

68. Warren Belasco argues that once white bread had been widely demonized as symbolic of social artificiality, "Baking brown bread nicely balanced the personal and political—a craft and a statement, a first step toward self-reliance." Belasco, *Appetite for Change*, 50.

69. Horton, *Country Commune Cooking*, 158.

70. Horwitz, *Communes in America*, 155.

71. Horton, *Country Commune Cooking*, 169–70.

72. Molly O'Neill, Foreword to Elizabeth David, *Summer Cooking* (New York: New York Review of Books, 2002), 5.

73. Peter Rabbit, quoted in Gardner, *The Children of Prosperity*, 38.

74. Horton, *Country Commune Cooking*, 13, 15, 14.

75. Ibid., 15. William Wallace Irwin, *The Garrulous Gourmet* (New York: McBride, 1952?), 3.

76. Horton, *Country Commune Cooking*, 15.

77. Ibid, 15, 54, 59.

78. Ibid., 27, 37.

79. True Light Beavers, *Eat, Fast, Feast*, 206.

80. Horton, *Country Commune Cooking*, 56, 127, 165.

81. Crescent Dragonwagon, *The Commune Cookbook* (New York: Simon and Schuster, 1972), 12. It's important to note that in Dragonwagon's commune, men were also regularly involved in cooking. Although it is the case that traditional gender roles persisted in many communes, men were more frequently involved in commune cooking than in traditional single family homes during this period. Communes, because they were large, tended to assign teams to kitchen duties and these teams were typically made up of both men and women.

82. Ibid., 19.

83. Dragonwagon, *The Commune Cookbook*, 24.

84. Horton, *Country Commune Cooking*, 60, 186.

85. Frances Moore Lappé, *Diet for a Small Planet* (New York: Friends of the Earth/Ballantine, 1971), 123.

86. Ibid., 130.

87. Mollie Katzen, *Moosewood Cookbook* (Berkeley, Calif.: Ten Speed Press, 1977), vii.

88. Nancy Harmon Jenkins, "A Restaurant of Ideas and Ideals," *New York Times*, October 24, 1990, C1; Belasco, *Appetite for Change*, 94–96.

89. Katzen, *Moosewood Cookbook*, viii.

90. Dragonwagon, *The Commune Cookbook*, 150.

91. True Light Beavers, *Eat, Fast, Feast*, 244.

92. Dragonwagon's parents were Ellen Zolotow, who wrote children's books, and biographer Maurice Zolotow.

93. For example, "At Total Loss Farm the Vermont commune made famous by Ray Mungo, I greeted Richard with 'Hi! I'm writing a commune cookbook!' He smiled mysteriously. 'So are we,' he replied. His family even had a contract, unlike me. We sat around in the kitchen and talked obliquely for an hour." The commune produced *Home Comfort: Life on Total Loss Farm*, published by Doubleday in 1973. Mostly collective memoir, the book includes a short recipe section that was the typical mixture of traditional mainstream American recipes, such as pumpkin pie, and more international and experimental fare—whole wheat battered tempura. Horton, *Country Commune Cooking*, 52.

94. Sigrid M. Shepard, *Natural Food Feasts from the Eastern World* (New York: Arco, 1976); Lillian Langseth-Christensen, *The Down-to-Earth Natural Food Cookbook* (New York: Grosset & Dunlap, 1973); Marguerite Patten, *Health Food Cookery* (London: Hamlyn, 1972); Gail L. Worstman, *The Whole Grain Bake Book* (Seattle: Pacific Search Press, 1980).

95. Eleanor Levitt, *The Wonderful World of Natural Food Cookery* (Great Neck, N.Y.: Hearthside, 1971), 15–16.

96. Levitt, *The Wonderful World of Natural Food Cookery*, 28, 154.

97. Ibid., 154.

98. Jean Hewitt, *The New York Times Natural Foods Cookbook* (New York: Quadrangle, 1971), 2.

99. Ibid.

100. Ibid., 5.

101. Ibid., 5.

102. Ibid. Health food cookbooks, like Lappé's, did typically assume a female reader with sole responsibility for feeding a family. While happy to introduce new foodways, these authors generally did not challenge existing gender ideologies or the cultural norm of the nuclear family.

103. Alice Waters, *The Chez Panisse Menu Cookbook* (New York: Random House, 1982)

104. Craig Claiborne and Pierre Franey, "Going by the Book," *New York Times*, December 5, 1982, SM156.

105. Waters, *Chez Panisse Menu Cookbook*, ix.

106. Julia Child, *My Year in France* (New York: Anchor, 2006), 18–19. Recalling her first taste of *sole meunière* at La Couronne in Rouen, she wrote, "at La Couronne I experienced fish, and a dining experience, of a higher order than any I'd ever had before."

107. Waters, *The Chez Panisse Menu Cookbook*, x.

108. Barbara Kafka, "Tres Fresh," *Vogue* 172, 11 (November 1, 1982): 368–71, 404.

109. Waters, *The Chez Panisse Menu Cookbook*, xi.

110. Ibid., x.

111. Ibid., 3.

112. Ibid., 7.

113. Brown, *The Tassajara Cook Book*, vi; Waters, *The Chez Panisse Menu Cookbook*, 5, 10.

114. Waters, *The Chez Panisse Menu Cookbook*, 16.

115. Ibid., 260. Jeremiah Tower also tells this story in *Jeremiah Tower's New American Classics* (New York: Harper and Row, 1986), 12.

116. Nathan Myhrvold, Chris Young, and Maxime Bilet, *Modernist Cuisine: The Art and Science of Cooking* (Bellevue, Wash.: Cooking Lab, 2011).

117. Michael Ruhlman, "Cook from It? First, Try Lifting It," *New York Times*, March 8, 2011.

118. Christopher Idone, *Glorious American Food* (New York: Random House, 1985), 1.

119. James M. Lawrence, "Does the World Really Need Another Food Magazine," *Eating Well*, premier issue (October 1990): 7.

120. Walter Scheib, *White House Chef* (New York: Wiley, 2007), 215.

CHAPTER 6. THE PALATE OF PERSONALITY: CHEFS AND COOKBOOKS AT THE END OF THE TWENTIETH CENTURY

1. Gourmet Magazine, *The Gourmet Cookbook* (New York: Gourmet, 1950).

2. Nora Ephron, *I Feel Bad About My Neck* (New York: Knopf, 2006), 18.

3. Nora Ephron, "Critiques in the World of the Rising Souffle (Or Is It the Rising Meringue?)," *New York Magazine*, September 30, 1968, 39.

4. Jeremiah Tower, *Jeremiah Tower's New American Classics* (New York: Harper & Row, 1986).

5. Ellen Brown, *Cooking with the New American Chefs* (New York: Harper & Row, 1985),

6. Thomas MacNamee, *Alice Waters and Chez Panisse* (New York: Penguin, 2007), 127.

7. Brown, *Cooking with the New American Chefs*, 10–11.

8. Wolfgang Puck, *The Wolfgang Puck Cookbook* (New York: Random House, 1986), xiv.

9. Lois Dwan, "At Spago, Who Needs Truffles?" *Los Angeles Times*, May 9, 1982, J1.

10. Marian Burros, "Cooking Is Becoming a Choice Career for Americans," *New York Times*, March 24, 1982, C1.

11. Michael Korda, *Another Life: A Memoir of Other People* (New York: Random House, 1999), 398–99; Charlotte Adams and James Beard, *The Four Seasons Cookbook* (New York: Holt, Rinehart and Wilson, 1971).

12. Andrew Dornenburg and Karen Page, *Becoming a Chef: With Recipes and Reflections from America's Leading Chefs* (New York: Van Nostrand Reinhold, 1995), 14.

13. Ibid., 14, xxiii.

14. Madeleine Kamman, Introduction to Dornenburg and Page, *Becoming a Chef*, xviii.

15. Mark Charles Miller, *Coyote Cafe* (Berkeley, Calif.: Ten Speed Press, 1989), xv; Anne Lindsay Greer, *Foods of the Sun: New Southwest Cuisine* (New York: Harper & Row, 1986), 13.

16. Miller, *Coyote Cafe*, 79.

17. Ruth Reichl, "The Coyote Cafe Finally Howls," *Los Angeles Times* April 5, 1987, K94.

18. James Beard, *The New James Beard* (New York: Knopf, 1981), vi, ix. Beard's new attitude is another example of the encouragement to "get loose," that Sam Binkley chronicles in the 1970s. Sam Binkley, *Getting Loose: Lifestyle Consumption in the 1970s* (Chapel Hill: University of North Carolina Press, 2007).

19. John R. Thelin, *A History of American Higher Education* (Baltimore: Johns Hopkins

University Press, 2004, 2011), 52. For a broader discussion of identity politics in the 1980s and 1990s, see Daniel T. Rodgers, *Age of Fracture* (Cambridge: Harvard University Press, 2011).

20. Miller, *Coyote Cafe*, preface.

21. Ibid., xi.

22. Brown, *Cooking with the New American Chefs*, 109, 75.

23. Michael Roberts, *Secret Ingredients* (New York: Bantam, 1988), 3.

24. Ibid., 8.

25. Pete Wells, "When He Dined, the Stars Came Out," *New York Times*, May 8, 2012.

26. Ibid.

27. Nika Hazelton, *American Home Cooking* (New York: Viking, 1980), 7.

28. James Villas, "From the Abundant Land: at Last, a Table of Our Own," *Town and Country*, 130–66, June 1976.

29. Larry Forgione, *An American Place* (New York: William Morrow, 1996), dedication.

30. Ibid., 3.

31. Ibid., 17, 150.

32. Stephen Langlois, *Prairie Cuisine from the Heartland* (Chicago: Contemporary, 1990), 1.

33. Betty Fussell, *Masters of American Cookery* (Lincoln: University of Nebraska Press, 2005), 43.

34. Josee Johnston and Shyon Baumann explore this rhetorical setting in *Foodies*, their study of gourmet attitudes in contemporary North America. Baumann and Johnston find that the notion of world food reinforces the idea of Western exceptionalism that subtly unsettles the equality of world cultures. As Johnston and Baumann write, "Exoticism is an important strategy for validating foods in an omnivorous culinary discourse." If, as is the case in urban America, diners have access to iterations of many cuisines, the work of distinction becomes more complex. Johnston and Baumann found that "the search for socially and geographically distant and norm-breaking foods allows foodies," the contemporary version of the gourmet, "to signal distinction without offending democratic sensibilities." Status among the connoisseurs no longer derives from eating the most expensive meal but from eating (and talking about) the most unusual. Josee Johnston and Shyon Bauman, *Foodies* (New York: Routledge, 2010), 122.

35. Lisa Heldke, "Let's Cook Thai," in Sherrie Innes, ed., *Pilaf, Pozole, and Pad Thai* (Amherst: University of Massachusetts Press, 2001), 176. Heldke identifies her behavior and that of others of her adventurous class: "I put a name to my penchant for ethnic foods—particularly the foods of economically dominated cultures. The name I chose was 'cultural food colonialism'" (177).

36. Caroline Bates, "Good Evening, Vietnam," *Gourmet* 61, 1 (2001): 46–47.

37. Dorothy Kalins, *Saveur* 1, 1 (Summer 1994): 11.

38. Ibid.

39. Ibid.

40. "Not in *This* Lifetime," *Saveur* 1, 1 (Summer 1994): 16.

41. "Never Eat at a Restaurant ..." *Saveur*, 1, 2 (September/October 1994): 17.

42. Peter Hellman, "Baking It," *Saveur*, 1, 1 (Summer 1994): 33.

43. Allison Engel, "The Cherry Orchard," *Saveur* 1, 2 (September/October 1994): 35.

44. *Saveur* 1, 2 (September/October 1994): 15.

45. Cynthia Hacinli "Fishing Camp Cooking," *Saveur* 1, 2 (September/October 1994): 97.

46. Robin Gourley, "Coocolate Cake," *Saveur* 1, 2 (September/October 1994): 51.

47. Ibid. 51; Ann Mendelson, "The 1970s," 61, 9 (September 2001): 153–57.

48. Hacinli, "Fishing Camp Cooking."

49. Dorothy Kalins, "Come into Our Kitchen" *Saveur* 1, 2 (September/October 1994): 9.

50. Dacquoise is a classic French dessert made from layers of hazelnut meringue and buttercream.

51. Unidentified reader, quoted by unidentified editor, "Sugar and Spice," August 2001, 20.

52. Paul Luna, "Texts and Technology 1970–2000," in Simon Eliot and Jonathan Rose, eds., *A Companion to the History of the Book* (Oxford: Blackwell, 2007), 385, 389.

53. Philip B. Meggs, *Meggs' History of Graphic Design* (Hoboken, N.J.: Wiley, 2006), 494.

54. Luna, "Texts and Technology 1970–2000," 390.

55. Ruth Reichl, "Letter from the Editor," *Gourmet* 59, 9 (September 1999), 24.

56. Ibid.

57. Letter from Jeff Inslee, "Sugar and Spice," *Gourmet* 61, 1 (January 2001): 23. Inslee was referring to Stern's "The One and Only" about the Downing Cafe in Downing, Wisconsin, *Gourmet* 60, 11 (November 2000): 126–30.

58. Jane Stern and Michael Stern, "Two for the Road," *Gourmet* 55, 6 (June 1995): 132.

59. Barbara Frey Waxman has defined the genre as work that "like the *bildungsroman*, traces the evolution of a youth into a mature food aficionado, into a food professional and (often) into a contented adult." "Food Memoirs: What They Are, Why They Are Popular, and Why They Belong in the Literature Classroom," *College English* 70, 4 Special Issue: Food (March 2008): 364.

60. Virginia B. Wood, "Foodie Fiction," *Austin Chronicle*, June 13, 1997.

61. Nora Ephron, *Heartburn* (New York: Vintage Contemporaries, 1996), 119.

62. Ibid., 6.

63. Laurie Colwin, *More Home Cooking: A Writer Returns to the Kitchen* (New York: HarperCollins, 1993), 81.

64. Ruth Reichl, *Tender at the Bone*, New York: Random House, 2010.

65. Anthony Bourdain, *Kitchen Confidential* (New York: Ecco Press, 2000), 5.

66. *Taste of Home*, premier ed., 1, 1 (February/March 1993): 2.

67. Ibid.

68. The selection of editors was explained in the first issue. The editors were chosen in two ways: 1) contacted people who had sent in recipes to company's other magazines 2) asked home ec. extension agents to identify the three best cooks in an area, then contacted them. "from this list we carefully selected the ones we felt would make the biggest contribution to future issues." *Taste of Home*, premier ed., 44.

69. Ibid., 18.

70. Phillip Stephen Schulz, *As American as Apple Pie* (New York: Simon and Schuster, 1990), 11.

71. Ibid., 12.

72. "Checking in with the Experts," *Taste of Home*, premier ed., 62.

73. Dorothy Pritchett, "Empty Nesters," *Taste of Home*, premier ed. 1, 1 (February/March 1993):13; Ena Quiggle, "Cashew Chicken," recipe, *Taste of Home* 1, 3 (June/July 1993): 29.

74. Anne Mendelson, "Should Chefs Write Cookbooks?" *Gourmet* 9, 10 (September 1999): 136.

75. Ibid.

76. Florence Fabricant, "The Man Who Would Turn Chefs into Household Names," *New York Times*, March 17, 1993, C1.

77. Mendelson, "Should Chefs Write Cookbooks?" 136.

78. In an article in *Gastronomica*, in which she considered twenty food blogs published by women, Paula Salvio found language and assumptions that reflected "a domestic ideology that resonates with white, middle-class, post-World War II discourses." Although using a modern form to express the role of food in their lives, female food bloggers seemed to be upholding less progressive ideals. Paula M. Salvio, "Dishing It Out: Food Blogs and Post-Feminist Domesticity," *Gastronomica* 12, 3 (Fall 2012): 31–39, 32.

79. Celia Barbour, "For Orange Zest, Substitute Kool-Aid," *New York Times*, March 21, 2007.

CHAPTER 7. ORIGIN STORIES: A NEW DISCOURSE IN TWENTY-FIRST-CENTURY COOKBOOKS

1. Raj Patel's *Stuffed and Starved* is probably the best-known book to explore the coexistence of surplus and starvation in world food markets. Raj Patel, *Stuffed and Starved: The Hidden Battle for the World Food System* (New York: Melville House, 2008).

2. Jeff Crump and Bettina Schormann, *Earth to Table: Seasonal Recipes from an Organic Farm* (New York: Ecco/HarperCollins, 2009), 6.

3. In June 2014, *New York Times* food writer Kim Severson likened the gluten-free trend to nouvelle cuisine in terms of its potential to bring permanent change to American cooking. Severson suggested, "For chefs, gluten-free eating could change forever the role of grains in the kitchen just as the French nouvelle cuisine movement led to lighter, simpler dishes that considered the health of the diner as well as the taste of the raw ingredients." Kim Severson, "Gluten-Free Eating Appears to Be Here to Stay" *New York Times*, June 18, 2014, D1.

4. Michael Steinberger, *Au Revoir to All That: Food, Wine, and the End of France* (London: Bloomsbury, 2010), 31–32.

5. Julia Child, "'La Nouvelle Cuisine': A Skeptic's View," *New York*, July 4, 1977, 32–34.

6. Ibid.

7. Jean and Pierre Troisgros, *The Nouvelle Cuisine of Jean and Pierre Troisgros*, trans. Roberta Wolfe Smoler (New York: Morrow, 1978).

8. William Bayer and Paula Wolfert, "The New Cookbooks: Tasters' Choice," *New York*, 82.

9. Ibid.

10. Michele Urvater and David Liederman, *Cooking the Nouvelle Cuisine in America* (New York: Workman, 1982), 18.

11. Ibid., 18–19.

12. Ibid., 28, 24.

13. James Beard, *The Four Seasons Cookbook* (New York: Holt, Rinehart, 1971), 12–13.

14. Stephen Langlois, *Prairie Cuisine from the Heartland* (Chicago: Contemporary Books, 1990), 2.

15. Larry Forgione, *An American Place* (New York: William Morrow, 1996), 6.

16. Walter Scheib, *White House Chef* (Hoboken, N.J.: John Wiley, 2007), 266.

17. First published in 2006, Michael Pollan's *The Omnivore's Dilemma: A Natural History of Four Meals* (New York: Penguin, 2006) sold 310,150 copies in 2008, when it was published in paperback, according to *Publishers Weekly*. Dermot McEvoy, "Bestselling Paperback Books of 2009," *Publisher's Weekly* 256, 12 (March 23, 2009).

18. Eric Schlosser, *Fast Food Nation: The Dark Side of the All-American Meal* (Boston: Houghton Mifflin, 2001); Morgan Spurlock, *Supersize Me*, Samuel Goldwyn Films, 2004.

19. For figures on the more recent growth of farmers markets, see the U.S. Department of Agriculture chart, which shows that markets increased from 1,755 in 1994 to more than 8,000 in 2013: USDA, *Farmers Market Growth*, Agricultural Marketing Service, 2012; Pollan, *The Omnivore's Dilemma*, 8.

20. For example, *King Corn*, a film (in which Pollan appears) attacks corn subsidies and high fructose corn syrup production. Curt Ellis, Ian Cheney, *King Corn*, dir. Curt Ellis, Ian Cheney, Aaron Woolf; New York: Docudrama Films, distributed by New Video, 2008.

21. Thomas McNamee, *Alice Waters and Chez Panisse* (New York: Penguin, 2007), 336–37.

22. Ibid.

23. About the "eat your lawn" movement, see Patricia Leigh Brown, "Redefining American Beauty, by the Yard," *New York Times*, July 13, 2006.

24. Michael Pollan, *In Defense of Food* (New York: Penguin), 2008; Crump and Schormann, *Earth to Table*, 6.

25. Evan Jones, "The American Scene," *Gourmet* 45, 8 (August 1985): 66.

26. Pollan, *In Defense of Food*, 196.

27. Michael Pollan, *The Botany of Desire* (New York: Random House, 2001).

28. Julie Guthman argues that Pollan's answer, to the "what to eat" dilemma, "albeit oblique, is to eat like he does." Guthman, "Can't Stomach It: How Michael Pollan, et al. Made Me Want to Eat Cheetos," *Gastronomica* 7, 3 (Summer 2007): 75–79, 78.

29. Julie Powell, *Julie and Julia* (New York: Little Brown, 2005), 15.

30. Rachel Laudan, "A Plea for Culinary Modernism: Why We Should Love New, Fast, Processed Food," *Gastronomica* 1, 1 (Winter 2001): 36–44, 42, 40, 39.

31. Pollan addressed his critics by acknowledging that the poor have few options to eat "well." Michael Pollan, "Why Eating Well Is Elitist," *New York Times*, May 11, 2006.

32. Laudan might suggest a likely third choice, to find some way to process the mushroom to make it edible. She reminds readers that many staple foods of world populations— maize, taro, wheat—are inedible or even poisonous in their natural state. Laudan, "A Plea for Culinary Modernism," 36–44.

33. Marilou Suszko, *The Locavore's Kitchen* (Athens: Ohio University Press, 2011), i, xx.

34. Ann Vileisis, *Kitchen Literacy* (Washington, D.C.: Covello, 2008), 6–11.

35. Ibid.; Amy Cotler, *The Locavore Way* (North Adams, Mass.: Storey Press, 2008), 2.; Jim Denevan, *Outstanding in the Field* (New York: Clarkson Potter, 2008), 10.

36. Suszko, *The Locavore's Kitchen*, xiv–xv.

37. Virginia Heffernan and Amanda Hesser, "A Conversation About Food, Cooking and Alice B. Toklas," May 19, 2011, *New York Times Opinionator Blog*.

38. Barbara Kingsolver, *Animal, Vegetable, Miracle* (New York: HarperCollins, 2007).

39. Kingsolver's book won the James Beard Award for General Fiction in 2008.

40. Kingsolver, *Animal, Vegetable, Miracle*, 2.

41. Roger Cohen, "The World: Heartburn; Fearful over the Future, Europe Seizes on Food," *New York Times*, August 29, 1999.

42. Kingsolver, *Animal, Vegetable, Miracle*, 4.

43. Brett Laidlaw, *Trout Caviar: Recipes from a Northern Forager* (St. Paul: Minnesota Historical Society Press, 2011), 5.

44. Dan Hofstadter, "A Spirited Garden," *Gourmet* 52, 9 (September 2002): 82.

45. Among many examples of excellent work with this theme are Alice Julier, *Eating Together: Food, Friendship, and Inequality* (Urbana: University of Illinois Press, 2014) and Krishnendu Ray, *The Migrant's Table: Meals and Memories in Bengali-American Households* (Philadelphia: Temple University Press, 2004).

46. For example, see Robert Putnam, *Bowling Alone: The Collapse and Revival of American Community* (New York: Simon and Schuster, 2001).

47. Laidlaw, *Trout Caviar*, 4–5; Russ Parsons, *How to Pick a Peach: The Search for Flavor from Farm to Table* (Boston: Houghton Mifflin, 2007), vii; Susan Wiggins, "Locavore Literature," *Gastronomica* 8, 2 (Spring 2008): 85.

48. Wendell Berry, "The Pleasures of Eating," in *What Are People For* (Berkeley, Calif.: Counterpoint Press, 1990, 2010), 145.

49. Kingsolver, *Animal, Vegetable, Miracle*, 13.

50. Tim Porter and Farina Wong Kingsley, *Organic Marin* (Riverside, N.J.: Andrews McNeel, 2008), 5; Pollan, *In Defense of Food*, 192, 183. Paul Rozin et al., "Attitudes to Food and the Role of Food in Life in the U.S.A., Japan, Flemish Belgium and France: Possible Implications for the Diet-Health Debate," *Appetite* 33 (1999): 163–80, 179.

51. Pollan, *In Defense of Food*, 200.

52. Kingsolver, *Animal, Vegetable, Miracle*, 351.

53. Cotler, *The Locavore Way*, 148; Crump and Schormann, *Earth to Table*, 4.

54. Michael Pollan, *Food Rules* (New York: Penguin, 2009)

55. E. Melanie DuPuis, "Angels and Vegetables," *Gastronomica* 7, 3 (Summer 2007): 34–44, 43.

56. Vileisis, *Kitchen Literacy*, 6, 10.

57. Pollan, *In Defense of Food*, 3.

58. For an example of "fuss" about food, Ken Albala finds that during the European Renaissance "melons should be eaten with no other foods," but that if they accidentally were, wine might serve as "a corrective." Kan Albala, *Eating Right in the Renaissance* (Berkeley: University of California Press, 2002), 255.

59. The best book about food scarcity in America is Janet Poppendieck's *Breadlines Knee-Deep in Wheat*, new ed. (Berkeley: University of California Press, 2014).

60. Crump and Schormann, *Earth to Table*, 2.

61. Pollan, *In Defense of Food*, 181.

62. David Julian McClements, César Vega, Anne E. McBride, and Eric Andrew Decker, "In Defense of Food Science," *Gastronomica* 11, 2 (Summer 2011): 76–84.

63. Gregory Ziegler, "In Defense of Food Science," *Food Technology* (May 2008): 164.

64. Crump and Schormann, *Earth to Table*, 1.

65. "Farm," *Portlandia*. IFC, Season 1, Episode 1, 2011.

66. Powell, *Julie and Julia*, 41.

67. DuPuis, "Angels and Vegetables," 34–44.

68. Tracie McMillan, *The American Way of Eating* (New York: Scribner, 2012).

69. Crump and Schormann, *Earth to Table*, 7; Denevan, *Outstanding in the Field*, 9–10.

70. Aaron Bobrow-Strain, "Kills a Body Twelve Ways: Bread, Fear, and the Politics of 'What to Eat?'" *Gastronomica* 7, 3 (Summer 2007): 45–52, 49.

EPILOGUE. WHAT SHOULD WE READ FOR DINNER?

1. Nora Ephron, *Julie & Julia*, Columbia Pictures, 2009; Julie Powell, *Julie and Julia* (New York: Little Brown, 2005); Alex Prud'homme, *My Life in France* (New York: Knopf, 2006).

2. Julia Child, Louisette Bertholle, and Simone Beck, *Mastering the Art of French Cooking* (New York: Knopf, 1961).

3. The *Fannie Farmer Cookbook* is still in print in both its updated form and as a facsimile edition of the original, while *The Joy of Cooking*, still in print in revised form, has also spawned a series of single-topic books such as *Joy of Cooking: All About Soups and Stews* (2000), *Joy of Cooking: All About Grilling* (2001), and *Joy of Cooking: All About Pies and Tarts* (2002).

4. Better Homes and Gardens, *Better Homes and Gardens New Cook Book* (Des Moines, Iowa: Meredith, 1953), 124.

5. Deborah Perelman, *Smitten Kitchen*, January 24, 2008, http://smittenkitchen.com/blog/2008/11/pie-crust-102-all-butter-really-flaky-pie-dough/ (accessed February 6, 13).

6. Deborah Perelman, *The Smitten Kitchen Cookbook* (New York: Knopf, 2012).

7. Mark Rotella, "The Bestselling Cookbooks of 2012," *Publishers Weekly*, February 8, 2013.

8. Letter from W. P. Anderson, *Gourmet* 3, 1 (January 1943), 2.

SELECTED BIBLIOGRAPHY

COOKBOOK COLLECTIONS

Beatrice McIntosh Cookery Collection, University of Massachusetts at Amherst.

Fales Library Food and Cookery Collection, New York University.

Feeding America: The Historic American Cookbook Project, Michigan State University Library (online).

Library of Congress, Community Cookbooks: Selected Titles from the General Collections (online).

——. Rare Book and Special Collections Division.

Radcliffe Institute, Arthur and Elizabeth Schlesinger Library on the History of Women in America, Culinary Collection

Newcomb College Institute of Tulane University, Culinary Collection.

COOKBOOKS

Adams, Charlotte and James Beard. *The Four Seasons Cookbook*, New York: Holt, Rinehart, and Wilson, 1917.

Beard, James. *Cook It Outdoors*. New York; Barrows and Company, 1941.

——. *The Fireside Cook Book*. New York: Simon and Schuster, 1949.

——. *The New James Beard*. New York: Knopf, 1981.

Better Homes and Gardens. *Better Homes and Gardens New Cook Book*. Des Moines, Iowa: Better Homes and Gardens, 1953.

Betty Crocker's Picture Cook Book. New York: McGraw-Hill, 1950.

Booth, Letha. *The Williamsburg Cookbook*. Williamsburg, Va.: Colonial Williamsburg Foundation, distributed by Holt, Rinehart and Winston, 1971.

Bracken, Peg. *The I Hate to Cook Book*. New York: Harcourt, Brace, 1961.

Brock, Alice May. *Alice's Restaurant Cook Book*. New York: Random House, 1969.

Brown, Cora, Rose Brown, and Bob Brown. *The Wine Cook Book*. Boston: Little, Brown, 1934.

Brown, Dale. *American Cooking*. New York: Time-Life Books, 1968.

Brown, Edward Espe. *The Tassajara Bread Book*. Boston: Shambala, 1970.

——. *Tassajara Cooking*. Boulder, Colo.: Shambhala, 1974.

Brown, Ellen. *Cooking with the New American Chefs*. New York: Harper and Row.

Browne, Charles, *The Gun Club Cook Book*. New York: Scribner's, 1946.

Bullock, Helen. *The Williamsburg Art of Cookery: Or, Accomplished Gentlewoman's Companion*. Williamsburg, Va.: Printed for Colonial Williamsburg, incorporated, on the press of A. Dietz and his son, 1938.

California Fruit Growers Exchange. *For Vigorous Health: Sunkist Recipes for Every Day*. Los Angeles: California Fruit Growers Exchange, 1935.

Cannon, Poppy. *The Can-Opener Cookbook*. New York: Thomas Crowell, 1951.

Chamberlain, Narcisse and Narcissa G. Chamberlain. *The Chamberlain Sampler of American Cooking*. New York: Hastings House, 1961.

(Chamberlain, Samuel), Phineas Beck. *Clementine in the Kitchen*. New York: Hastings House, 1949.

Child, Lydia Maria. *The Frugal Housewife*. Boston: Carter and Hendee, 1830.

Child, Julia, Simone Beck, and Luisette Bertholle. *Mastering the Art of French Cooking*. New York: Knopf, 1961.

The Christian Woman's Exchange of New Orleans. *The Creole Cookery Book*. New Orleans: T.H. Thomason, 1885.

Corson, Juliet. *Miss Corson's Practical American Cookery and Household Management*. New York: Dodd, Mead, 1885.

Coudert, Jo. *The I Never Cooked Before Cook Book*. New York: Stein and Day, 1963.

Cotler, Amy. *The Locavore Way*. North Adams, Mass.: Storey Press, 2008.

Crump, Jeff and Bettina Schormann. *Earth to Table: Seasonal Recipes from an Organic Farm*. New York: Ecco/HarperCollins, 2009.

Dallin, Lynn. *Stay Out of the Kitchen Cookbook*. Garden City, N.Y.: Doubleday, 1968.

Davis, Adelle. *Let's Cook It Right*. New York: Harcourt, Brace, 1962.

De Knight, Freda. *Date with a Dish: A Cook Book of American Negro Recipes*. New York: Hermitage, 1948.

Denevan, Jim. *Outstanding in the Field: A Farm to Table Cookbook*. New York: Clarkson Potter, 2008.

Dragonwagon, Crescent. *The Commune Cookbook*. New York: Simon and Schuster, 1972.

Editors of American Heritage. *The American Heritage Cookbook and Illustrated History*. New York: American Heritage, distributed by Simon and Schuster, 1964.

Ellsworth, Mary Grosvenor. *Much Depends on Dinner*. New York: Knopf, 1939.

Esquire Magazine, *Esquire's Handbook for Hosts*. New York: Grosset & Dunlap, 1949.

Eustis, Celestine. *Cooking in Old Creole Days*. New York, R.H. Russell, 1904.

Fales Library. *101 Classic Cookbooks, 501 Classic Recipes*. New York: Rizzoli, 2012.

Farmer, Fannie Merritt. *The Boston Cooking-School Cook Book*. Boston: Little, Brown, 1896.

Fisher, Abby. *What Mrs. Fisher Knows About Old Southern Cooking*. San Francisco: Women's Co-op Printing Office, 1881.

Fisher, M. F. K. *The Art of Eating*. Cleveland: World, 1954.

——. *Serve It Forth*. New York: Harper & Brothers, 1937.

Forgione, Larry. *An American Place: Celebrating the Flavors of America*. New York: William Morrow, 1996.

Fox, Minnie. *Blue Grass Cookbook*. New York: Fox, Duffield, 1904.

Frigidaire Frozen Delights. Dayton, Ohio: Frigidaire, Corporation 1927.

Frigidaire Recipes. Dayton, Ohio: Frigidaire Corporation, 1929.

General Foods Corporation. *Correct Salads for All Occasions*. Minneapolis: General Foods Corporation, 1931.

Gibbons, Euell. *Stalking the Blue-Eyed Scallop*. New York: David McKay , 1964.

——. *Stalking the Wild Asparagus*. New York: David McKay, 1962.

Goudiss, C. Houston and Alberta M. Goudiss. *Foods That Will Win the War and How to Cook Them*. New York: World, 1918.

Gourmet Magazine. *The Gourmet Cookbook*. New York: Gourmet, 1950.

Green, Mary. *Better Meals for Less Money*. New York: Holt, 1917.

Greer, Anne Lindsay. *Foods of the Sun: New Southwest Cuisine*. New York: Harper & Row, 1986.

Hazelton, Nika. *American Home Cooking*. New York: Viking, 1980.

Hewitt, Jean. *The New York Times Heritage Cook Book*. New York: Putnam, 1972.

——. *The New York Times Natural Foods Cookbook*. New York: Quadrangle, 1971.

Horton, Lucy. *Country Commune Cooking*. New York: Coward, McCann & Geoghegan, 1972.

Idone, Christopher. *Glorious American Food*. New York: Random House, 1985.

Jensen, Bernard. *Vital Foods for Total Health*. Los Angeles: Bernard Jensen, 1952.

Jones, Evan. *American Food: The Gastronomic Story*. New York: E.P. Dutton, 1975.

Jones, Ita. *The Grubbag: An Underground Cookbook*. New York: Vintage, 1971.

Junior League of Charleston. *Charleston Receipts*. Charleston, S.C.: Walker, Evans & Cogswell, 1950.

Katzen, Mollie. *Moosewood Cookbook*. Berkeley, Calif.: Ten Speed Press, 1977.

Ladies Aid Society of the Fulton Presbyterian Church. *The Reappear: A Book of Choice Recipes*. Santa Rosa, Calif.: C.A. Wright, 1908.

Laidlaw, Brett. *Trout Caviar: Recipes from a Northern Forager*. St. Paul: Minnesota Historical Society Press, 2011.

Langlois, Stephen. *Prairie Cuisine from the Heartland*. Chicago: Contemporary Books, 1990.

Lappé, Frances Moore. *Diet for a Small Planet*. New York: Friends of the Earth/Ballantine, 1971.

Larsen, Carl and James Singer, eds. *The Beat Generation Cook Book*. New York: 7 Poets Press, 1961.

Laurel, Alicia Bay. *Living on the Earth*. New York: Vintage, 1971.

Lemke, Gesine. *How to Make Good Things to Eat*. Chicago: Libby, McNeil and Libby, 1900.

Leslie, Eliza. *Directions for Cookery in Its Various Branches*. Philadelphia: Carey & Hart, 1840.

Levitt, Eleanor. *The Wonderful World of Natural Food Cookery*. Great Neck, N.Y.: Hearthside, 1971.

Lewis, Edna. *The Edna Lewis Cookbook*. Indianapolis: Bobbs-Merrill, 1972.

——. *The Taste of Country Cooking*. New York: Knopf, 1976.

Lobel, Cindy R. *Urban Appetites: Food and Culture in Nineteenth-Century New York*. Chicago: University of Chicago Press, 2014.

Lynch, Reah Jeanette. *"Win the War" Cook Book*. St. Louis: St. Louis County Unit, Women's Committee, Council of National Defense, 1918.

MacDougal, Allan Ross. *The Gourmet's Almanac*. New York: Covici-Friede, 1930.

Miller, Mark Charles. *Coyote Cafe: Foods from the Great Southwest*. Berkeley, Calif.: Ten Speed Press, 1989.

Owen, Jeanne. *A Wine Lover's Cook Book*. New York: M. Barrows, 1940.

Ornish, Dean. *The Spectrum: A Scientifically Proven Program to Feel Better, Live Longer, Lose Weight, and Gain Health.* New York: Ballantine, 2007.

Panama Rose (Ira Cohen). *The Hashish Cookbook.* San Francisco: Gnaoua Press, 1966

Parloa, Maria. *First Principles of Household Management and Cookery.* Boston: Houghton, Mifflin, 1882.

Parsons, Russ. *How to Pick a Peach: The Search for Flavor from Farm to Table.* Boston: Houghton Mifflin, 2007.

Pellegrini, Angelo. *The Unprejudiced Palate.* New York: Modern Library, 2005.

Perelman, Deborah. *The Smitten Kitchen Cookbook.* New York: Knopf, 2012.

Peters, Lulu Hunt. *Diet and Health with Key to the Calories.* Chicago: Reilly and Lee, 1918.

Porter, Tim and Farina Wong Kingsley. *Organic Marin.* Riverside, N.J.: Andrews McMeel, 2008.

Puck, Wolfgang. *The Wolfgang Puck Cookbook.* New York: Random House, 1986.

Randolph, Mary. *The Virginia Housewife: or Methodical Cook.* Baltimore: Plaskitt, Fite, 1838.

Rankin, Louise. *An American Cookbook for India.* Calcutta: Thacker and Spink, 1933.

Roberson, John and Marie Roberson. *The Famous American Recipes Cookbook.* Englewood Cliffs, N.J.: Prentice-Hall, 1957.

Roosevelt, Nicholas. *Creative Cooking.* New York: Harper & Brothers, 1956.

Rorer, Sarah Tyson. *Mrs. Rorer's New Cook Book.* Philadelphia: Arnold, 1902.

Scheib, Walter. *White House Chef.* New York: Wiley, 2007.

Shenton, James P. et al. *American Cooking: The Melting Pot.* New York: Time-Life, 1971.

Simmons, Amelia. *American Cookery.* Hartford, Conn.: Simeon Butler, 1798.

Suszko, Marilou. *The Locavore's Kitchen.* Athens: Ohio University Press, 2011.

Tipton, Edna Sibley. *Reducing Menus for the Hostess of To-day.* New York: Appleton, 1925.

Toms, Agnes. *Eat, Drink and Be Healthy.* New York: Devin-Adair, 1963.

Tower, Jeremiah. *Jeremiah Tower's New American Classics.* New York: Harper & Row, 1986.

Troisgros, Jean and Pierre. *The Nouvelle Cuisine of Jean and Pierre Troisgros.* Trans. Roberta Wolfe Smoler. New York: Morrow, 1978.

The True Light Beavers. *Eat, Fast, Feast.* Garden City, N.Y.: Doubleday, 1972.

Turgeon, Charlotte. *The Saturday Evening Post All-American Cookbook.* Nashville, Tenn.: Nelson & Curtis, 1976.

——. *Time to Entertain.* Boston: Little, Brown, 1954.

Tyree, Marion Cabell. *Housekeeping in Old Virginia.* Richmond: Randolph & English, 1878.

Urvater, Michele and David Liederman. *Cooking the Nouvelle Cuisine in America.* New York: Workman, 1982.

Van Dyke, Louis and Billie Van Dyke. *The Blue Willow Inn Bible of Southern Cooking.* Nashville, Tenn.: Rutledge Hill, 2005.

Verta Mae (Smart-Grosvenor). *Vibration Cooking.* Garden City, N.Y.: Doubleday, 1970.

Vileisis, Ann. *Kitchen Literacy.* Washington, D.C.: Covello, 2008.

Waldo, Myra. *The Complete Book of Gourmet Cooking for the American Kitchen.* New York: Putnam, 1960.

Walter, Eugene. *American Cooking: Southern Style.* New York: Time-Life, 1971.

Waters, Alice. *The Chez Panisse Menu Cookbook.* New York: Random House, 1982.

Whitehill, Jane. *Food, Drink, and Recipes of Early New England.* Sturbridge, Mass.: Old Sturbridge Village, 1963.

Williams, Martha McCulloch. *Dishes and Beverages of the Old South*. New York: McBride Nast, 1913.

Wolfe, Linda. *The Literary Gourmet*. New York: Random House, 1962.

Women of General Foods Kitchens. *The General Foods Kitchens Cookbook*. New York: Random House, 1959.

Wood, Morrison. *With a Jug of Wine*. New York: Farrar, Straus, 1949.

SECONDARY SOURCES ABOUT FOOD AND COOKBOOKS

Adamson, Helen Lyon. *Grandmother in the Kitchen*. New York: Crown, 1965.

Albala, Ken. *Eating Right in the Renaissance*. Berkeley: University of California Press, 2002.

Anderson, Lara. *Cooking Up the Nation: Spanish Culinary Texts and Culinary Nationalization in the Late Nineteenth and Early Twentieth Century*. Woodbridge: Tamesis, 2013.

Appadurai, Arjun. "How to Make a National Cuisine: Cookbooks in Contemporary India." *Comparative Studies in Society and History* 30, 1 (January 1988): 3–24.

Barr, Luke. *Provence, 1970: M. F. K. Fisher, Julia Child, James Beard, and the Reinvention of American Taste*. New York: Clarkson Potter, 2013.

Basbanes, Nicholas A. *A Gentle Madness: Bibliophiles, Bibliomanes, and the Eternal Passion for Books*. New York: Henry Holt, 1995.

Bourdain, Anthony. *Kitchen Confidential*. New York: Ecco Press, 2000.

Bower, Anne L. *African American Foodways: Explorations of History and Culture*. Urbana: University of Illinois Press, 2007.

———. *Recipes for Reading: Community Cookbooks, Stories Histories*. Amherst: University of Massachusetts Press, 1997.

Buckler, Helen. "Why Live Without Cooks?" *Saturday Review of Literature*, January 25, 1930.

Douglas, Mary. "Deciphering a Meal." *Daedalus* 101, 1, *Myth, Symbol, and Culture* (Winter 1972): 61–81.

Driver, Elizabeth. "Cookbooks as Primary Sources for Writing History: A Bibliographer's View." *Food, Culture and Society* 12, 3 (September 2009): 257–74.

Ferguson, Priscilla Parkhurst. "Culinary Nationalism." *Gastronomica: The Journal of Food and Culture* 10, 1 (2010): 102–9.

Fussell, Betty. *Masters of American Cookery*. Lincoln: University of Nebraska Press, 2005.

Gold, Carol. *Danish Cookbooks*. Seattle: University of Washington Press, 2007.

Gvion, Liora. "What's Cooking in America? Cookbooks Narrate Ethnicity: 1850–1990." *Food, Culture & Society* 12, 1 (March 2009): 53–76.

Hartman, Stephanie. "The Political Palate: Reading Commune Cookbooks." *Gastronomica: The Journal of Food and Culture* 3, 2 (2003): 29–40.

Heldke, Lisa. "Let's Cook Thai." In Sherrie Innes, ed., *Pilaf, Pozole, and Pad Thai*. Amherst: University of Massachusetts Press, 2001.

Lewis, George H. "The Maine Lobster as Regional Icon: Competing Images over Time and Social Class." In Barbara G. Shortridge and James R. Shortridge, eds., *The Taste of American Place*. Lanham, Md.: Rowman and Littlefield, 1998.

Lieffers, Caroline. "'The Present Time Is Eminently Scientific': The Science of Cookery in Nineteenth-Century Britain." *Journal of Social History* 45, 4 (2012): 936–59.

Lincoln, Waldo. *Bibliography of American Cookery Books, 1742–1860*. Worcester, Mass.: Davis, 1972.

Jordi, Nathalie. "Samuel Chamberlain's Clementine in the Kitchen." *Gastronomica: The Journal of Food and Culture* 7, 4 (Fall 2007): 42–52.

Lorsy, Ernst, "Escoffier." *Gourmet* 4, 1 (January 1944): 10.

Lowenstein, Eleanor. *Bibliography of American Cookery Books*. Worcester, Mass.: American Antiquarian Society, 1971.

McMillan, Tracie. *The American Way of Eating*. New York: Scribner, 2012.

Mitchell, Christine M. "The Rhetoric of Celebrity Cookbooks." *Journal of Popular Culture* 43, 3 (June 2010): 524–39.

Neuhaus, Jessamyn. *Manly Meals and Mom's Home Cooking: Cookbooks and Gender in Modern America*. Baltimore: Johns Hopkins University Press, 2003.

Newlyn, Andrea K. "Challenging Contemporary Narrative Theory: The Alternative Textual Strategies of Nineteenth-Century Manuscript Cookbooks." *Journal of American Culture* 22, 3 (1999): 35–47.

Pollan, Michael. *In Defense of Food*. New York: Penguin, 2008

——. *Food Rules*. New York: Penguin, 2009.

——. *The Botany of Desire: A Plant's Eye View of the World*. New York: Random House, 2001.

——. *The Omnivore's Dilemma: A Natural History of Four Meals* (New York: Penguin, 2006).

Reddinger, Amy. "Eating 'Local': The Politics of Post-Statehood Hawaiian Cookbooks." *Nordic Journal of English Studies* 9, 3 (September 2010): 67.

Reichl, Ruth. *Tender at the Bone: Growing Up at the Table*. New York: Random House, 2010.

Ridley, Glynis. "The First American Cookbook." *Eighteenth Century Life* 23, 2 (May 1999): 114–23.

Rombauer, Irma and Marion Rombauer Becker. *The Joy of Cooking*. Indianapolis: Bobbs-Merrill, 1951.

Scott, Elizabeth M. "'A Little Gravy in the Dish and Onions in a Tea Cup': What Cookbooks Reveal About Material Culture." *International Journal of Historical Archaeology* 1, 2 (1 June 1997): 131–55.

Seligson, Marcia. "What We Need Now Is Another French Cookbook." *New York Times*, November 10, 1969

Sherman, Sandra. "The Whole Art and Mystery of Cooking": What Cookbooks Taught Readers in the Eighteenth Century." *Eighteenth-Century Life* 28, 1 (2004): 115–35.

Shprintzen, Adam David. *The Vegetarian Crusade: The Rise of an American Reform Movement, 1817–1921*. Chapel Hill: University of North Carolina Press, 2013.

Solomon, Eileen. "More Than Recipes: Kosher Cookbooks as Historical Texts." *Jewish Quarterly Review* 104, 1 (Winter 2014).

Supski, Sian. "Aunty Sylvie's Sponge: Foodmaking, Cookbooks and Nostalgia." *Cultural Studies Review* 19, 1 (1 February 2013).

Szathmary, Louis. *American Gastronomy*. Chicago: Regnery, 1974.

Theophano, Janet. *Eat My Words: Reading Women's Lives Through the Cookbooks They Wrote*. New York: Palgrave Macmillan, 2002.

Tipton-Martin, Toni. *The Jemima Code: Two Centuries of African-American Cookbooks*. Austin: University of Texas Press, 2015.

Villas, James. "From the Abundant Land: at Last, a Table of Our Own." *Town and Country*. 130–66, June 1976.

Zafar, Rafia. "Elegy and Remembrance in the Cookbooks of Alice B. Toklas and Edna Lewis." *MELUS* 38, 4 (Winter 2013): 32.

INDEX

acidosis, 54, 253n25

Adams, Charlotte, *Four Seasons Cookbook*, 187, 217–18

Adobe PageMaker, 201

Adobe Photoshop, 201

advertising, 5, 44, 48–49, 103, 236

aesthetics, 176–77, 181

affluence, signs of, 55–56

African American cooking, 26–29, 30, 41, 78, 130–31, 139–42, 141

Albala, Ken, 273n58; *Eating Right in the Renaissance*, 245n2, 251n73

Alice's Restaurant Cook Book (Brock), 158–59

Allhof, Fritz, 256n28

amateur-pro cooking status, 124

Americana cookbooks: accuracy, 138; adaptation for modern kitchens, 137–38; audience, 138; in the bicentennial year, 7, 140–41; Cold War culture, 7, 132; versus Eurocentric gourmet cooking, 132; format, 132; and the historic preservation movement, 132, 262n83; Native American portrayal, 134; origin story of America, 133, 137; recipes, 135–36; regional representation, 133–34, 137; Southern cooking, 135; and tourism, 137–38, 262n83; variety versus conformity, 136–37

American Cookery (Simmons), 9–10, 245n3

American Cooking (Brown), 128–29, 134

American Cooking: Southern Style (Walter), 130–31

American Cooking: The Melting Pot (Shenton), 129–30

American culture, 2, 5

American Food: The Gastronomic Story (Jones), 139–40

American Heritage Cookbook and Illustrated History, 134–35, 261–62n75

An American Place, 192

American Stove Company, 63

The American Way of Eating (McMillan), 237–38

A Midwife's Tale (Ulrich), 233–34

Andrews, Colson, 205

Animal, Vegetable, Miracle (Kingsolver), 228, 232–33, 235

antebellum era cookbooks, 10, 11, 18, 41–42

antigourmet, 116–20, 200, 205, 206

appliances/tools: chafing dish, 21–22; cookstove, 246n1; electric extractor (juicer), 55–56; versus gourmet cooking, 117–18; heat regulators, 63; as mechanical servants, 64–65; refrigerator, 50–51, 59, 62, 246n1

The Art of Eating (Fisher), 102

As American as Apple Pie (Schulz), 206–7

asparagus, 141–42

athleticism, 65, 253n43

Aunt Dinah, 29

ACKNOWLEDGMENTS

MANY PEOPLE AND INSTITUTIONS supported the work that became this book. My first and biggest thanks are to Robert Lockhart, Senior Editor at the University of Pennsylvania Press. He shows remarkable wisdom and patience in seeing what a book might be and helping the author get the manuscript there. The two anonymous readers for the Press offered truly constructive criticism that inspired me to approach the project in a new and better way and I am grateful for the attention they gave my work.

The Culinary Historians of New York awarded me an Amelia Scholars grant that funded my first research trip for this book. The encouragement of the members of that convivial group have also been very sustaining as I wrote. I also thank the Radcliffe Institute's Arthur and Elizabeth Schlesinger Library for a travel grant that enabled me to visit the astounding collection of cookbooks there. Suffering from mild morning sickness at the time, I was unable to face any recipes dealing with lobster, but I think I read everything else in the collection.

Four grants from the Professional Staff Congress of the City University of New York supported research trips and writing time for this project. A fellowship leave of one year from Queensborough Community College enabled me to spend all day every day reading and writing about cookbooks. During part of that year, a research fellowship at the Five Colleges Women's Studies Research Center gave me the rare gifts of a beautiful quiet place to write and a scholarly community to discuss ideas with. I am especially grateful to the artist E. B. Lehman for her hospitable stewardship of the Center during the time I was there. Jennifer Fronc and Lindsey Churchill were very supportive colleagues during that semester and I have been delighted to follow the progress of their work ever since.

At the CUNY Center a Science and Society fellowship helped me develop ideas in Chapter Two. I am grateful to the lively group of social scientists, philosophers and literary scholars who gave my work their attention. A residency in the New York Public Library's Wertheim Study has sustained my work on this book from beginning to end. I thank my many known and unknown colleagues in the Study for their silent solidarity as we all tapped away at our projects.

The New York University colloquium "Feast and Famine" were kind enough to host me twice to talk through parts of this book and I deeply value the comments (and delicious lunches) I received from the Food Studies Program at those gatherings. I met Farha Ternikar at Feast and Famine and she also deserves sincere thanks for inviting me to talk about my work at Le Moyne College and for becoming a great friend in the process. Another NYU friend, Sara Franklin, has given great support as a reader and conversant as we share a very particular fascination with the late Twentieth century cookbook publishing industry.

My stalwart friends historians Kathleen Feeley and Cindy Lobel have rolled up their sleeves to work on this book and helped me shape a frenzy of ideas into something that looks like text. They were both working hard on wonderful books of their own while I was writing this one, so I am especially grateful for the time they took to help me. Andrew Haley has also given me excellent advice on how to start the whole thing, which turned out to be the hardest part.

Special thanks are due to my aunt, Elizabeth Christenfeld, whose brilliant way of talking about food and culture led me never to doubt that cookbooks were a viable subject for a history. Last, I give thanks to my family, Preston and Petra Johnson, for being patient and supportive and sharing meals with me every day.